SYSTEMS OF SURVIVAL

JANE JACOBS

SYSTEMS
OF SURVIVAL

*A Dialogue on
the Moral Foundations
of Commerce
and Politics*

Random House
New York

Grateful acknowledgment is made to HarperCollins
Publishers for permission to reprint excerpts from
The Way of Life According to Lao Tzu edited by
Witter Bynner. Copyright 1944 by Witter Bynner.
Reprinted by permission of HarperCollins Publishers.

Library of Congress Cataloging-in-Publication Data

Jacobs, Jane
Systems of survival : a dialogue on the moral foundations of
commerce and politics / Jane Jacobs.—1st ed.
p.   cm.
ISBN 0-394-55079-X
1. Business ethics.   2. Political ethics.   I. Title.
HF5387.J32   1992
174'.4—dc20   92-50157

Manufactured in the United States of America

468975

Book design by Carole Lowenstein

To 1712 Monroe Avenue,
555 Hudson Street,
and 69 Albany Avenue

. . . the old oracle said,
"All things have two handles:
beware of the wrong one."

—RALPH WALDO EMERSON

PREFACE

This book explores the morals and values that underpin viable working life. Like the other animals, we find and pick up what we can use, and appropriate territories. But unlike the other animals, we also trade and produce for trade. Because we possess these two radically different ways of dealing with our needs, we also have two radically different systems of morals and values—both systems valid and necessary.

This is an unconventional approach to moral understanding. Philosophers and religious teachers have traditionally analyzed and emphasized the virtuous life for individuals and precepts for virtuous ruling, frequently both combined. People concerned nowadays with the ethics of working life—as in law, business, science, legislative bodies—tend to deal with happenstance ethical particulars, randomly mingling personal and private virtues into the mix. Neither approach coherently sorts out the startling moral contradictions in working life and the reasons for them.

As individuals trying to be good, we aim at being both loyal and honest, for example. But in working life, these two virtues are often in conflict; that is, we must be loyal at the expense of honesty or, conversely, honest at the expense of loyalty to our organization or fellow workers. Does this mean, as is so often concluded, that we can be "good" only in our private lives and that moral behavior must bend or break when we participate in the world's work?

No, that demoralizing notion is nonsense. Clear rules—if we heed them—tell us when honesty takes precedence and when loyalty does if the two conflict. Understanding the reasons for contradictions in the two systems of morals and values throws light on many conundrums: for example, why government-run businesses bog down in waste, inefficiency, and disappointed hopes, no matter what the system of government; when it is ethical to lie and deceive; when industriousness becomes a monstrous vice; what snobbery tells us; why there are no just resolutions for some types of debt defaults; why the practice of law embodies peculiar ethical problems; whether it is true or false that the mystiques of male bonding and loyalty come down to us from prehistoric hunting life; why governments cannot resist meddling in agriculture; why science flourishes only in societies that have achieved commercial vitality, but art can flourish magnificently in societies that lack commerce as well as in those that pursue it; what are the roots of class distinctions; whether organized crime models itself on government or business; and many other puzzles.

I have not invented the two moral and value systems I shall expound. The human race has accomplished that feat during millennia of experience with trading and producing, on the one hand, and with organizing and managing territories, on the other hand. I have merely sorted out this material, analyzed the probable origins and continuing functional reasons for it, and identified types of functional and moral quagmires into which organizations and institutions sink when they confuse their own appropriate moral system with the other.

Intuitively, many of us already understand much of the material with which I shall deal, but often not with sufficient clarity. For one thing, many of us have taken on casts of mind so skewed toward one set of morals and values that we have little understanding of the other, and little if any appreciation of its integrity too. If you do not already recognize a bias you may have absorbed from education, experience, interests, or ambitions, perhaps you will discover it here. The precept "Know thyself" includes knowing the scales with which one weighs actions and attitudes in the great world of work outside oneself.

The form I have chosen for my exposition is dialogue, primarily because this device suits the subject matter, as one of my characters says. So within the limits of my skill, this is the last you will hear of an author's voice. But expository dialogue usually employs a know-it-all who instructs fledglings, disciples, or stooges. My characters, instead, are equals, struggling together to make moral sense of working life.

This choice is not a whimsy. I am convinced we need continual but informal democratic explorations on the part of people who must thread their ways through governmental, business, or volunteer and grass-roots policies, or must wrestle with the moral conflicts and ethical puzzles that sprout up unbidden in all manner of occupations. Former Marxist societies, as they seek to reconstitute themselves, desperately need to clarify right and wrong in business and politics. But so do we. I hope that what my characters work out will help provide useful and suggestive guidelines.

CONTENTS

SYSTEMS OF SURVIVAL

❖

CHAPTER ONE

Armbruster's Summons

COFFEE FOR KATE. Beer for Hortense. Brandy for Jasper and Quincy. Ben dug into his sweater pocket for a kumquat to flavor his mineral water.

Armbruster wondered if he and his guests would be able to agree only that they disagreed and poured himself a scotch. He had mailed his invitations "to explore breakdowns of honesty" on the first anniversary of his retirement as publisher of Caitlin Books. Although he had never been more serious, the date he had absentmindedly set for this gathering led two guests to expect an evening of amusing April Foolery. None knew the others, although Jasper, Kate, and Ben had all been published by Armbruster's small firm and he had worked closely with each.

Jasper had been Armbruster's most successful author and looked it in his rosy-tan cashmere jacket. Every year for almost two decades he had dependably delivered a crime novel, and all but two were still in print. Dismay at the recent onset of his fiftieth year had impelled him to try writing his memoirs, for which he expected the evening to furnish a funny paragraph. He was curious, too, to see how Armbruster lived. The apartment, in a fine old building off Manhattan's Gramercy Square, was more modest than he had expected.

Kate, just turned thirty, was the youngest guest. Her breezy book on

animal memory, *Instinct or Recollection?,* had enjoyed a modest popular
success but hurt her professionally. Her colleagues in a Long Island
university denigrated it as lightweight, and her along with it. She had
been jockeyed into an exasperating bureaucratic slot on an interdisci-
plinary project involving rabbit neurobiology, where she had no time for
her own cherished research on squirrel behavior. Although she looked
tired and rumpled in a pink wool dress, she was resolved to enjoy a
lighthearted respite from budget battles, grant applications, and back-
biting.

Ben's latest book, *Numbered Days for the Planet,* a surprise best seller,
had depressed Armbruster, but Ben himself seemed cheerful enough. As
an advocate of recycling he bought his clothes at garage and yard sales,
which accounted for the short, bunchy hang of his trousers. Always on
the prowl for recruits to his causes, Ben never turned down an invitation.

Quincy, now risen to eminence in a major New York bank, had at
one time been the loan officer with whom Caitlin Books had dealt.
Although his business relationship with Armbruster was long in the past,
the two had remained friends who enjoyed each other's conversation
over occasional lunches. Quincy planned to make his visit brief. He was
working ten-hour days and had come straight from his desk, shedding
neither the clothes nor the air of a man prepared to preside in a
boardroom.

Hortense was Armbruster's niece. She was a crisp-looking lawyer of
forty-three, about the same age as Ben, with a practice in divorce,
separation, child custody, and family support cases, along with legal aid
work for battered wives and juvenile offenders. Although Armbruster
respected her competence, he had invited her mainly out of kindness.
An automobile crash had widowed her four years previously, and now
that her twin sons had entered colleges in California and Oregon,
neither made it back to New York for holidays. Armbruster surmised
she was lonely. But Hortense, who loved reading, delighted in any free
time coming her way and would have preferred spending the evening
with Robert Caro's latest volume on Lyndon Johnson. She had accepted
out of kindness, supposing Armbruster to be at loose ends and needing
encouragement of some sort.

After the little bustle of introductions and getting settled, Armbruster
clinked the ice in his drink purposefully and delivered a preamble. "I've
become disturbed about dishonesty in workplaces. Although I didn't

realize it at the time, my worry dates from a euphoric moment in Hanover immediately after my retirement. I'd accepted a brief consulting engagement there to straighten out confused international rights for a German American family's authorized biography of its late admirable head and was about to follow my exertions with a holiday in Switzerland. I took my fee to a local bank for transfer to my bank here. Commonplace sort of transaction, but this was one of those occasions when the commonplace suddenly seems extraordinary. It hit me that I'd handed over my fee to a total stranger in a bank I knew nothing about in a city where I knew almost nobody, and those few unworldly to an extreme, in exchange for nothing but a flimsy paper with a scribble in a language I didn't understand. What I had going for me, I reflected, unworried, as I dashed to catch my train for Zurich, was a great web of trust in the honesty of business. It struck me with awe how much that we take for granted in business transactions suspends from that gossamer web.''

Ben, who had been fidgeting with the kumquat from his empty glass, interrupted. ''What you were struck with, Armbruster, was complacency and it isn't justified. Consumerism and the business that serves it, honestly or not, are destroying our planet at a rate—''

''Yes, let me go on. I've come to agree with you, Ben, I was being complacent, but in my case about the web of trust upon which so much business depends. Although it was serving me well at the moment, the great web is in a deplorable state. Of course I read in the press about the same kinds of chicanery and avarice you do, but it was a personal experience that brought home to me with a jolt that people who surely ought to know better are conspiring with dishonesty when it seems to benefit them. I was taking part in a two-day symposium at a big midwestern university. I won't single it out by name because I've learned that unfortunately what was happening there is not unique. All too common. The symposium was organized by the biology department, Kate; I even looked for you there. The subject was how to combat public mistrust of science. In midmorning on the first day a disturbance swept the room. Much whispering, buzzing, passing notes, people excusing themselves. A recess was called. I took it on myself to amble about and pry. In departmental offices professors, graduate students, and clerks were falling over one another rummaging about. They were cleansing the place of pirated software. It seems that somebody from economics had called a friend in environmental studies, Ben, who called a friend in biochemistry with word that police were cracking down on stolen software.

"It turned out later in the day that the police were interested in a clique of computer science students who had worked up a thriving illegal operation, reproducing copyrighted software and peddling it throughout the university at prices all too literally a steal. Next day, with the heat off, the stolen material was being reentered into computers. Everything was back to normal. Knowingly buying and using stolen material was normal! This is loss of rudimentary bearings."

"Your software flap sounds rather mild," said Hortense. "I thought you were going to regale us with a cocaine scandal."

"The point I'm making is formidable," said Armbruster. "This thievery was being connived at by everybody. It wasn't a worried university that set the police on the scent. They were acting on outside complaints from two software design firms."

"What evidence did they have?" asked Jasper.

"The usual. Undercover police bought discs, then made the arrests."

"Armbruster, let's make some distinctions," said Kate. "Leaving aside the few students who were profiting from piracy, probably nobody was motivated by greed. By rights, the faculty and students should have funds for the tools they need. They probably don't. That's why the piracy was tolerated. As an author, I recognize I'm not a disinterested party where copyright protection is concerned. But neither are you. All your working life you've relied on the sanctity of copyrights. That's your vested interest."

"I refuse to apologize for espousing honesty," said Armbruster. "I daresay we all have vested interests in other people's honesty."

"Look at it from the arrested students' point of view," said Hortense. "They likely feel aggrieved at being victims of entrapment. The police weren't being honest when they passed themselves off as harmless customers. I'm just passing on to you the way my resentful juvenile offenders react to such masquerades."

"I take it you're reminding me, Hortense, that we have a complicated subject here. I know that. Nevertheless, we do depend on moral norms of everyday working behavior. If the norms go, for whatever reasons, what have we to rely on?"

Armbruster replenished the drinks and then continued. "When I returned home I went to the library and fed my worries from back issues of the newspapers." He flourished a sheet of notes. "Reports of embezzlements; false advertising; fraudulent labeling; dishonest accounting; collusive bids; false business-tax returns; workers' time sheets cooked up to defraud buyers, pad their bills; kickbacks to union officials in return for wage contracts cheating workers; dishonest repair shops; insider trading and other illegal stock manipulations; unauthorized use of customers' bonds for collateral on the part of a broker (that one came out in bankruptcy proceedings); a big patent-infringement case, which the infringer lost; pretenses at conforming with factory safety regulations involving bribes to inspectors; lies about toxic-waste disposal by factories and also waste-disposal service companies; cover-ups of dangerous reportable accidents by managements of chemical factories and also nuclear power plants; sales of condemned meat and tainted fish; a mail-order house that takes the money and doesn't always ship the goods; insurance frauds including falsified appraisals.

"With the exception of some of the embezzlers who were individuals victimizing their employers, these were all crimes committed by business owners or managers, bent on victimizing other enterprises, or else their own workers, their own customers, their own suppliers, or the public at large."

"What do you expect?" asked Ben jauntily. "Businesses try to get away with as much as they can."

"Not so," said Armbruster. "Dishonesty has to be taken seriously. Investigations, prosecutions, and actions like patent-infringement suits are the very reasons you're aware of business crimes, Ben. Commercial life is viable only if crime of all sorts is kept in hand."

"I can tell you a tale," said Jasper. "I used it as background in one of my novels, but I'll spare you my embellishments. This is a true story of how our great midtown garment industry was almost done in at one point because crime got out of hand. Several different theft rings were involved, the largest operated by a Mafia crime family with its own ostensible manufacturing firm right inside the district, shipping garments from its storage rooms to retailers across the country. The closest it came to manufacturing was sewing its own labels on stolen goods— much as other robbery rings screw new license plates onto cars shipped from their garages. Some clothing and fur coat retailers may have known or suspected that they were receiving stolen goods, but probably most thought they were merely getting bargains.

"Here is how it worked. By day, of course, thousands of workers filled the streets and loft buildings. By night the district seemed deserted except for couples here and there smooching in dark doorways. The smooching was camouflage. These couples were actually lookouts, equipped with walkie-talkies to alert thieves inside the buildings in case police showed up.''

"Didn't the garment companies have night watchmen?" asked Kate. "Or at least burglar alarms?"

"Sure, but the thieves turned off the alarms and the watchmen were immobilized by bribes and fear. Watchmen and other building employees were organized to supply information about which manufacturers, at given times, had large inventories on hand, ripe for plundering. This went on for years. At first the thieves were circumspect—took such small quantities from big inventories that the losses were not much noticed. They were supportable. But with success the criminals grew bolder and greedier. The scale became so large that finally it was not supportable. The losses drove some companies out of business. Others were moving from the city to escape the same fate. It was rapidly becoming an unviable place for business, as Armbruster puts it. Finally the situation forced the city to mount a giant police raid planned as secretly and carefully as a war operation. It was a success. Among dozens of criminals caught, convicted, and sent to jail were the head of a Mafia crime family and a senior police detective who had been on the robbers' payroll.''

"Why didn't he tip them off this time?" Ben asked.

"He was kept in the dark. His superiors had finally grown suspicious of him because of failed raids in the past, some of which he had supervised or helped organize.''

"Just like a spy story where an intelligence agency suspects that it's infiltrated by a mole," said Hortense.

"Very similar," Jasper agreed. "To get back to Armbruster's point about viability of business, some of our city neighborhoods that are not as important as the garment district are now so lawless that all business—all legitimate business—in them has either failed or fled.''

"The conventional idea is that unemployment and poverty are major causes of crime," said Hortense. "That's certainly true in part. I see that cause and effect in some of my juvenile-crime cases, and in family breakdowns. But you suggest the reverse is true too: crime can be a cause of unemployment and poverty.''

"Right," said Armbruster. "You're rediscovering the vicious circle." He consulted his notes again. "A public policy research group noted in 1989 that small New York businesses were creating new jobs at only a third the national rate. The researchers concluded that a chief reason was the direct costs of crime to the small businesses, added to the high indirect costs of expensive security measures.

"But that's only violent crime. Let me remind you that the catalogue of white-collar crimes I read you a few minutes ago didn't include so much as a fistfight. White-collar crimes are as expensive to commerce as crimes of violence, perhaps more so. Too many insurance frauds make insurance premiums insupportable, the same as too much insured incompetence. A business using false accounting to pretend it's solvent when it isn't can set off a whole string of losses, including bankruptcies among innocent suppliers. A few careless welds, negligently inspected and fraudulently certified, can cost millions in equipment breakdowns. I meant it as fact, not metaphor, when I said viable commerce hangs from a gossamer web of morality and trust."

"But pursuit of profit always gets out of hand," said Ben. "Look at exploitative logging, mining, one-crop factory farms. The longer-term common good and the environment take second place or may not be considered at all. The harm done gets worse and its scale and scope increase with the help of technology. Old-time whaling fleets were bad enough; modern ones became absolutely devastating, and very quickly. Advanced technology is the reason we now get disasters like Three Mile Island, Bhopal, Minamata Bay, Chernobyl, Valdez—"

"What do all such shocking events have in common?" Armbruster interrupted. "Shocking breaches of trust. Well before each such disaster a specious web of trust has been contrived. After the breakdowns we learn of the broken promises, lies, and cover-ups."

"Bad luck comes into it," said Quincy, speaking up for the first time.

"The bad luck spins out of morally indefensible shortcuts and gambles," said Armbruster. "You advocate more stringent public policies, Ben, but any policy is a fiasco if it isn't backed up by honesty."

"Sloth has a part in triggering the disasters," said Kate. "Also inadequate training. Honesty's important, but that certainly can't be the whole story."

Quincy nodded. "I take issue with your sweeping diagnosis, Armbruster. You're overlooking honest misjudgment, identifiable as such only with hindsight. There we have a major cause of financial disasters. Their costs dwarf all those Ben mentioned, combined—as I've only too much reason to know. Undoubtedly you recall the debt defaults of poor

Third World countries. Our own bank was badly victimized. All the large commercial banks were, along with smaller ones that assumed portions of the debts through ordinary consortium arrangements. We made those loans with good intentions and honest dealing. If acts of sloth or dishonesty played any part, that was inconsequential. Nevertheless, the resulting fiasco, when borrowers defaulted almost en masse, threatened to destroy the banking system itself—with all the repercussions that catastrophe would have entailed. Technically speaking, the rescue operation did compel accounting irregularities, but even that was well and responsibly handled. In sum, if transgressions other than honest misjudgments were responsible, I'm unable to put my finger on them.''

"I don't get it," said Kate. "What do you mean about accounting irregularities?''

Quincy switched his attention from Armbruster to Kate, and his tone from casual authority to patient condescension. "Normally, you must realize, when a bank borrower defaults on interest payments, the bank writes down the value of the loan on its books. Do you understand?'' Kate nodded and Quincy continued. "If it's clear the principal isn't going to be repaid, the loan is written off as a dead loss—you understand?—less whatever can be recovered from forfeited collateral or sold at a discount to optimistic speculators in bad IOUs. The write-downs and write-offs are conventions of honest accounting.''

"For good reason, eh?" put in Armbruster. "If you didn't keep track, you'd wake up some morning and find you'd gone bust without being aware it had happened.''

"Yes, as you say. But these defaults were too massive to treat in the ordinary way. Besides calling bank solvency into question, the write-downs and write-offs would have abruptly and dangerously constricted assets and hence the banks' abilities to serve the continuing needs of commerce and industry. In this crisis, the emergency measure agreed upon, with full cooperation of the government and bank regulators, was to lend defaulting countries funds for interest payments that they could not meet otherwise.''

"As I understand it," said Armbruster, "those loans for interest payments never got to the borrowers. In effect, you bankers were making loans to yourselves—advanced more money but simultaneously took it back as owed you. These were paper transactions only.''

"Why did you do that?" asked Kate. "Throw good money after bad?''

"Because on the books, interest was thus still being paid. Technically, therefore, the loans were not in default—"

"What stopped you from lending interest payments to yourself forever, then?" asked Ben.

"Obviously the new loans were further increasing the defaulters' debts, hence further enlarging unpayable interest. Pyramiding couldn't continue indefinitely. We were cooking the books, to put it crudely. Indeed, one German banker had the temerity to say bankers in his country would go to jail for what we were doing. But this was an emergency measure only, comparable to constructing a boom, say, to contain an oil spill after the fact. It served until we could take more orderly measures for growing out of the bad loans."

"Meaning?" asked Kate.

"Until gradually, over the course of years, we could conventionally write down or write off the loans as we were able, which is precisely what we've been doing." He sighed, then turned to Armbruster. "With apologies, I should be on my way. I can't spare time for friendship these days. If you'll all excuse—"

"Please," said Hortense. "I don't mean to be nosy, but if this all worked out as you say, why do you sound as if it's still worrying you? You do give that impression. Is it because of the fiddle with the accounting?"

Quincy managed a wintry smile and subsided in his chair. "It is, somewhat. I dislike it as a quasi-legitimate precedent for circumventing difficulties. Who knows where that can lead?" He sighed again. "But no, a more immediate concern is that the foreign defaults still hurt. Allocating profits to postponed write-downs has made it devilishly difficult to deal with subsequent massive losses from real estate loans and leveraged buy-outs gone bad, plus ordinary recession losses."

"The whole system's so rotten," said Ben, "people can't be honest and upright even if they want to. Not and get things done. I take honesty seriously even if the law isn't making me, but I have to bend like everybody else. Last summer—but no use going into that."

"If your point is that society forces us into dishonest behavior, by all means do go into it, Ben," said Armbruster. "Unless it embarrasses you?"

"Oh, it embarrasses me. But I'm kind of proud of it too. How's that for moral confusion? All right, I'll tell you. Last summer I spent a couple of weeks helping a tiny Canadian organization that's been trying to stop the government from building a logging road up a wooded mountain. The province owns the forest and sells timber-cutting rights, the way Washington sells grazing and timber rights on federal land out West.

"This protest group I was helping calls itself PPOWW, for Preserve and Protect Our Wilderness Watershed. Kind of cute, huh? But it had no pow, no clout at all. First they tried petitions and lobbying. No effect. Then they raised money and commissioned a professional environmental assessment. I've read it. A good, responsible job; it concluded the watershed is fragile and would be subject to erosion and potential mudslides. The logging that should be permitted is so minimal it wouldn't justify the road costs. But the government undercut PPOWW's study with its own, which came to different conclusions."

"Who are they, these pow people?" asked Hortense.

"Most of them have modest farms in the valley below. Some just have good vegetable gardens and a few fruit trees—like the local nurse's family or the fellow who's the garage mechanic and general machinist. The schoolteachers were all on PPOWW's side, also three craftsmen and a cartoonist and a pair of software designers. The owner of the only café was against PPOWW because she's always cynical and contrary, they say, and anyhow was hoping for business from loggers. A few other people were hoping to pick up jobs when logging started, but nearly everybody, including the kids, was attending meetings and signing petitions. About fifteen really active members do most of the work and fund-raising and were feeling desperate because the valley depends on water from the heavily shaded slopes above. There isn't much rain, but there's heavy winter snow cover that mostly melts in place; the surplus leaks out slowly through the summer. Also, in summer, morning mists get caught in leaves and needles and form drops that fall like little summer rains. On logged slopes the mist isn't captured.

"I went out to take a look. Spruces and cedars with wildlife of all kinds, even black bears and eagles. I fell in love with the place. Up behind the fields and orchards are what they call water-boxes, which are kind of reservoirs where accumulating seepage is withdrawn into pipes. The people depend on this for household water, also irrigation when they need it. Water's naturally limited, so land without rights to a water-box is almost worthless for farming or even a house site. If the slopes are logged, people won't be able to depend on reliable summer seepage. They're also scared about mudslides, which can swallow up houses and gardens and kill people. Besides, they're attached to the woods, and I don't blame them. They have a grisly vision of the roads and big machines tearing things up.''

"Weren't other people working on this?" asked Hortense. "Ornithologists, backpackers, wilderness lovers—doesn't Canada have people and organizations like that?''

"Lots, but they already have lots of fights on their hands, you wouldn't believe how many, and they're almost all volunteers and can stretch only so far. PPOWW has had three disadvantages.

"First, before the valley was settled, the ridge where the top levels out and some of the slopes were logged of the biggest and oldest trees, with ox and horse teams, so it isn't the forest primeval. It doesn't have that grandeur and ancient mystery of thousands of untouched years. That's what rouses up the big mass actions.

"Second thing, the logging company does a public relations job that has nearly everybody snowed except the people on the spot. It claims it logs only fifteen percent or less of any given watershed, pays attention to soil conditions and erosion dangers, and 'wastes none of the province's precious timber resources'—that's how they go on—and leaves no usable debris behind and replants immediately. It says its logging even counters the greenhouse effect by making way for new, young growth to take up more carbon dioxide than old trees. It says it takes timber before it falls anyhow or forest fires consume it. It pulls out all the right words, like 'sustainable' and 'renewable' and 'organic.' The government backs all this by coming down hard on the need for logging and sawmill jobs and timber exports.''

"It doesn't necessarily sound too bad," said Kate. "Forests do regenerate if the logging is done properly. This one already did recover once, evidently.''

"Hey, are you with me or against me?" asked Ben. "Wait till you hear. You have to understand this whole area is out of the way. That's the third disadvantage, and it's serious. People in the valley aren't really isolated, like old-time hillbillies. They have families and friends outside and city customers and all, but just the same they're really the only ones who see what's actually going on and understand the threat.''

"That rings true," said Hortense. "Even people in a threatened city neighborhood find it's hard to make unthreatened neighborhoods comprehend the bad consequences of impending highway or other development schemes.''

"I was given a tour by PPOWW of other forests where logging had been done recently," Ben continued. "We concentrated on tracts this same company's been through. It took all day, dawn until night. One spot was a really good, careful job and shows they can do it right if they want."

"That's likely the one they show off," said Hortense.

"Yeah, but in all the others they cut corners one way and another. That fifteen percent figure is a joke. People hear it and visualize eighty-five percent of a watershed left untouched. But the company interprets it to mean fifteen percent a year! Using that standard, in ten years you could log a hundred and fifty percent—just to give you an idea of how ridiculous this is. The company takes about as much as it wants as fast as it wants and talks its way out of complaints. 'We voluntarily exceeded conservation standards in that watershed by logging only nine percent,' and not mentioning they logged almost forty percent in the three previous years. They play tricks with how they define a watershed, too. If they're denuding it too fast even for their own fake interpretations, oh, that's just part of a bigger watershed. Then there's the waste. The government sets stumpage fees—that's what they call cost of cutting-rights—so low they're almost a giveaway. So the company has no incentive to be thrifty. They take out the most profitable stuff, of course, but ruin most of what's left because it's in the way. There are huge piles of dead, mangled trunks and other debris, so it looks like some giant played jackstraws. That makes careful replanting a joke, just going through the motions to say they did it. All this is what terrified PPOWW.

"When the lobbying and petitions and their own study didn't do any good, they thought about a lawsuit on account of illegal damages already done to public resources."

"Sounds a possibility," said Hortense. "A citizens' suit."

"They were frightened out of it. The legal advice they got was that it would be long-drawn-out and expensive and winning it chancy, and if they lost they'd be liable for costs so heavy they'd never be able to raise them in their whole lives. They might lose their homes and farms. They had no idea what to try next, and this is where I got into it. Some of them'd read my book and wrote to me, and I agreed to get together with them when I got out to the coast on a California trip.

"Well, when I got time to think about it by myself after the tour they gave me, I reasoned we needed to show the public the contrast between one of those vandalized, heartbreaking tracts and PPOWW's own woods. It was just tailor-made for television, but since it was so remote and all, we needed an event.

"The next day I hashed it over with some of the active members. We decided on an invasion of volunteers to plant seedlings in a desolate jackstraw tract. We worked up a kind of scenario. So a couple of members set to work right away, organizing the volunteer planters and their transportation and seedlings, while I drove back to the city to do some conniving there along with three other members—two farmers and a very savvy woman who's a potter."

"Did you actually get television people interested?" asked Hortense. Ben nodded. "Come on, that doesn't sound plausible. Everybody and his brother has some cause they want aired. It's not all that easy."

Ben looked embarrassed. "Umm, here's where I junked honesty. I had to lie. It's kind of elaborate. Are you sure you want to know?"

"By all means," said Armbruster.

"Out there the really bad thing protestors can do is drive iron spikes into the trees. They're like big, long, thick nails but with small heads. If you drive them in the right depth, the bark grows over quickly and the trees look innocent. It's been done, and they say logging companies use metal detectors if they're suspicious. I don't know if that's true, but spiking is mostly talk because it's like being terrorists. When a spiked trunk gets to the mill and hits the saw, hell breaks loose. Pieces of the saw and chunks of wood go flying with terrible force. Besides the machinery damage, maybe it could kill a sawyer. That's why PPOWW wasn't going to do any such thing, but the television people didn't know that. We got them thinking our tree-planting invasion was a spiking invasion—desperate, lawless stuff. You know how the media are."

"You lied to them, I take it," said Jasper.

"Deliberately made them jump to the wrong conclusion, the same as lying. When we reached the city—that was the next morning; we drove all night—the three who came with me went to a construction supply place and bought ten dozen spikes. I went to a bar and restaurant where television people hang out at lunchtime. I've gone there with them, and quite a few of them know who I am because of talk shows about my books. Sure enough, I fell into small talk with a couple of reporters, and then in came my friends, very noticeable because they were wrestling two heavy cartons. I introduced them to the reporters and explained who they were and they sat down with us. They put on a good act. Two were nervous and furtive and one of the farmers was brash and braggy. He let slip what they had in the boxes under the table. They said they'd better push on and asked if I wanted to come with them. I said no, just 'see you later.' ''

"The reporters bit?" asked Jasper.

"They bit. I got coaxed into saying how desperate these people were—which was true enough—and how they had something or other planned but I wouldn't vouch for what. Then I got persuaded into agreeing to guide a reporter, a cameraman, and a sound man to where whatever-it-was would happen day after tomorrow."

"Wouldn't the logging company get wind of this?" asked Jasper. "How could you be sure the television people wouldn't let it out?"

"Okay if they did," said Ben. "We wanted the company to know. That was part of our scenario. In fact, we made sure they did. When I knew the trip with the TV van was sewed up, I phoned back to the valley. As soon as the members with the spikes got home, they got that message and made sure the news of their purchase reached the ears of the café lady and the people who wanted logging jobs. Of course that alerted the logging company, and to make sure, one of our people put in an anonymous phone call to the mill, a bit of friendly, frightened information. Everybody had the right dope about the time of the invasion, but the wrong place. That was another lie.

"Even the tree planters didn't know where they were actually going until they got there. We ran this like a military operation. Secrecy, obedience, discipline, with some people giving orders and others taking them, don't ask questions, just do it. I was worried all the time we'd louse it up somehow, what a crazy gamble.

"But it went off like clockwork. Timing was everything. On the day, the television people and I started out very early, before dawn. In midafternoon we reached the bad, logged tract we'd picked out for them to film. It wasn't the worst one, that was too far from the PPOWW woods, but it was bad enough. And there was our band of tree-planting volunteers, working away in the midst of the devastation. The cameraman started filming that as long as he was there. The reporter was disappointed, but I jollied her along with assurances there was probably going to be more for her to see.

"As soon as the van had passed by, a few miles from the site, a watcher of ours along the road phoned back to the valley, and a couple of our guys waiting for that call drove to the different place where a company foreman and four of his men had set up a barrier and were standing around wondering why no spikers had shown. Our fellows sashayed up, passed the time of day, and casually let drop where the action really was. The foreman and three of his men—they left one behind at their barrier—jumped in their pickup, good and mad at being fooled about the location. Just when we wanted them.''

"A baited trap,'' murmured Jasper.

"Right. Picture it. Here they were, our brave little band of public-spirited volunteers, peacefully doing their good work while the camera whirred, and suddenly there's this bunch of angry, yelling men in hard hats, pelting in on them. All on film. The tree planters looked terrified, dropped their seedlings and spades, and ran to their cars, and the loggers took after them. The cameraman was real pleased with all this pictur-esque action and shouting. Then I persuaded him and the reporter and sound man, as long as they were so close, to go with me to the PPOWW woods so they could see what the hullabaloo was all about.

"Woods are the most photogenic in either the early morning or late afternoon when the light slants in, so for this we'd picked a beautiful spot on the east side of the valley, catching the afternoon sun. Details, details. The contrast to where he'd just been filming galvanized the cameraman. He even caught an eagle in flight—we couldn't plan that. Then he went back to the vandalized tract again and got some sad, lifeless pictures in the twilight.

"The contrast, just the way we hoped, was stunning on television. Flabbergasting. All the more so when it was coupled with a company executive in his office in Toronto, a couple of thousand miles away, spouting the usual hypocrisy, with pictures giving him the lie while he was talking. Then a quick take of the provincial minister responsible for forestry denouncing selfish, ignorant extremists. I was that staple media character, the expert from away who is asked a question or two, and my replies were used for voice-over narrative putting the fight into its environmental context and describing the watershed's fragility. What a package! It was only a four-minute sensation on the evening news the next day but it made viewers so mad that PPOWW began getting some effective help at last. One of the big environment groups applied for a temporary injunction on the road work.''

"What became of those spikes?'' asked Jasper.

"Ha! Nobody knows nothin'. No denials, even. They just vanished. Not entirely, though, you might say. They're a mystery, hanging in the air like lore, or a symbol.''

"But can't you tell us where they are hidden or how they were disposed of, or whatever?" Jasper pressed.

"Nope, I don't know. Only one person does. I gave you a hint who and you've forgotten it, that's all I'll say. At least the government and the logging company seem to have backed off from the PPOWW woods for the time being. They realize they have a nest of hornets on their hands. So we accomplished that much. But nothing's really changed. The whole thing's a moral mess, and that includes me and the PPOWW people, when you come down to it. We lied to the television people—"

"Got them to jump to the wrong conclusion," said Jasper. "Not exactly the same thing. Diplomats do it all the time and nobody thinks the worse of them for it."

"Look, it was a lie," said Ben. "And I'm not about to compound it by oiling over that fact like a weasling diplomat. Furthermore, we deliberately created an impression that loggers beat up on peaceable tree planters. I won't say I regret it if the PPOWW woods are saved, which they still may not be. But what I'm saying is: How can people stay honest, even if they want to, when the whole system's rotten?"

"If you think the system's corrupt," said Quincy, "think about the former Communist countries and what their system has put them through. Their environmental miscalculations have much outdone ours."

"That's supposed to cheer us up?" asked Ben.

"Flailing around like this is getting us nowhere," said Armbruster.

"I'm afraid that goes for me," said Quincy, who had risen and was putting on his overcoat. "Except for the software larceny and Ben playing fast and loose with the truth, we're no closer to identifying malfeasance. A big subject. I enjoyed your story, Ben. Refreshing to be in those woods instead of the default jungle." He gestured toward his briefcase. "Homework to do."

As the door closed behind Quincy, Armbruster shrugged. "We seem to have lost our other man of practical affairs."

"Other man?" asked Hortense. "Who?"

"Fellow who couldn't come. You may have seen his name, Stover, the past few days. The congressman he baby-sits got caught in a conflict of interest and Stover's been implicated in the attempted cover-up. Too bad. It seems the cover-up was more disgraceful than what was being concealed."

"So often the case," said Hortense primly.

"I'm concerned about more than white-collar crime and other dis-

honesty,'' said Armbruster, ''although that's what got me started thinking. I'm concerned that government-run businesses are such swamps of
waste and futility, and not just in Communist countries but everywhere.
I'm worried about the growth of ethnic warfare and terrorism. Hortense, why don't lawyers, of all people, keep their ethics straight? All
these mergers and takeovers and the economic dinosaurs they've created—is that progress or destruction? Why can't we believe anything
our political leaders tell us? And now it turns out that we're going to
face fantastic bills and maybe fantastic dangers disposing of stored nerve
gas sufficient to wipe out all life on earth many times over. One would
suppose enough to wipe it out once would have been sufficient. Are
things being run by the sorcerer's apprentice? Is everything out of
control?''

Hortense looked at Armbruster with concern and said soothingly,
''You're upsetting yourself over very difficult practical matters. Let's
get back onto your subject of morality.''

''But the two are one and the same—morality and practical matters,'' replied Armbruster. ''Or so tangled together they might as well
be one and the same. Everything said here has made that point. There's
the practicality of letting a stranger transfer a check for you, the
practicality of copyright protection, the practicality of doing business in
the garment district, the impracticality of doing it in lawless neighborhoods, the practicality of maintaining a water supply for Ben's pow
people, the logging company's notion of practical ways and means to
take out timber, the practicality of foreign lending, the practicality of
resorting to dishonest accounting when the need arises. Impossible to
separate those practical matters from moral considerations. Yes, I was
flailing about, Hortense, but I've a hunch that the key to understanding
no end of practical matters—and impractical messes they get into
too—may very well be the subject of morality.''

''Looking for a key—the key—to understanding all perplexities; that
way lies madness,'' said Jasper. ''Or to give madness another name, that
way lies ideology. We need more of that?''

''The last thing I'd suggest is concocting another ideology,'' said
Armbruster. ''Nor am I interested in conspiracy theories to explain the
world, another name for madness. And I'm not searching for what could
be if only things were run my way. I'm strictly thinking about what goes
on, and I'm hazarding that morality may afford a handle, on the assumption—I may be wrong—that morality is not another name for chaos.''

''Even chaos has patterns,'' said Kate thoughtfully. ''At least that seems to be true in the physical world, although mathematicians and physicists have recognized that only recently.''

''So I've come to the conclusion,'' Armbruster resumed, ''that we must try to think in a systematic fashion about morality in practical working life. And that's why I asked you here. Since this is my proposal I'm making myself chairman of an exploration committee, and I hope you, my friends, will be the committee. The only ground rule is that we cleave to behavior people use, or are supposed to use, in their work. This is going to be puzzling enough without straying into strictly personal behavior.''

''Do I understand you brought us here to set us to work on a committee?'' demanded Jasper. ''If I had known that, I would never have come! I am not even sure what you are driving at, but with all respect, Armbruster, it sounds absurd.'' He glanced around at the others. ''Five acquaintances meet to solve your idea of the great problems of society? Five didactic talking heads that do not know what they are talking about? I can imagine your contempt if I brought you that idea for a novel, and you would be right.''

''This is no novel,'' said Armbruster. ''This is a tradition older than the novel. Dialogue—didactic talking heads, if you will—goes back to Plato and possibly to the dawn of consciousness about right and wrong, whenever that was. The form—disagreements, speculations, second thoughts, questions, answers, amended answers—it's suited to the problematic subject matter. Let's give it a try. What harm can it do?''

''We are not qualified,'' said Jasper. ''So why us?''

''Why not us?'' said Armbruster. ''If more-qualified people are up to the same thing, more power to them. But we don't know that, do we? No doubt you think I'm obsessed. Very well, I'm asking you to indulge me. I find wheedling distasteful, but won't you agree merely to gamble a bit of time?''

''I can think of several better ways of spending my time,'' said Ben. ''What's there to gain by this gamble, as you call it?''

''It may be pointless. But at the least, perhaps we'll clarify our own understanding of how the world works, and that's worth something.''

''Sure,'' said Jasper sarcastically. ''You name it, and we'll deliver for you. No thanks.''

''What I had in mind,'' said Armbruster, ''is that each of us who chooses might bring in a report. Then we can discuss it. Don't look so hostile. I realize that being writers, you'll go to any lengths to postpone and evade writing. I don't mean written reports. I suggest you speak from notes or merely from the top of your head if that's what you prefer. I'll tape what's said, whether report or discussion. In fact, although I should have mentioned it earlier and I hope you don't object, my machine's been running.'' He reached for the bookshelf behind his back and placed a large recorder on the table.

"After giving this some thought,'' he went on, ''I propose our first report should simply aim at identifying our system or systems of moral behavior concerned with work. What sorts of rules safeguard the security of moving money around? We know honest accounting is one but we also know it's fragile. Anything else? Why do we accept that it's all right for police to assume dishonest masquerades, as Hortense put it, and if so, why don't we accept that anybody can do the same? Obviously we do have norms, whether spoken or not. I'm not suggesting you probe into anything outlandish or esoteric. Nothing in the vein of tribesmen dedicating their spears to the Great Bear, if they do. Just some thinking about the commonplace norms we purport to depend on. Any volunteers?''

After a silence, Kate spoke up diffidently. ''I'm interested in your mention of systems, Armbruster. I like uncovering systems; it's what I've enjoyed most in my work, and I miss it in the job I'm stuck with for the time being. But mind you, I can't promise—''

"You're a shrewd one, Armbruster,'' said Ben. ''You dangled the bait of systems and Kate snapped it up. I deal with systems too, but that's a false lead to what you seem to be after. You've misidentified the problem. Those people with the pirated software, they knew they'd done wrong. That's why they went into their little panic. We already know it's wrong to pollute the air, soil, and water. The problem isn't recognizing what's wrong; it's doing what's right, or enforcing it. Right is right and wrong is wrong, and—''

"Oh, I couldn't disagree more!'' Hortense exploded. ''Right and wrong depend on circumstances. I see that constantly in my law practice. And that's only to speak of our own society. Why, even our own subcultures differ in standards of acceptable behavior. We all know that. Right and wrong start with 'that depends' and go on from there. The possibilities are infinite.''

"There you have it,'' said Armbruster, beaming at Hortense. ''You, Hortense, are a moral relativist. And you, Ben, are a moral absolutist. Logically, you might both be wrong, but it's inconceivable you can both be right. Given that interesting disagreement on fundamentals, can't you at least attend to whatever Kate comes back with? Then you can pick it apart to your heart's content or drop the whole thing if you want. Just give it a try, one day of listening and talking, no further commitment. How long do you need, Kate?''

''This is a new idea to me. How about two or three months? I'll ring you up.''

''Two or three months!'' snorted Armbruster. ''Come now, Kate, what's the least time? Remember, we're not expecting a polished production.''

Kate poured herself another cup of coffee and, asking ''May I?,'' went out to the kitchen to reheat it in Armbruster's microwave. On her return she took her time sipping it. ''Well,'' she finally said, brightening up, ''to tell you the truth I'm fed up with my own job these days and I do have leave coming. I'll take it now; it will be a nice break. I'll need a couple of days to make arrangements for while I'm away; then if I hole up with no interruptions, I could try for . . . three or four weeks? But really, Armbruster, maybe all I'll have to report is frustration.''

''Done,'' said Armbruster. ''Let's say four weeks from Sunday. Starting at ten in the morning? Bring your own lunches and I'll provide drinks.''

''By the way,'' said Ben as they were putting on their coats, ''what you said about tribesmen. You might be interested to know that the Micmacs called the Great Bear the Keeper of the Game and believed all the plants and animals were a sacred gift to be used sacredly, with care. If we'd enforce that moral example, just about everything else would fall into place. I don't see what can be so complicated about that.''

''Sanctimonious cant,'' said Hortense huffily. ''Women know all about it. Putting victims on a pedestal, the better to exploit them in good conscience.''

CHAPTER TWO

A Pair of Contradictions

Relieved to see all four on the appointed morning, Armbruster expansively showed off his new coffee maker, which managed its own heating, and fiddled with his tape recorder while Kate passed out typed sheets.

"You can keep these in front of you for reference," she said. "I'll explain later why I call them syndromes." She paused as they glanced down the lists.

MORAL SYNDROME A

Shun force
Come to voluntary agreements
Be honest
Collaborate easily with strangers and aliens
Compete
Respect contracts
Use initiative and enterprise
Be open to inventiveness and novelty
Be efficient
Promote comfort and convenience
Dissent for the sake of the task

Invest for productive purposes
Be industrious
Be thrifty
Be optimistic

MORAL SYNDROME B
Shun trading
Exert prowess
Be obedient and disciplined
Adhere to tradition
Respect hierarchy
Be loyal
Take vengeance
Deceive for the sake of the task
Make rich use of leisure
Be ostentatious
Dispense largesse
Be exclusive
Show fortitude
Be fatalistic
Treasure honor

Jasper was first to speak. "This is mystifying. Why are you presenting us with two sets of morals? And look how they dispute each other! What are you up to? This makes no sense."

"I realize these lists aren't self-explanatory," said Kate. "But give me a chance to explain. That's what I intend—"

Before she could finish her sentence, Ben burst in. "This advice, or whatever it's supposed to be, is immoral! What do you mean, 'Promote comfort and convenience'? We're already destroying the planet with that behavior!" He ran his finger down the sheet. "Be ostentatious!" He looked up. "Have we been dragged here to praise consumerism?"

"Hear me out," said Kate. "I promise this isn't frivolous. Armbruster, you're right. It's possible to explain a lot with these two lists. What was it you said about governments running businesses badly? These lists gave me a handle on that. Other things surprised me—like where does art come from, and how come agriculture gets so many subsidies but it's in perpetual crisis anyhow, and when industriousness is vicious. If we dig into these precepts further than I've been able to so far, they may explain a lot."

Ben, who had not been listening, began another tirade. "Furthermore, why doesn't responsibility come into your absurd rules or whatever they are—"

"Glad you noticed that right off," Kate answered. "Where's cooperation, courage, moderation, mercy, common sense, foresight, judgment, competence, perseverance, faith, energy, patience, wisdom? I omitted these because they're esteemed across the board, in all kinds of work. In conduct of personal life, too, for that matter, not just in working and public life."

"I like what C. S. Lewis said about courage," Jasper put in. "He called it the master virtue because it makes practice of all the others possible."

"Maybe," said Kate, "but I'd think cooperation is probably the most important of the universals. We're social animals, and everything we are or have hangs on cooperation. These two lists I gave you are the residues left after I subtracted universals—cooperation, courage, patience, and so on. The first point to notice about the residual precepts is how contradictory they are. Plain irreconcilable."

"Where did you find these lists?" asked Armbruster.

"I compiled them myself," said Kate. "It wasn't all that easy, either. I'll thank you not to huff and puff them away on sight, Ben. I'm in no mood to suffer fools gladly."

"Let's plan to be patient with each other," said Armbruster. "A universal virtue, as you say, applying to all kinds of work, and especially exploration."

"Maybe I'd better tell you how I went about this," said Kate. "First, I immured myself in the library, opening to closing. Read, read, read, and took notes."

"Read what?" asked Hortense.

"Hit and miss at first, but sharpened up as I went along. Biographies; business histories; scandals; sociology, although that was less help than I expected, except for some of the Europeans. I dipped into general history and, in spite of what you said, Armbruster, about ignoring tribesmen's spears, skimmed some cultural anthropology. Nights at home I clipped newspapers.

"I drew on three kinds of evidence. Whenever I ran across behavior that was extolled as admirable, I cast it in the form of a precept. If a businessman was praised because his handshake was as good as his bond, I cast it in the precept 'Respect contracts.' If another was admired for tenaciously carrying out a commercial idea successfully in the face of contrary conventional advice and discouragement from experts and bankers—Edwin Land, inventor and producer of the Polaroid camera, for instance—I cast that as 'Be open to inventiveness and novelty,' 'Use initiative and enterprise,' and 'Dissent for the sake of the task.' I should emphasize, though, that not one of these precepts is here because it turned up as a unique or even a rare instance. Every one showed up over and over, in varying contexts. If a soldier was extolled for redeeming the honor of his regiment by rallying it when it was about to retreat, I cast it as 'Treasure honor,' and so on.

"I did the same with behavior that was laid out as expected or proper, as in job-training manuals, and such useful sociology as I did find. These are the kinds of rules or tips cast in such precepts as 'Be industrious,' 'Be honest,' 'Be efficient,' 'Collaborate easily with strangers and aliens,' in Syndrome A, and 'Be obedient and disciplined,' 'Respect hierarchy,' 'Be loyal,' in Syndrome B. A lot of the universals show up too in what's expected or proper.

"My third type of evidence was behavior that was deemed scandalous, disgraceful, or criminal. I identified what was being transgressed, such as honesty; or if extortion, say, was the crime, I cast it as 'Shun force,' and 'Come to voluntary agreement.' If conflict of interest was the gist of a scandal, I cast it as 'Shun trading.' I also made note of what sorts of work or positions in life were associated with a given precept."

"Why didn't you say 'Don't take bribes' when you made a precept out of conflict-of-interest scandals?" asked Ben.

"I did have that as a precept at one point," said Kate. "But then when I kept running across much the same underlying moral principle in contexts that couldn't quite be described as bribe-taking, I cast it as the more embracing precept 'Shun trading.' Stick with me and you'll see why. Precepts I first drew from one of my three kinds of evidence were reinforced when they turned up, as they did more often than not, in one or both of the other kinds of evidence I used.

"It's coincidence, as far as I can see, that there are fifteen items in each syndrome. Ben, you seem to think I included trivial and even deplorable stuff. But when I repeatedly ran across evidence for a precept, I included it regardless of any preconceptions I had. That's a habit of people who study animal behavior, and you have to take me with my habits, Ben. I pay attention to traits of a species, even when I don't know of reasons for them. In the haste imposed on me, I may have missed important precepts, but I doubt it, because the time arrived when I wasn't catching new fish, just netting repetitions.

"Then I holed up at home and tried to make sense of my notes. First I sequestered off the universals; I've already mentioned that. The unsorted residue seemed a mess of contradictions. Honesty and deceit both prescribed? What to make of that? Novelty and tradition? Fortitude and comfort? Ostentation and thrift? Dissent and obedience? So on and so on!"

"Acceptable behavior depends on circumstances," said Hortense.

"I wasn't ready to concede that anything goes," said Kate. "Especially since my reading convinced me how much store people set by admirable behavior. Even hypocrisy tells us that much. It also irritated me to suppose I was dealing in nonsense. I don't believe the behavior of a successful species is meaningless. And in spite of all our flaws, all our failures and tragedies and shortcomings, humankind is highly successful considered as a species. So I drew on universally esteemed perseverance and faith, and suppressed the universally deplored temptation to despair, shuffled my notes, and stared at them by day and dreamed of them by night.

"My first glimmer of order came when I noticed that specific precepts were repeatedly associated with specific others: loyalty with obedience and respect for hierarchy, for instance; industriousness with thrift and efficiency. Aha! Precepts came in linked clusters! Each kind of occupation I'd noticed had its clusters, and those clusters overlapped with other clusters. Combining the overlaps resolved the clusters into these two lists I gave you.

"This was exciting because I was thrilled to discover that neither list was internally contradictory. Honesty didn't turn up with deceit, nor ostentation with thrift, and so on. Therefore, neither list indicated that anything goes."

"At least that's something," said Ben, shooting a triumphant glance at Hortense.

"So I still had all the perplexing contradictions, but now they were resolved into two systems, each with its own integrity. Next, I compiled occupations associated with each list. Here, I must admit, I found a few anomalies—some occupations firmly associated with both lists instead of one."

"What are they?" asked Hortense.

"Law, you'll be interested to know, Hortense. Not making or enforcing law—that's with the B list only. But private legal practice uses precept clusters from both syndromes. Also agriculture. I'll set them aside until later."

Armbruster made a note and Kate looked at him inquiringly. "Just one of my habits when editing," he said. "Making running notes of loose ends when they turn up. You have to take me with my habits. Please continue."

"The A syndrome was easy. The occupations associated with it overwhelmingly concerned commerce, and production of goods or services for commerce; and, in addition, most scientific work. Moral Syndrome A was what you had going for you, Armbruster, when you handed over your check to a stranger in the Hanover bank. So I think of A as the Commercial Moral Syndrome. But I suppose we could as well call it Bourgeois. By and large, these are the classic bourgeois values and virtues."

"Then you should acknowledge that these precepts or values or norms, or whatever, are Western values," said Ben. "This is Eurocentrism. It applies, at best, only to a very limited part of the human race."

"That's a funny thing for somebody to say who thinks that right and wrong are the same under all circumstances," said Kate. "I suggest you're relying on word-association instead of thinking. You hear the word 'bourgeois,' and 'Western values' automatically pops out. Come off it, Ben! I'm not dealing in metaphysics, or even in abstractions. This is about concrete, nitty-gritty commercial life. It's about giving honest weight, finding customers, and competing successfully with other commercial people. These precepts rule wherever commercial life is viable, East or West. They apply to Islamic innkeepers, Buddhist batik makers, Hindu brass craftsmen, or Shinto brake manufacturers, just as they do to Christian, Jewish, or atheist auto mechanics and potters out there in your PPOWW valley.

"That brings me to the word 'syndrome.' It comes from the Greek, meaning 'things that run together.' We customarily use it to mean a group of symptoms that characterize a given condition. In this case, the condition characterized by these symptoms is practice of viable commercial life.

"The B syndrome was more enigmatic. I wondered, What do these occupational groups have in common: armed forces and police, aristocracies and landed gentries, government ministries and their bureaucracies, commercial monopolies—that seemed an anomaly at first, but it isn't—law courts, legislatures, religions and especially state religions? If this list is a syndrome too, I asked myself, then what condition does it characterize?

"It finally struck me. They're all concerned with some aspect of territorial responsibilities. The condition is the work of protecting, acquiring, exploiting, administering, or controlling territories.

"Think about your behavior in the PPOWW battle, Ben. I seem to remember you used deceit for the sake of the task; discipline and obedience and respect for hierarchy—some people giving orders, others taking them, don't ask questions, do it. Ostentation—that was quite a show you put on. Loyalty. Your charade with the spikes carried the implied threat of exerting prowess, physical force, even though you didn't exert it, and you sounded pretty gleeful about the threat continuing to hang in the air, like lore. You also sounded vengeful. A nice, plump cluster of items from Moral Syndrome B. And sure enough, you and PPOWW were battling in the cause of stewardship over a piece of territory. Not territory in the abstract. Again, we aren't dealing in abstractions. Real, concrete territory. I suppose we might call this the territorial syndrome. Taken as a whole, it also describes the classic heroic virtues and values."

"So Ben wasn't being morally confused after all when he felt proud of what he and his group pulled off," said Hortense. They all smiled at Ben.

"But I don't like identifying the syndrome as heroic," Kate continued. "All the occupations associated with it aren't heroic. A lot consist of humdrum bureaucratic work in government. We could call it the government, or ruling, syndrome, but that's too limited. There are Ben's battlers, for instance, confronting government and fighting with rulers. Also it doesn't at all characterize some of the activities that governments undertake, like weather-forecasting services, for instance. Those subscribe, like other hard sciences, to the commercial precepts."

"The words are giving you trouble because your thinking is fuzzy," said Jasper. "What you have done sounds clever but it does not persuade me. Nothing is triter than constructing pairs: yang and yin; black and white; old and young; masculine and feminine; good and bad; left and right; hot and cold; sick and well; quiet and noisy. So easy and so specious. In my experience, and in yours, too, if you stopped to think, reality always exhibits gradations, degrees, mixtures, shades of gray. Realities do not fit into pairs of tidy boxes. I suspect you took a quick and easy way out and slid by the complexity of real life in your desperate desire to impose hasty order on the confusion of your notes."

"Wait," said Armbruster, who had swung around and was searching the bookshelf behind him. "Before you write off Kate's pair, you ought to know or recall that she has corroboration from a thinker who was anything but trite and slipshod. Listen to what Plato said, Jasper. Here, right at the beginning of the *Republic,* he has Socrates asking Cephalus, who has evidently done well for himself commercially, about the moral life associated with his wealth. Cephalus says it is a benefit, meaning virtue, not to have lied to or deceived anyone, even unwillingly. Socrates picks this up as meaning 'justice or right is simply to speak the truth and to pay back any debt one may have contracted.' Cephalus agrees.

"But then Socrates immediately goes on to cast doubt. Can't these same actions be sometimes wrong, he asks, because, and I quote again, 'everyone would surely agree that if a friend has deposited weapons with you when he was sane, and he asks for them when he is out of his mind, you should not return them.' Nor is one doing right, he suggests, 'to tell the whole truth to a man in such a state.' "

"But he's syndrome hopping!" exclaimed Kate. "The first answer was from commercial precepts, but the second has nothing to do with commerce. It's a form of policing."

"A bit later," Armbruster went on, turning the page, "Socrates proposes, among other paradoxes, that the man who is a good guardian of the camp is also able to steal the plans of the enemy. Following this line of reasoning, he arrives at the shocking statement that justice, then, seems to be a craft of thieving, 'of course to the advantage of one's friends and to the harm of one's enemies.' "

"More Syndrome B morality!" cried Kate. "Here, look, 'Deceive for the sake of the task.' I put it in. But it's outrageous to get a good commercial answer and then make out it's faulty because it's not a good answer for policing or waging war. This is gratuitous, mischievous confusion."

"Precisely Plato's point too," said Armbruster. "He, or rather his speaker, Socrates, subsequently takes pains to distinguish between two great, major groups of occupations and their purposes, precisely to disentangle their contradictory virtues from one another. I emphasize two groups, Jasper. He said both are necessary: the commercial occupations to supply everybody's physical needs and also support the guardians, presumably by taxation."

"Guardians?" asked Kate.

"They're your Moral Syndrome B people, Kate. Police, soldiers, government policymakers and rulers. Socrates explains they're necessary to protect the state from corruption within and enemies outside. I propose, Kate, you call Syndrome A 'commercial,' as you wanted, and you call Syndrome B 'guardian,' in deference to Plato, even though guardianship as Plato expounded it may be a bit narrow."*

"If I remember correctly," said Hortense, "Plato was speaking in allegory. He was using the Republic, the city-state, as an allegory of how the virtuous individual should conduct his life. His republic was an abstraction. It represented the soul of man, to be guarded against impiety, sloth, greed, lust, arrogance, envy, cowardice, and so on, including the vice of seeking after worldly honors. He used weaknesses and evils in the conduct of the state to illustrate the vices individuals should guard themselves against. That's how I remember it."

Armbruster regarded Hortense with surprise. "Yes," he said, "and he also did the reverse, singling out vices in the individual as analogues to evils in commerce and government. It seems to me he was trying to embrace all morality, both private and public, in one unified theory—a more ambitious project than ours. My point is merely that Kate's discovery has illustrious precedent."

Kate failed to return Armbruster's admiring smile. "I'm embarrassed," she muttered. "I apologize. Now I see I should've begun with the old philosophers. But when we read them in school they went over my head. I was so bored, I hardly remember. Well," she sighed, "I guess I've been reinventing the wheel . . ."

"Not at all," said Armbruster briskly. "Plato was being cursory, especially with respect to commerce, in comparison with the precepts you've compiled. And you disagree with him outright when you include ostentation and largesse in the guardian syndrome, although you're certainly with him on the leisure. No, no, my object was not to dishearten but rather to encourage you, and to suggest that Jasper withhold judgment."

Jasper, however, seemed lost in his own thoughts. "Say, Armbruster," he inquired, "did Socrates leave it that justice is a craft of thieving, or did he produce a definition that makes more sense?"

"He finally did get around to defining justice and injustice both." Armbruster paused to locate a page about halfway through the *Republic*. "As to whether it makes more sense—well, it's puzzling. He flatly

*For convenient reference, the precepts, under these titles, are reprinted in the Appendix.

states that justice—I'll quote—'is to perform one's own task and not to meddle with that of others.' He seems to say that this makes possible the practice of other virtues, including wisdom, courage, and moderation, which he's expounded in the buildup to his big denouement about justice.

"To give an example of unjust behavior he cites a cobbler exchanging tools and work with a carpenter, or one man working as both a cobbler and carpenter. From this, he goes on to generalize that the two ranks of guardians—rulers and their police and soldier auxiliaries—shouldn't switch jobs with each other or with the commercial people, nor should anyone mingle these kinds of work together. He calls such behavior 'the greatest wickedness' and says it does the 'most harm' to the community, hence constitutes the greatest injustice, and therefore the opposite behavior must be justice. And this time he isn't playing with paradoxes or trying to shock. He seems to mean it.''

"Ridiculous!" said Hortense. "It's no big deal for a cobbler to switch to carpentry. Or do both, like capable homesteaders in pioneer days. That's injustice? Or a demobilized soldier who takes up cabinet making? Armbruster, this has to be allegorical, not literal, but I can't imagine what sense it makes as allegory either.''

"Maybe he had a personal hang-up," said Jasper. "A cobbler made him a shoddy pair of shoes, and he found out—''

"I looked it up once in a learned commentary," said Armbruster. "Your supposition, Jasper, is more plausible than the tortuous and farfetched speculations about Plato's meaning that I found there. After the commentator had done his arcane best with the passage, he wound up by judging Plato's argument 'weak.' But that the argument should be weak is puzzling in itself, because Plato thought justice supremely important, that's clear, and he was no slouch at making a strong case for his opinions. It's beyond me, Jasper. Maybe enlightenment will dawn if we proceed, maybe not. Let's get on with Kate's findings about her syndromes. You do have more to say about them, I take it?''

"Oh my, yes. This is only a start. We have to look into reasons for these two syndromes.''

"I thought we got the reasons," said Hortense. "One to support daily needs; the other to combat corruption and enemies.''

"Right, as far as that goes," said Kate, speaking again with enthusiasm. "Basically or sketchily, yes; but that tells too little about the why's and wherefore's that I picked up while I was tracking down precepts. I plan to go into those, as far as I got.''

CHAPTER THREE

Kate
on the
Commercial
Syndrome

"THE SEQUENCE of these precepts doesn't imply order of impor-
tance," Kate began. "I'm merely moving from the simpler to the
more complex for my own expository convenience, and for yours as
listeners. All the precepts are important, and all are connected.

"*Shun force,* to start with, is simple in principle but not always
easily accomplished because commercial wealth is found in the midst
of things. It's accessible to customers, suppliers, the public. It travels
on common carriers. So it's tempting, and likely it always has been,
to robbers, sacking armies, hijackers, and sneak thieves. Jasper told us
the first night here how ruinous this vulnerability can be if it's not
protected. So many pirates lurked off the coasts of medieval England
that London merchants went to the expense of financing a fleet of
fighting ships and gave it to the Crown. That's supposed to be the way
the English navy started."

"Why give it to the Crown?" asked Jasper.

"Because 'Shun force' has a second meaning. It also forbids commercial people themselves to use force."

"You mean, if they did they'd be scared of each other?" asked Ben.

"Of course. They'd have good reason to be. The precept, in this
second meaning, gives substance to the second item, *Come to voluntary
agreements.* Even children know that this is what 'I'll trade you' means.

When violence or intimidation enters a transaction, it's no longer trade. It's taking by force.

"*Be honest,* in its turn, gives substance to voluntary agreement. To be sure, as Armbruster pointed out with that Augean stables list of white-collar criminality, some commercial organizations practice dishonesty and some get away with it, too, much as some predators on commerce get away with violence. But by definition, dishonesty is kept down to supportable levels wherever commerce remains viable. My guess is that the earliest form of commercial fraud and cheating was with weights and measures. One oddity I ran across in the library was a translation of letters of recommendation addressed to the gods. Ancient Egyptians prepared or commissioned the letters for their tombs. One standard popular bit ran like this: 'I neither increase nor diminish the measure of grain, I am not one who shorts the palm's length'—that refers to the hand, a unit of measurement for dry goods, like cloth, for instance—'I am not one who shorts the field's measure, I put not pressure upon the beam of the balance, I tamper not with the tongue of the balance.' Evidence like that, along with the fact that the earliest forms of standardization imposed by governments seem to have been standardized weights, implies that the ancients took commercial dishonesty as seriously as we do, if not more so."

"Since we have engaged to stay for the day, can we get on to something less obvious than the stunning news that honesty is the best policy?" said Jasper.

"I don't know that it is that obvious after my stolen-software experience," said Armbruster. "But Jasper does have a point; you're laboring the obvious a bit."

"Sorry, I'll try to be brisker, but I have a point of my own to make before moving on. Notice that we now have basic reasons that commercial people need symbiotic help from guardians: to combat violent predators on commerce, of course, but also to mandate honesty and give the mandate teeth by ferreting out dishonesty in commercial life, investigating, exposing, disgracing, prosecuting, and punishing it—in short, suppressing it down to supportable levels even if the ideal of eliminating it completely isn't realistic, alas.

"The next precept, *Collaborate easily with strangers and aliens,* links tightly with honesty. Here's an account by a traveler in Asia Minor back at the time Greeks and Turks were furiously at war, the Greeks trying to free themselves from the Ottoman Empire. This is the headman of a backwater Turkish village speaking. 'We Turks have the land and we have the fruit trees but we have no capital and we don't know how to sell our fruit. Every spring the Greek merchants come to our village and together we make an estimate of our crop. They lend us the money to pay for collecting and packing the fruit and for our own needs. In the autumn we send the fruit to Smyrna or Panderma. It never happens that a Turk will sell his crop to any merchant but the one who lent him the money, and it never happens that the merchant fails to send back the balance of the sale price of our fruit. If we trust each other in this way, why can't . . . leaders trust each other too? . . . We are being ruined by these foolish wars.'

"In any commercial life more complicated than a hamlet market," Kate went on, "and it would have to be an isolated hamlet at that, commercial people are compelled to deal with strangers and almost-strangers as suppliers or customers, and often enough with aliens. This requires enormous trust, like Armbruster's trust in the stranger at the Hanover bank. But trust is feasible only where honesty is usual.

"Commercial people invent devices to facilitate trust among strangers, always have. Receipts are likely the oldest forms of business documents. Long ago receipts or bills of account were put into trade just as if they themselves were the valuables they represented; they were exchanged as if they were money. That was possible only because honesty could be presumed and commercial life was being operated on the premise that it is as disgraceful to defraud strangers and aliens as it is to cheat a friend.

"That premise is the foundation of the quality we call cosmopolitanism, from the Greek words *cosmos* and *polis,* meaning 'universal people.' The principal places in which strangers do business together are big commercial cities. The cosmopolitanism of these cities is no accident. It's an instance of functional necessity becoming a cultural trait. To make mundane, everyday deals with strangers and aliens, for no reason except that they're customers or suppliers, demands tolerance for people outside one's own background and personal preferences and, often enough, even respect for them as well. Cosmopolitanism spills over into other fields, such as the arts, but its roots are commercial." She paused to locate a note.

"Here, Mariam Slater, she's an anthropologist, wrote this about Nairobi as it was in 1960. 'Each ethnic group meets almost exclusively its own kind in private arks of family, club or place of worship. The visitor quickly learns to spin a tight cocoon in an atmosphere in which an Ismali does not speak to his Baluchi or Hindu neighbor except in the marketplace.' "

"I wouldn't tag that as a cosmopolitan spirit," said Hortense.

"No, it wasn't. But the point is that insofar as ethnic collaboration existed at all in Nairobi, its locus was specifically and only the market-place. Here's something you'll like, Jasper," Kate continued. "Cosmo-politanism and insularity are contrasts, but not a tidy, discrete pair. They're two poles, rather, with shadings and degrees and mixtures all the way from one pole to the other.

"Those shadings and degrees are in great part a reflection of perma-nence and impermanence of relationships. That's an interesting subtlety expounded by Norbert Elias, a great German sociologist who exhaus-tively studied the old French royal courts. He contrasted the permanent court relationships—until the French Revolution swept them away—with the impermanent relationships that the French bourgeoisie were taking in their stride during the same period. He said of the courtiers that each stood 'by and large in a lifelong relationship with every other member of his society . . . inescapably dependent on each other as friends, enemies or relatively neutral parties. They must therefore observe extreme caution at each encounter with each other. Prudence or reserve are dominant features. . . . Because every relationship in this society is necessarily permanent, a single unconsidered utterance can have a permanent effect.' That's the insularity pole. The same observa-tions hold true of humble insular societies, too, where family grudges and feuds are tenacious, sometimes handed along for generations, or where being born on the wrong side of the tracks can be the most important element in a person's identity for life.

"Elias contrasts the court life with the relatively free-and-easy bour-geoisie, who 'usually deal with each other over far more specific and short-lived purposes. . . . The relationship comes quickly to an end if the material opportunities each offers to the other no longer seem favorable enough. . . . Permanent relationships are confined to private life.' That's the cosmopolitan pole. Realities give most of us in commer-cial cities something between the two. When trust among strangers and aliens breaks down in large commercial cities, insularity is no practical substitute for the loss. Many people flee such places if they can. It's serious; it's nothing less than the failure of commercial civilization, where trust among strangers and aliens is vital.

"Now I'm moving along to the precept *Compete*. Its most obvious direct link is with voluntary agreement, which presupposes choice. Effective choice demands competition. Choice is impossible, and voluntary agreement a sham, if one of the parties to the agreement holds a monopoly. I hope you're noticing, Jasper, how every precept in this syndrome links directly with other precepts, and indirectly with all of them. That's the clustering and overlapping I mentioned earlier. I emphasize, this isn't just a linear set of rules and values. Taken singly, the precepts are banal. But you can't reject them singly without devastating the syndrome as a whole.

"Competition also links with honesty and shunning force, because of the sheer costs of dishonesty and force. The sign on the door of my neighborhood supermarket says, SHOPLIFTING COSTS US ALL. That's true. The costs of shoplifting have to be figured into prices. I won't go on about that because we touched on it sufficiently, I think, while we were flailing around our first evening."

"But that must mean that, taken as a whole, a country with high crime and dishonesty rates suffers in international commercial competition," said Hortense thoughtfully.

"To be sure," said Kate, "although that wouldn't necessarily be the most important competitive factor. Probably not, but it figures in. I'll get back to more about competition later." Armbruster made a note.

"*Respect contracts* gives substance to voluntary agreement. That's obvious. But in my hasty dip into law, I gathered that contracts and contractual law somehow create individual rights; however, I'm still hazy about it."

"I can help clarify that," said Hortense.

"Please. I'm out of my depth."

"People doing commercial work need contracts, whether they're written or not," said Hortense. "They need assurance the courts will enforce contracts if need be—another honesty safeguard requiring guardian help—and will do so justly. 'Justly' means according to what the contract says."

"Not always," said Jasper. "Make a contract with a killer to murder somebody, or an arsonist to burn down a building, and it will not be enforceable by a court. Far from."

"Of course," said Hortense. "Actions in conflict with recognized public policy are not protected by contracts or the courts. That was a point Shakespeare made in *The Merchant of Venice*. To us, the chief oddity of the contract between Shylock and Antonio is that anyone would think for a moment of taking to court a contract demanding the forfeit of flesh from a defaulter.

"To get back to enforcement of an intrinsically legal contract: among other things, 'justly' means that nobody's rank or status permits him to terminate a lease on whim, evade a legitimate debt, welsh on a promise to deliver, withhold agreed-on wages, and so on. What the contract says is of the essence; the social status of the parties to it is irrelevant.

"Now picture this," she went on enthusiastically. "Picture a society where commercial need for contracts is growing but the law doesn't take that into account. Commercial contractual law is missing. In early medieval Europe, that was the situation. The established law courts—the courts of the guardians—were shaped by feudal law, which is the rule of rank, hierarchical law. So for a long time, hundreds of years, commercial people were pretty much on their own legally. They not only invented the kinds of contracts they needed; they also set up binding arbitration courts. You could say they were inventing their own guardians, to fill a gap. They built up precedents and the whole contraption was known as the Custom of Merchants.

"Admiralty law started the same way. Originally it was the rules and rulings sailors, shipowners, and merchants invented to deal with salvage rights, insurance on cargoes, liability for losses, and so on. Admiralty law's a delight. You can smell the salt air and feel the stormy waves. Matters like the tides and the seaworthiness of vessels skirting reefs come into adjudications. Admiralty lawyers travel a lot and know distant ports firsthand. I really wish that's what I'd gone into, but it's not welcoming to women.

"Eventually, admiralty and contractual law were absorbed into rulers' formal legal systems. Consulates have a similar history; they were first set up by merchants in cosmopolitan trading cities as a kind of home away from home, to give help when it was needed. It's now thought the Jews invented them and then other ethnic groups of foreign merchants took up the idea too. Eventually, states took them over."

"States aren't inventive, like commercial people," said Kate. "But I thought Rome had commercial law."

"It did. So did the Greeks. But you must understand that all ancient concepts of rights were connected to status. Rights were thought of as the by-products of duties, and duties were attached to status. For instance, the head of a Greek or Roman household had duties owed to that status; therefore he also had rights not possessed by other household members, nor by men who didn't head households. It was the same with other aspects of status, such as military rank, religious authority, slave ownership, citizenship, whatever. So, as biological, individual, natural creatures, people in ancient Greece and Rome had no rights. That was the feudal European concept, too. It's also the Confucian concept. The Roman commercial law you mentioned, Kate, was available only to people whose duties required it. Incidentally, it was called the Law of Foreigners, even when Romans themselves were using it. It omitted a lot of rigmarole and ritual attaching to noncommercial law. But it didn't introduce individual rights as we understand them in the tradition of commercial law we've inherited."

"I thought individual rights were natural rights," said Ben.

"That's the sort of fiction we call myth," said Hortense. "Useful symbolically. But as a practical matter, society confers or withholds rights. The medieval European Custom of Merchants let the genie of individual rights out of the bottle—or opened the Pandora's box of their nuisances and evils, as people who deplore individual rights would have it.

"The contractual law we inherited from those medieval merchants contained radical conceptions. Not only did it apply alike to all individuals, no matter who they were or what their social status might be, but it was available to individuals for no other reason than that they were individuals, making contracts. That second notion is so inseparable from our contractual law that we even have the fiction that a corporation is a person. That's so corporations, like individuals, can make contracts and carry on commercial life under protection of civil law. To realize how radical the Custom of Merchants was, we only need to think about some of the battles to extend the jurisdiction of contractual law.

"For instance, slaves lack rights as individuals. After slaves in the United States were freed, the Fourteenth Amendment to the Constitution theoretically gave them access to all the rights of individuals available under contractual law. But by custom, hierarchical law, the rule of rank, still prevailed, so freedmen and their descendants seldom enjoyed the benefits of contractual law. Every time a black homeowner was driven from his legally purchased house in a white neighborhood he was being treated as if hierarchical law, derived from social status, prevailed. Every time effective barriers were thrown up against black-owned businesses, and they were, more often than not, or against employment of qualified blacks, or they were excluded from labor unions and apprenticeships controlled by unions, it was as if contractual law did not exist for African Americans. As someone has said, even buying a loaf of bread is a contract. So is being served a meal in a restaurant. A bus ticket is a contract, but if you have to stand instead of sit because of your color, that's the rule of rank, not contract. So many of what we call civil rights are actually rights to make contracts as equals.

"A generation ago," Hortense continued indignantly, "large numbers of American women began to create businesses of their own. To their outrage and disbelief, many discovered they were blocked from signing commercial leases or borrowing commercial funds on their own responsibility. Banks and landlords demanded a male cosigner, usually a husband or father. By custom, sexism was excluding women from individual rights under contractual law. Another variety of sexism has often denied homosexuals the benefits of contractual law; those battles still continue.

"Neither rulers nor philosophers invented individual rights. Nor did nature invent them. Not Rousseau or Thomas Paine or Thomas Jefferson, much less the barons who extorted Magna Carta from King John on grounds of the rights their rank entitled them to. The strange idea of rights unconnected to status was what medieval serfs referred to when they said, 'City air makes free.' By getting to the city and subscribing to its extraordinary customs, they wiggled out of hierarchical law and into contractual law. I don't need to tell you individual rights still frighten many governments. They also frighten economic oligarchies. It's no wonder the very idea had to emerge outside of government—and even then as a by-product of other practical purposes."

"If you're still worried that your pair of syndromes is old hat, Kate, relax," said Armbruster. "You definitely won't find equal contractual law or individual rights in Plato."

Kate picked up a new sheaf of notes. "Contractual law allows ordinary people to *Use initiative and enterprise*—makes it feasible as a practical matter. Initiative and enterprise are highly esteemed in commercial life, as well they should be. Wherever commerce flourishes over extended time, new products and services keep entering trade. And so do new ways of producing, distributing, and communicating. These all require initiative and enterprise.

"We're into a big cluster of precepts now: *Be open to inventiveness and novelty, Be efficient, Promote comfort and convenience,* and *Dissent for the sake of the task.*

"All of these link directly and tightly with competition, which I said I'd get back to. Commercial life affords so many ways to compete. A company can build a successful commercial position upon efficient ways of producing. It can develop entirely new things to purvey, or significantly improve old things. Competing for customers—whether they are other producers or ultimate consumers—often entails promoting convenience and comfort for them.

"Elias, the sociologist of court life I mentioned earlier, notes that in prerevolutionary French cities the homes of established tradesmen, artisans, and merchants looked modest. But they incorporated more comforts and conveniences than the grand and ostentatious residences of aristocrats. Comforts and conveniences are quintessential bourgeois preoccupations, both for themselves and for customers. That preoccupation may perhaps provide the principal motor driving commercial life. It's the reason, for instance, that I have use of a clothes-washing machine, where the elves do the work for me, and the comfort of a hot shower.

"Ben, surely you recognize how many comforts and conveniences have become necessities, even for the ascetic likes of you: refrigeration, operating-room anesthetics, telephones, copying machines, computers, faxes, modems . . . or jumping back in time, how about printed books instead of scanty, expensive manuscripts, clocks and watches instead of hourglasses and sundials, warm gloves instead of chilblains—"

"You're cheating," Ben broke in. "You're pretending to be a cool observer but you're a special pleader. What about aerosol cans, what about forests felled for junky comic books full of violence, what about sealed windows that force energy-wasting air-conditioning in even the best weather, what about gas-guzzling cars, what about tobacco, what about wasteful, ostentatious packaging?"

"Touché," said Kate. "I got carried away because commercial preoccupation with comfort and conveniences down through the years means we aren't living lives of drudgery shivering in the rain with a hoe or beating out the laundry on a rock.

"The whole cluster of precepts I last mentioned demand *Dissent for the sake of the task.* We're so brainwashed into thinking of dissent only in political or philosophical terms. But consider that every single improvement in efficiency of production or distribution requires dissent from the way things were previously done. So does every new kind of material used in production. So does every innovative product—even the deplorable ones. Innumerable practical acts of dissent. Like individual rights, this is radical stuff—subversive of things as they are.

"Furthermore," Kate went on, "when this commercial type of dissent is successful, it is often quickly and obviously so. That can seldom be said of purely intellectual, spiritual, or ideological dissent, which is apt to be influential—when it's influential at all—on posterity rather than contemporaries. Dissent of both kinds takes wrong turnings. But when intellectual or ideological dissents are impractical, it can take breakdown after generations of turmoil, hardship, and conflict to demonstrate that fact.

"Now we come to another cluster: *Invest for productive purposes, Be industrious,* and *Be thrifty.* These are tightly linked with dissent, because changes in the way things are done commercially, and especially additions of new products or services into trade, demand productive investment. To be sure, just continuing in traditional ways requires some productive investment too, because tools wear out. But mere replacement costs are as nothing compared with the time, risk, and effort devoted to experimenting, and the costs of changed production or distribution or communication equipment. Making productive investments requires a surplus over current consumption—in other words, it requires thrift. And producing surpluses requires industriousness.

"Nobody wins esteem in commercial life by being an able-bodied idler or freeloader. Pity, maybe; moral esteem, no. But I think the harshness of the bourgeois attitude toward idlers goes deeper than the connection of industriousness with thrift and investment. It may be rooted in the fact that trade and production are viable only when people apply themselves in continuous effort, not sporadic fits and starts."

"Isn't that true of successful effort of any sort?" asked Armbruster.

"By no means," said Kate, "as we'll see when we look at the guardian moral syndrome." Armbruster made a note.

"Those three precepts, to be industrious, thrifty, and invest productively, compose a famous trio. Marx called them exploitation of the workers, profiteering, and unjust ownership of the means of production. Max Weber called them the Protestant work ethic, an unsatisfactory term, as he himself granted, because it's parochial and misleading."

"It's past lunchtime," said Armbruster. "You've touched on all your precepts except *Be optimistic.* That shouldn't be complicated."

"Not complicated, but superficially paradoxical. I think it's connected with fear of violence and dread of insecurity generally. Business people are forever trying to protect themselves from nasty surprises. They try to penetrate the future with forecasts, surveys, and voracious consumption of news. Newspapers began with what we now call their business sections. The earliest seems to have been a newsletter put out by the Fuggers, a German banking and mercantile family, to keep themselves and their clients well informed. The foundations of the family's banking enterprise, incidentally, were laid down by an early-fifteenth-century artisan, a weaver, who expanded from weaving into merchant trading and from trading into banking.

"Commercial people then and now take security measures with insurance policies, pledges of collateral, letters of credit from customers and bills of lading from suppliers, and so on. All that paperwork! The earliest writing, on clay tablets, seems to have been notations of how many jars of wine and cruets of oil were on hand, and seals laying out who they came from or what belonged to whom. So writing done by ordinary people for everyday life seems to have started with commercial accounting.

"Offhand, you'd expect obsession with security to be associated with pessimism, withdrawal, and fear of the future, maybe chronic, bitter suspicion of it. Certainly not anything as cheerful as optimism. But look at it this way. People who take practical steps to forestall surprise and misfortunes are, by definition, optimists. They aren't resigned to misfortune, they aren't fatalistic. Furthermore, the precautions are often successful. So they lead commercial people to assume that after a mistake or an unpreventable disaster there'll likely be a second chance or a third. It's not necessarily true. Commercial life is full of failures. But because the insurance money comes in, or the courts order redress, the second chances do work out often enough to sustain a comforting belief in the paper forts."

"Outrageous complacency," said Ben. "Meantime, the planet—"

"I'm with you about environmental complacency," Kate interrupted him. "But face the fact that commercial optimism, and the courage it gives to forge on, are much esteemed, and then think about the implications of that fact for strategies of environmental protection. As a generalization, people with a commercial cast of mind find it almost impossible to believe they're headed willy-nilly into irreversible environmental disaster. They can't believe there's no way out. It doesn't ring true emotionally. Instead, what does grab commercial people, emotionally as well as practically, is ingenious ways to forestall disaster.

That's why business papers these days are full of reports about recycling discarded tires into rubberized road pavements; de-inking newsprint to save pulpwood, and somebody's even newer invention that doesn't require de-inking; possible methods of storing solar heat so that electricity could be generated even in the dark; retaining tropical forests by emphasizing nut production and using them as sources of pharmaceutical and medical research—that sort of thing.

"When ingenuity is the approach to conserving resources and repairing past mistakes, at least you have commercial life and its powerful force of optimism working with you. You don't, simply by crying gloom and doom. Of course the ingenuities, unless they're merely wishful, demand initiative, invention, dissent, industriousness, thrift, productive investment, and the spurs of competition—in fact, the whole moral syndrome."

"Let's keep talking during lunch," said Armbruster. "I've a question for you right off, just wait a minute."

He restarted his coffee maker and put out plates and a pitcher of cider while Ben unwrapped a parcel of sprouts and dates, Hortense found a spoon for her yogurt, Kate pulled two peanut butter sandwiches from among news clippings in a manila envelope, and Jasper, to the accompaniment of oh's and ah's from the others, opened an elegant lacquered box of sushi and a small bottle of sake.

"Early on," said Armbruster, seating himself with an apple and a generous slice of Gouda, "you told us science belongs to this commercial syndrome, but you haven't referred to science since, except in some glancing references to technology. What did you have in mind when you said that?"

"We're always saying 'the arts and sciences,' at least in the university we are, as if they were twins. But they have different parentage and differ in many other important ways as well. For instance, the arts can flourish magnificently in cultures and subcultures with little commerce to speak of. They often have. Science, on the contrary, develops only feebly in a culture until trade and production have already been developing vigorously. Oh, I don't mean that science is absent in noncommercial societies, or that an impulse toward it isn't ancient, maybe even universal. Or at least as universal as curiosity. All the same, scientific investigation proliferates and scientific knowledge ramifies and accumulates as a sequel to flourishing commercial life."

"Does that mean we can expect the Japanese to become leaders in science?" asked Hortense.

"I think so," said Kate. "And probably Koreans, too."

"But why the connection?" Armbruster pressed.

"It's partly circumstantial. Trade, production, and the technologies they use stimulate all manner of scientific curiosity; simultaneously, inventive commercial life provides diversifying tools for pursuing the curiosity.

"But more important, science needs the same values and precepts as commerce. Honesty is the bedrock of science. Moral rules for research are: don't lie, don't deceive or cheat under any circumstances; if you're making reasoned guesses, say so and lay out your reasons.

"Voluntary agreement is the agreement that counts among scientists. Forced agreement to findings or conclusions is worse than useless. Science thrives on dissent for the sake of the task. Any theory is thus only provisionally true in science. It's understood that theories can't be proved; they can only be disproved. An accepted theory is merely one not yet proved false—and the possibility always exists that it may be.

"T. H. Huxley, Darwin's great defender, said, 'Science and her methods gave me a resting place independent of authority and tradition.' Obedience, adherence to tradition, and subservience to authority aren't morally esteemed in science. Instead, science is open to novelty. It's inventive. It demands initiative and enterprise. It is an unremittingly industrious occupation. Scientists believe, perhaps excessively, in investment for production of information at the expense of current consumption.

"As for thrift—it's interesting that a major tenet is what's called 'parsimony of explanation,' meaning the leanest and simplest explanation—the thriftiest—that accounts for the data is preferred over more extravagant, elaborate, or convoluted explanations. Of course that isn't literal thrift but it shows a cast of mind that values economy of means, and this cast of mind also rules good technology.

"Science requires and values easy collaboration with strangers and aliens—that's how scientists pool what they learn and build on one another's work. Like trade, this collaboration hops, skips, and jumps without regard to confinements of territory. In pre-modern Japan, men with an interest in science who dared associate on their own initiative with the occasional alien geographer or navigator who penetrated the realm—or even read and studied alien scientific thought and findings—were sometimes driven to suicide by social disapproval or were hunted down by the police. Cold war hawks here persecuted scientists suspected of associating with Communists. Exclusiveness and secrecy were even more treasured by the Soviet government, which didn't help Soviet science.

"Guardian values and rules, in their entirety, are so contradictory to the rules and values of science that it's worrying to see guardian assumptions creeping in as an accompaniment to government-dispensed research grants, which are now far and away the biggest sources for scientific research. Researchers sniff out what subjects and approaches will please the guardians and tailor their own interests accordingly. Worse, they neglect unexpected puzzles they encounter if delving into them won't be on the beam. This is serious because pursuing unexpected side issues has proved fruitful. The unanticipated discovery of penicillin's lethal effects on bacteria is a famous instance. Also, the value guardian grant-givers place on hierarchy becomes reflected in research laboratories themselves. He who can bring in the grants is king. Sometimes the guardian values are so blatant as to be stunning." She tapped a clipping. "In 1990, researchers at Stanford University who had received a grant from one of the agencies of the federal Department of Health and Human Services balked at an attached provision that barred them from publishing any of their preliminary findings without first obtaining permission from their federal grant officer, whose decision was to be final and binding on them. The department justified the provision on grounds that the findings might be erroneous or might have 'adverse effects on the federal agency.' Six days after the Stanford researchers refused to accede, the grant was withdrawn from them and awarded to researchers at St. Louis University Medical Center, who were more amenable.

"Stanford then sued the federal department on grounds that the demanded provision was unconstitutional. The judge of the U.S. District Court in Washington, where the case was heard, agreed. He said in his opinion that the provision was 'impermissibly vague,' and asked rhetorically what constitutes an adverse effect on a federal agency, and 'Who will decide whether the conclusions drawn by Stanford are erroneous—the non-scientist contracting officer?' Upholding the provision, he said, 'would be an invitation to government censorship wherever public funds flow.' "

"That seems to settle that," said Armbruster.

"Not necessarily," said Kate. "The department is so adamant in its wish for control and obedience that it's appealing the case. And there's that troubling loophole of 'impermissibly vague.' What if next time such a contract contains a lot of fine print to eliminate the vagueness? Or, more realistically perhaps, what if increasing numbers of researchers absorb the lesson that an 'understood' docility will be rewarded? The underlying trouble here is that guardian controllers of research funds either are not aware that the commercial moral syndrome guides science or, if they are aware, give short shrift to the integrity of that syndrome. It isn't the guardian syndrome they themselves work by, with its contradictory values of obedience, hierarchy, loyalty, and exclusiveness; also deceptiveness for the sake of the task, which in the case of the Department of Health and Human Services seems to include protecting the department's political, public relations, or other interests. Could be an interest in answers they've already settled upon and want the research to verify. That's all that a lot of people think science is good for.''

"I've a question," said Jasper. "How does religion come into your commercial syndrome? You did mention the Protestant work ethic.''

"She said it was an empty catchword," said Ben.

"No, no, not empty," said Kate. "What happened seems to me similar to what Hortense told us about medieval commercial practices' taking root and flourishing outside established law, then later being assimilated as civil law by the courts. In this case they were eventually assimilated into religious doctrines. You must realize, first, that in medieval Europe the Christian church forbade usury. It was a sin.''

"Usury is loan-sharking," said Ben. "Good thing to be down on, I'd say."

"That's our meaning of usury, but to medieval Christians usury meant lending money in return for interest, no matter what the rate. Gradually a few loopholes were condoned, the major one being that if a loan was put at serious risk—say, to finance a chancy venture like a trading voyage with its hazards of shipwreck and pirates—then interest could be justifiable as recompense for the risk of total loss. Other religions have forbidden lending at interest; to this day that remains Islamic doctrine, although in practice ample loopholes now exist, mainly under the concept that loans represent 'buying into' an enterprise, with interest rationalized as a share of its profits.

"In sixteenth-century Europe, some religious reformers, followers of Calvin especially, dissented from the church view of usury, as they did from many other points of church doctrine. Calvinism—the Dutch Reformed church and the Presbyterian church and its offshoots, including Congregationalism, the variety of Presbyterianism the Puritans brought to America—held that lending at interest was not only morally respectable but praiseworthy in the eyes of God.

"Furthermore, they held that wealth was the consequence of godly industry, thrift, and productive investment. Previously, possession of wealth had been theologically accounted for as a gift from God for His own inscrutable purposes, or alternatively as the Devil's doing.

"Thousands of Calvinist sermons and tracts drummed those reform ideas into Protestant flocks and extolled the benefits of wealth from productive investment, thrift, and industriousness, provided that some of the proceeds were given charitably for the work of the church and that the sin of avarice was avoided. A clergyman named Baxter strikes me as a champion killjoy but his published sermons were popular. He exhorted the righteous to 'keep up a high esteem of time and be every day more careful that you lose none of your time than you are that you lose none of your gold and silver. And if your recreations, dressings, feastings, idle talk, unprofitable company or sleep be any of them temptations to rob you of your time, accordingly heighten your watchfulness.'

"But the Calvinist divines had more congenial tidings, too. While they condemned waste of wealth on vainglory, luxury, and profligacy, they approved the use of riches for comfort. They urged a decent comfort of the home as praiseworthy. And all the Protestants weren't insanely extreme about industriousness. The ruling bodies of the Dutch Reformed and French Huguenot branches of Calvinism condemned excessive labor on grounds it robbed time and energy from the service of God. From time to time they even backtracked on the advisability of usury. Not all Protestant movements were as radical as the Calvinists, either. Luther and his followers didn't condone lending at interest."

"You're a long time getting around to Weber," said Jasper.

"Weber was trying to explain the remarkable success of northwestern Europe in commerce and industry. He proposed giving credit to what he called the Protestant work ethic. But here we get into knotty problems of cause and effect. Weber's critics soon pointed out that no place was more enthusiastically Calvinist than Scotland, where Presbyterianism had been enthroned as the state religion, and no population was more willing to endure sermonizing than the Scots. Yet Scotland remained poor and for the most part backward in commerce and industry. Critics also pointed out that Geneva, where Calvin had been based, was already—before his time—probably the most bourgeois city in Europe. The Dutch cities where Calvinism took root quickly and firmly had also anticipated Calvinists in their actual commercial practices. In sum, Weber's critics suggested he'd got things backward: that commercial ways shaped Calvinism, not the reverse. Weber himself then wavered on this point of cause and effect, which is a credit to his science-minded respect for dissent and to his own honesty.

"What happened, as I said, seems to be that religious reformers were catching up with existing commercial morality and legitimizing it. But that's not to say that Protestantism had no significant influence on commercial behavior, Scotland notwithstanding. Wherever commercial precepts and practices were strong, religious approval must have further reinforced them.

"Moreover, religion also concentrated on trying to prevent commercial greed from getting out of hand. The sin of avarice was expounded and excoriated. And once the Calvinists accepted commercial behavior as one facet of divine order, this influenced secular conceptions about the nobleness of mundane work and enterprise. For instance"—she dug among her notes—"Emerson said this: 'A man coins himself unto his labor, turns his day, his strength, his thought, his affections into some product which remains as the visible sign of his power.' Notice the commercial turn of phrase 'A man coins himself,' and along with it the spiritual tone of 'calling' and dedication. It's a far cry from saying bourgeois values are base or business is a racket."

"Let me give you a quote now," said Ben.

> "The golf links lie so near the mill
> That almost every day
> The laboring children can look out
> And see the men at play.

"How does child labor fit into this amazingly high-minded picture of yours? Or a guy condemned to turn the same five bolts over and over all his life on an assembly line?"

"One way they fit in is that both are now obsolete in commercially advanced societies," said Kate. "But your question does touch on an interesting paradox. The very industriousness of commercial life—of course, along with attention to productive investment, thrift, efficiency, comfort and convenience, dissent from traditional ways of doing things, and the rest of the moral syndrome—eats away at grinding drudgery.

Commercial life creates novel and enterprising ways of evading it, not only on assembly lines and in mills but in homes, too, and on farms.''

"You have given more thought to these precepts than I expected when you dropped them on us,'' said Jasper. "But your fixation on a pair of moral syndromes still troubles me. So arbitrary. If there are two independent sets of precepts, then why not three? Or for that matter, why not four, or seven?''

CHAPTER FOUR

Why
Two
Syndromes?

Y OU TELL us you found these precepts, Kate, and having been found
they obligingly resolved themselves into a pair,'' said Jasper. ''You
claim this is not your creation but enlightenment from higher authority—in this case, the facts of life. But dogmatists always believe they
have found higher authority of some sort when they are selecting and
arranging material to suit themselves. After you gloated over your tidy
pair, did it enter your mind to wonder why only two?''

Kate grinned. ''I was planning to tell you if you didn't ask. It's
probably my best idea. I think we have two distinct syndromes because
we have two distinct ways of making a living, no more and no less.''

''I'd have thought we had no end of ways,'' said Hortense. ''What
do you mean, only two?''

''Don't say only two,'' Kate replied. ''Two is lavish, extraordinary,
phenomenal, unprecedented. We're unique in having the two. All the
other animals have one only. Here, I'll lay it out for you.

''First, we're able to take what we want—simply take, depending,
of course, on what's available to be taken. That's what all other animals
do, including even some highly developed social ants, who capture
aphids to serve as milking herds, or beavers, who log to construct dams
and lodges, or wood rats, who collect and hoard baubles, or Norway
rats, who take voyages on ships from port to port.

"A band of hunters and gatherers in the wild, working their territory for what's available, would be the early human exponents of this way of getting a living.

"But in addition, we human beings are capable of trading—exchanging our goods and services for other goods and services, depending, again, on what's available, but in this case what's available for exchange rather than taking. Moreover, available for exchange by voluntary agreement, the essence of trading. A prototype might be a little open-air market where people lay out their wares in confidence they won't be seized by takers and then haggle and barter with customers.

"Of course, everybody doesn't have to make a living. Some people get by on gifts, charity, or inheritances. But that means somebody else worked up the wherewithal. How did they manage that? We're back to two ways of doing so—taking or trading."

"But did you search for other ways?" asked Jasper.

"Racked my brains. If you think of any, please tell me." She waited in silence, then ostentatiously drummed her fingers until Armbruster spoke up.

"I can't think of others. Apparently none of us can. But I wish you wouldn't look so smug."

"It might be pleasant or interesting or fruitful to have other ways," said Kate. "But I can't imagine what they would be. This is a given human condition, one of our many built-in limitations. To wish we had additional ways is like wishing we had additional eyes in the backs of our heads. We don't, and that's that."

"Got you now," said Jasper. "You're discounting ingenuity. It's done with mirrors."

"Only by ingeniously making do with the eyes nature gave us. Sure, we've built no end of ingenuities into trading and taking. But the fact remains, getting a living is built upon them. I've come to think of the two moral syndromes as survival systems, worked out by long experience with trading, on the one hand, and taking, on the other."

"If you're right," said Armbruster, "you've been systematizing a stratum of behavior that underlies what we conventionally accept as morality. Some of your precepts obviously correspond with legal or ethical views of right and wrong. Others don't. Yet you've put them all more or less on a par. I think that's what sticks in our craws, Kate. Or anyhow, it does in mine."

"Maybe the syndromes are existential morality, Armbruster," said

Kate. "That's rather what I mean by survival systems. I like your metaphor of a substratum."

"Morality under any name, pooh!" exclaimed Ben impatiently. "Both your syndromes are awful. One's greedy, penny-pinching, philistine, consumerist, and criminally heedless of the common good. The other looks to be cruel, ruthless, dishonest, and power-mad. Any good things in either one are spoiled by the bad. Can you prove you're right?"

"I just explained before lunch that theories can't be proved. They can only be disproved. It's the same with a hypothesis, a reasoned guess, which is what I've put forward. My hypothesis is that we have two contradictory ways of getting a living; therefore we have two contradictory moral syndromes, one to suit each way and its derivatives. You're welcome to shoot holes in this and disprove it."

"I can do that right off," said Ben. "You've ignored a third method, one that's not based on domination or on dog-eat-dog competition. It's based on the common good. I'm thinking of the system that's summed up by this principle: 'From each according to his abilities, and to each according to his needs!'"

"An elegant principle," said Armbruster, "but such a flop in practice: the Soviet Union, Yugoslavia, China, Cuba, Albania, Poland, East Germany, Bulgaria, Romania, Czechoslovakia, Tanzania, Nic—"

"That could be on account of bad leaders, bad luck, stupid planning, and vindictive embargoes by capitalist countries," Ben broke in.

"Everything's disappointing in practice, Armbruster," said Jasper. "What those countries had before they tried communism was plenty disappointing in practice."

"Furthermore, this third kind of morality does work," Ben resumed. "Look at the Israeli kibbutzim, for instance. All kibbutz property is held in common by the members of the community. And they stick to the principle that everybody contributes what he can and each gets what he needs and nobody is richer or poorer than the others and nobody holds the power. Doesn't that disprove your two ugly syndromes?"

"No," said Kate. "In fact, it's one more example of adherence to the commercial syndrome. Successful kibbutz communities are outstanding for industry and thrift. They plow capital back into their work. They pay close attention to serving customers honestly and efficiently and conveniently. They depend on voluntary agreements with customers and suppliers and they compete fairly and squarely with other enterprises. They respect contracts. They're inventive and open to new kinds of work—at least the successful ones are. Those that haven't attended to innovating are now failing or languishing in debt. How they differ from other kinds of commercial enterprises isn't by flouting the commercial moral syndrome. The community eliminates competition—but only among its own members—for prestige, goods, and power. It's much like a large, cohesive extended family with its own businesses in which all the members alike pull together for the good of the family and take care of one another. But in its way of getting a living for members, it takes the commercial syndrome very seriously, lives by it.''

''This kind of arrangement extends far back in time,'' said Hortense. ''Some convents and monasteries have had many of the same characteristics, and so have other self-supporting religious communities like the Shakers and Doukhobors. Also some of the socially radical producing communes that sprang up and flourished for a while in nineteenth-century America, and the idealistic producing communes set up in the 1960s, although they were mostly ephemeral.''

''Nests within the state, one and all,'' said Kate, ''without the responsibilities and functions of states, or even municipalities of any size. Your inference that they found a substitute or alternative for the guardian moral syndrome therefore doesn't wash, Ben, any better than your supposition that they were able to get a living by finding an alternative to the commercial syndrome.''

''What about Sweden, then?'' asked Ben. ''It's not a nest in a state; it's a state itself.''

''It's a welfare state,'' said Kate. ''Also not uncommon, although Sweden is unusually generous and complete in the social services it provides and its income redistributions. This is courtesy of government largesse, which, please note, Ben, is an item included in the guardian syndrome. The government gets its wherewithal directly and indirectly from the country's successful commercial life, which adheres to commercial precepts. In fact, it adheres to them so well that some of the biggest Swedish companies have now moved eighty percent or more of their production outside Sweden to keep down costs and so continue functioning. Very high taxes on business to support the largesse are part of the trouble; so is high labor turnover and chronic absenteeism, or that's what departing companies say.'' She dug around for a clipping. ''I wasn't going to bring this up until the time came to discuss largesse, but here's a sober report that says, 'There is no disputing the physical and

factual evidence that high-cost Sweden is an unattractive place to manu-
facture goods or start up new businesses. Nor is there any disputing the
disquiet this has caused.'

"Some Swedish civil servants may wish they could rule commerce by
command and control everything, but they don't. Take the forests.
They're mainly privately owned, and not by logging companies. Most
Swedish forest owners nowadays resist logging unless it's done exceed-
ingly carefully, if at all. They value the forests for aesthetic, recreational,
environmental, and ecological reasons, just like your PPOWW people,
Ben. But their conception of good territorial stewardship is at odds with
that of the government, which wants to promote logging to increase
timber exports, jobs, and tax yields, and mulls over methods for getting
its way by taking what it wants, either by forcing punitive taxes on
recalcitrant forest owners or offering special tax benefits—largesse—to
those that comply. Does this conflict about territorial stewardship sound
somewhat familiar, Ben?

"But we ought to save the question of the behavior of states until
we've examined the guardian syndrome. And now I have a confession
to make. I ran out of time before I could analyze all the guardian
precepts and the reasons for them, if any. I made pretty good headway
on a few, but only a few. From my point of view, it would be ideal if
one of you would collaborate with me. I could do the few items I've
already worked up, and give my notes and any preliminary thoughts on
others to whoever is willing to work on this. Hortense, would you like
to?"

"How about me?" asked Jasper.

"You, Jasper," exclaimed Kate. "I thought you considered it all
nonsense, no grounding in reality with its shades of gray instead of tidy
pairs, et cetera."

"I am still suspending judgment on that," said Jasper. "But I have
become interested in your technique. It is much like detective work. Be
amusing to try my hand at it. Besides," he added wickedly, "I can now
see that if I am going to find solid arguments for my position, I will have
to dig them out for myself. I warn you, collaboration with me may undo
your hypothesis."

"Fair enough," said Kate.

Ben groaned. "Kate got hooked by Armbruster with his bait of
constructing systems. Now she's hooked Jasper with the bait of playing
detective."

"We all have our preferred ways of constructing order," said Armbruster. "Very well. Either a disjointed or a collaborative report next, from Jasper and Kate. Four weeks from today? Same routine? But I'll supply lunch."

The subsequent small talk as they prepared to leave, picked up by the recorder, which Armbruster had forgotten to switch off, included a request from Ben to Hortense for a date to talk over a puzzling bit of environmental legal advice.

❖

CHAPTER FIVE

Jasper
and Kate
on the
Guardian Syndrome

JASPER, spreading out a neat fan of folders, briskly took the floor at the next session. *"Shun trading,"* he announced. "First precept and it is a puzzle. Had to assemble clues from across the years.

"In the days of chivalry a man was unfit for knighthood if he had a parent, grandparent, or great-grandparent on either side who had been a merchant or craftsman, 'in trade,' as they said. Shameful, base, contaminating. But why? The doings of craftsmen and merchants are so innocent compared with making wars, pillaging, extorting, persecuting, executing, censoring, holding prisoners for ransom, and monopolizing land at the expense of serfs, peons, or slaves—all honorable activities for people who would sooner have died than sink into trade.

"Not a quaint and passing fancy of medieval chivalry, either. A widespread attitude. So tenacious. As recently as the early nineteenth century a Polish aristocrat who dared meddle in trade was supposed to lose his rank and the landholdings and privileges that went with it. Same rule and same penalty held at the same time in Japan; independently arrived at, mind you, because Japan was closed to foreign ideas at the time and always had been except for ancient cultural acquisitions from China and Korea.

"Notice also that principled aloofness from trade is standard today in reigning royal families and not uncommon among tradition-minded gentry and aristocrats.'' He opened a blue folder and waved a news clipping. ''Here is a French marquis supporting himself and repairing and renovating his château from what he earns by renting it out for weddings and conferences. His wife does the catering. But they recoil from admitting they have a business. They say instead that they are promoting cultural events. What is more, the French government takes the distinction seriously. It gives the business a tax break, for being cultural, that it would not get for being commercial.

''Ben, I suspect you take it on faith that nonprofit activities are morally superior to profit-making commercial enterprises.'' He paused for a possible denial, which was not forthcoming. ''In some social circles, people are still at pains to distinguish inferior new money from superior old money cleansed of commercial taint by the passage of generations and time.''

''Snobbery!'' burst out Hortense. ''Sheer meanspirited snobbery. You find it laid out in no end of English novels, including modern ones.''

''It's not unknown in American novels,'' said Armbruster. ''Take Faulkner, with his flawed but honorable old families and his despicable commercial parvenus.''

''Any upper-class attitude has cachet, Hortense,'' Jasper resumed. ''But why was the attitude adopted by the people who gave it cachet? That question is at the heart of the puzzle. More than social snobbery is involved here. Judgments like *base, shameful, unfit, contaminating,* and *tainted* carry heavy moral freight.''

''It's hypocritical, too,'' said Hortense stubbornly. ''The richest man in England today, so it's said, is the Duke of Westminster because he's paid handsomely by tenants who make commercial use of his hereditary ducal landholdings in central London. It always was hypocritical. Those lords and gentlemen of yours, Jasper, they did selling, buying, and hiring. They sold grain and wool and animals from their lands, and coal from under them. They took rents from entire villages and market towns. They likely even leased out rights to hook salmon from their streams and shoot grouse in their scrubland, the way some of their descendants do today. Furthermore, they were big customers. They employed masons and artists and armorers and gamekeepers and falconers and servants of all kinds, and they were big buyers of foreign luxuries. What do you mean, they shunned trading? That was cant, not a description of realities.''

"Ah, arm's length!" said Jasper. "The important point was that they and their family members did not personally engage in buying and selling. Agents, stewards, and tenants did that and they absorbed the taint. Besides, they had the loophole of patronage. It was morally admirable to bestow or receive sinecures, livings, honoraria, pensions, and presents in return for services. All those counted as largesse, not as trade.

"Euphemisms and hypocrisy, if you like, Hortense, but euphemism and hypocrisy underline the puzzle. Why was plain, straightforward, direct trading dishonorable? This is not easy to winkle out. Historians and social observers have plenty to say about the attitude itself but not the reasons for it. They take it as a given—as if it were so natural it did not require explanation. Maddening."

"Maybe that's because they're guardian-minded themselves," said Hortense.

"Or because they don't have an answer," said Kate. "Few people are like Newton, who said to himself, 'Why is that?' when he saw the apple drop instead of sailing off. For most people, finding an answer, right or wrong, precedes recognizing that a valid question even exists."

"Which is likely the reason," said Hortense, "that so many parents think children's questions are not only tiresome but foolish when they don't have answers. 'Stop asking foolish questions!' "

"Be that as it may," said Jasper, "I could turn up only one speculation: that the trading taboo was a form of security against sieges or sanctions, the idea being that it made military sense for old-time aristocrats to have self-sufficient manors or fiefdoms instead of growing dependent on outside suppliers or customers. And of course economic self-sufficiency for military reasons has often been a policy of statesmen; there is that much to be said for the idea. But otherwise it is no good because it ignores too many clues."

"Such as?" asked Armbruster.

"For one thing, the trading taboo applied as stringently to landless knights or military freebooters as it did to aristocratic or noble families with landholdings. Also, it does not account plausibly for the deep moral power of the taboo. Does not explain why it went to the core of personal self-respect and honor. At most, it makes a case for trade being imprudent, not loathsome, and it would be as easy to argue that trading was prudent and sensible, which of course it often was—witness the loopholes of arm's length and patronage, as well as the poverty and weakness into which many backwater, relatively self-sufficient manors sank.''

"I take it you think you've a better speculation," said Armbruster. "Well, come out with it."

"I propose the taboo originated as a different type of military safeguard. Defense against treachery. Look at it this way. The hidden tunnel into the fortifications; the plan for the coming attack; information on a surprise tactic; the place hostages are hidden; discontents an enemy might cunningly cultivate if he knew of them; identification of a spy in the enemy's councils, a mole, as we say today; and so on. Warriors possess valuable military knowledge. Always have, still do. Even a corporal, or nowadays a cable clerk, can possess valuable secrets, but the higher a person's military rank, the more valuable can be his potentially damaging stock-in-trade, as a rule.

"So here is my first point. Trading secrets to the enemy is fundamentally like any trading. Both parties strike a bargain voluntarily for mutual benefit."

"You're talking about selling out," said Ben.

"Right, you've got it. We all know what selling out means. We all know it is base, shameful, tainted, contaminating.

"Now, here is my second point. In view of the danger, the personal disgrace of trading could not have been drummed in too thoroughly and early in the moral upbringing of children destined for military life. It is hard to think of a precaution more effective. Of course this is just my hypothesis, as Kate would say. But here is my third point. This practical and moral meaning of the taboo checks with its moral meaning in guardian work today. Nothing hypothetical about that."

"You mean for armed forces today?" asked Hortense.

"Yes, that. But even if war and preparations for war ever become obsolete, the precept to shun trading would still stand firm as a guardian virtue. Take something as unmilitary as building inspection by municipal governments. The commodity an inspector has for potential sale to a crooked contractor is impunity for mixing too little expensive cement with too much cheap sand, say. If the inspector sells out, we call it bribe taking and a breach of trust. But as between the two malefactors, we have a voluntary agreement for mutual benefit. Corrupt trading."

"That's one reason guardians themselves need guardians," Kate interrupted. "Supervisors and detectives inside government, of course, but also an alert citizenry and press, because guardian supervisors or detectives can also be corrupt themselves, or stupid."

"Impunity for wrongdoing is what a policeman has for potential sale," Jasper continued. "Or a judge, a customs officer, an environmental protection agent. Or take your kind of work, Hortense. A lawyer in private practice is free to accept any client she chooses and trade her advice, knowledge, and forensic skill for a fee. A respectable trading transaction. But as soon as that lawyer accepts an appointment to a regulatory agency, or wins election to a legislative post, the same kind of behavior, maybe even with one of her same old clients, converts to criminal bribe-taking.

"The precept to shun trading applies across the board in guardian work. And the only really effective defense is general moral respect for the precept—Armbruster's gossamer web again. Careful corrupt officials can slide through the danger of getting caught if they are satisfied with an IOU as payment. The IOU can be promise of a cushy commercial job after resignation from government service. Very hard to pin down that sort of bribe, that sort of trading.

"We have our modern versions of the old aristocratic arm's-length buffers," Jasper went on. "So some officials are forbidden to take a job in a business they have regulated, or a job lobbying former guardian colleagues, until a year or two has elapsed after they have left government service. Another modern arm's-length device is blind trusts for stocks, bonds, and real estate of officials who have important discretionary powers. Big potentials for selling out are built into the work of legislators, as we know because periodically the sellouts erupt as scandals. This is what your friend Stover got caught up in, Armbruster, when he unsuccessfully tried to arrange a cover-up for his corrupt congressman.

"Ferreting out and disgracing or jailing malefactors helps keep guardian sellouts in hand. But as I said, the bastion that really counts, and so is indispensable, is respect for the precept, respect strong enough to overcome temptation. When that is missing within any guardian institution taken as a whole, no legalistic approach can adequately substitute.

"Old-time Christian clergy used to dispense indulgences—spiritual impunity for wrongdoing—in return for donations to churches or other religious organizations. The donations were not for the personal benefit of clergymen, or were not supposed to be. All the same, even these buffered spiritual trades with rich sinners became such a scandal they undermined the church's moral authority. So during its counterreformation, the Roman Catholic church's response to the Protestant reformation, the church cracked down on the practice."

"Let me see if I have your argument straight," said Armbruster. "You tell us the precept to shun trading likely arose first in military life to make treachery unthinkable—even though it did occur, of course. You implied that since the same social groups both fought and ruled, the precept became entrenched in the general work of ruling and persisted as a moral safeguard against other forms of selling out."

Jasper nodded. "That is what I make of the clues. And I am adding that the good functional reason for the taboo got overlaid by social prejudices with no moral or functional content. But under the snobbery and other silliness, the original moral point was there all the same, and it is still there for virtuous people doing guardian work."

"Maybe another reason for the original taboo could have been to safeguard government property," said Hortense. "I'm reminded that four thousand years ago the Code of Hammurabi made a distinction between the property a Babylonian officer of the king held because of his official position and the property he owned privately. He was forbidden to trade in property that went with his position, or to shift its ownership to someone else in his family. But he was explicitly permitted to deal in his own property. No taboo or taint was attached to that, it seems."

"Like saying nowadays an officer can sell his own house or give it to his daughter," Kate suggested, "but not his housing on an army base. Or that a naval captain can buy and sell sailboats for himself but not the ship he commands."

"Or that a priest can't sell off the parish church or a chief of police put the police station up for sale and sink the money in a car dealership for his retirement," said Hortense. "What's interesting about such a law is that it was necessary. It must mean that a distinction so self-evident to us had to be sorted out once upon a time."

"What was the Babylonian penalty for ignoring the distinction?" asked Jasper. "Do you remember?"

"Yes, it wasn't so bad. The offending officer had to forfeit the money he'd gotten illegally. The really severe penalty, execution, was decreed for a governor or magistrate who took property belonging to a lower officer for himself or made money from hiring out his lower officers to anybody."

"Another temptation," said Jasper. "A guardian abusing the obedience owed him by underlings. We still run into that." He paused and looked at Ben. "I am kind of surprised you are not in government, Ben. Have you been, or ever thought about it?"

"You probably think I'd be happy working in an environmental protection agency. Wrong. For sure I wouldn't sell out. But half measures, bureaucratic time-wasting, oily press releases, expensive studies meant to delay action—no, all that doesn't appeal to me. I'd be interested only if real clout went with the job, real power for the fast, drastic improvements we've got to have. As it is, the pathetic progress isn't thanks to governments. It comes of uphill work exposing and pushing governments."

"You've anticipated the next precept, *Exert prowess,*" said Jasper. "It means having power and using it effectively. Prowess, by the way, was one of the four major virtues in the code of chivalry."

"What were the others?" asked Armbruster.

"Honor, loyalty, and largesse. 'Courtesie,' knowing your way around in court, was often elevated to a fifth. But there is more to be said about prowess. For knights, it meant bravery and skill in combat. That is still its meaning in the military. I do not need to remind you, in this terrible twentieth century, how much the military meaning of prowess continues to hold sway.

"In civil affairs, successful rulers and their regimes rely heavily on persuasion and custom to get their way. But notice, when persuasion fails, every effective government falls back on physical force. Do not pay your taxes and you can be slapped with punitive fines; then do not pay the fines and you can end in jail. A court of appeals is dignified and peaceful; right, Hortense? But get obstreperous, make even a small ruckus, and in a trice the physical force, the prowess, of the court marshals comes into play. Enforcement, backed up by the sheer physical power to prevail, is praiseworthy in guardian work. By definition, good government cannot be good if it is ineffectual, the point you made, Ben. We often overlook that fact when we concentrate on excessive recourses to physical force on the part of bad governments.

"Now Kate is going to take up the next couple of precepts."

"Prowess links directly with *obedience and discipline,*" said Kate. "Don't forget this is a syndrome, a collection of symptoms running together. Suppose you did have that government job, Ben, and suppose that after much debate and effort you had been armed with laws and effective enforcement policies and staffs to eliminate pollution by factories. But then suppose some of your inspectors began undercutting the policy, in this case not because they were corrupt but because they got to know some of the managers or their work forces, sympathized with their struggles to make a living, and eased up on harassing them. Would you want to put up with their personal conceptions of right and wrong, their moral beliefs in mercy and moderation, at the expense of bad air and poisoned water?''

"You're needling me. Of course not. We wouldn't have a program, we'd have a jungle.''

"Ah yes, jungle," said Kate, fishing around for a news clipping. "The very word used by a police inspector in this report. It tells of a policeman who refused his assignment to protect an abortion clinic and its staff and clients from interferences by antiabortion demonstrators. He was given a departmental police trial, convicted of insubordination, and dismissed from the force. Then he exercised his right to an appeal, the public proceeding reported here. He claimed he was conscientiously opposed to abortion and therefore had a constitutional right to refuse the duty. The inspector arguing for upholding his conviction said that when the man joined the force he surrendered his right to put conscience above obedience to orders, and added that if the police force didn't hold to that principle, the public wouldn't know what to expect from policemen. Policing would disintegrate, he said, into 'a state of anarchy, a jungle.' ''

"Obedience doesn't excuse crimes against humanity," said Hortense. "That was the point of the war trials against Nazis and later the trials of people like Eichmann. I think that proviso to obedience is fairly widely understood.''

"Perhaps that was the reasoning of this disobedient policeman if that's the way he viewed abortion," said Kate. "But in any case, this qualification to the guardian rule of obedience is seldom accepted in guardian practice. Ben thinks that denuding fragile watersheds is a crime against humanity and posterity, and I agree with him. More to the point, some policemen agree with us too. But you're living in a dreamworld if you think that will prevent police from arresting protestors obstructing government-authorized logging roads, when the police are given orders to make arrests. At most, all the protestors can hope for is that the police, if sympathetic to them, will be gentle in their use of physical force.

"I'm going to make only one point now about the precept to *Adhere to tradition* and come back to other points later. Tradition helps serve as a substitute for conscience in guardian work. That may be tradition's most important moral meaning. Normally, it sets limits to what's done. Adhering to tradition reassures a scrupulous or doubting recipient of orders who has no practical choice but to obey them. When guardian commands do flout tradition, they're at least apt to receive more than ordinary scrutiny and require more than ordinary justification. That's more true in peacetime, of course, than in war, when anything in the cause of victory, tradition be damned, is often acceptable. I suspect one reason revolutionary governments have become cruel so easily and swiftly after ascendancy is that they've lost the brakes of tradition. Throw tradition out and there goes its friction.''

"Why, that's exactly how precedent serves the law," said Hortense. "It's a brake. It helps protect us from arbitrariness and the whims and idiosyncracies of judges; juries, too.''

"Tradition perpetuates messes," Ben interrupted. "It's stultifying. It makes me sick to hear the two of you glorifying tradition. Remember the Bourbons, whose downfall came because they never learned anything and never forgot anything. Governments drag their feet instead of realizing they've got to change course. And when they say they will, their attachments to their cumbersome old bureaucratic—''

Kate interrupted him. "I hope you're remembering how different that is from vigorous commercial life, where dissents to how things have been done in the past are esteemed, and inventiveness and initiative are often richly rewarded, and flexibility and speed are ordinary. Last time, I mentioned some reasons that commerce needs help from guardians. The reverse is just as true, and not only because trade and production supply everyday necessities and pay taxes. Any country is stultified and backward if it lacks inventive, enterprising commercial life. You dwell on the trouble commerce makes, Ben, and you wish government would put everything right. But where else than from commerce can you get inventiveness and outflank traditional ways?'' Without waiting for an answer, she continued, "Tradition, prowess, and obedience all link tightly with the next precept.'' She gestured to Jasper, who took over.

"*Respect hierarchy*. It is the chief principle of organization for guardians," said Jasper. "Armed forces are the prototypical hierarchies: chains of command extending in formal, unbroken order from supreme commanders down through the officers and ranks to corporals and privates.

"By this time you may have noticed a motif. Guardian morals and values come largely—not entirely, but largely—from origins in the military. Kate and I were both struck by this. It was a suggestive clue I used when I was seeking the probable source of the trading taboo.

"Judges have hierarchies," he went on, "culminating upward in supreme courts. Government administrative agencies and departments are responsible to ministers, in turn responsible to heads of government."

"But that holds for commercial organizations too," protested Hortense. "Factory foremen give orders to workers and take orders from their own bosses, who report to their bosses, and so on, up to whoever's the chief executive. And unless he's the owner himself, he's responsible to a board of directors with a chairman, and the directors are supposed to be responsible to stockholders. What's so different?"

"Even in the case of a highly regimented business—"

"Regimented; acting like a regiment; military talk," put in Armbruster.

"Even a regimented business is no regiment," said Jasper. "It would be boring to plod through all the differences, but I will remind you of a few. Ambitious executives or skilled workers who find financial backing can quit and set up enterprises of their own."

"That's how most companies get their start," Kate interposed. "Their founders get experience in somebody else's company, then strike out independently."

"Guardians in real regiments cannot set up independent regiments of their own," Jasper went on. "In the rare instances when such a thing can be done, it is only because the government is disintegrating, and competing warlords or territories are trying to take over.

"Another thing, if the board of a commercial enterprise wants, it can sell off units to another commercial enterprise, or it can buy up formerly autonomous units. Often enough, it can set up joint ventures with foreigners on its own initiative, or move operations into foreign territories without involving the government and its hierarchies.

"But most important, Hortense, think about the huge numbers of small businesses in commercial life, not sharing a higher command structure among them. Of course these distinctions and differences do not apply to Marxist or other centrally planned economies, which actually do try to transfer the hierarchy principle into commercial life.

"Am I right, Hortense, in supposing that guardian work is ruled by rank and therefore by hierarchical law—instead of contractual law and its by-product of individual rights?"

"It depends. If governments want to, they can grant citizens or even aliens the right to sue officials as legal equals. In that case, government condescends to submit itself to contractual law. And the rule of rank within guardian organizations can be tempered with safeguards for individuals—like the right to a trial for insubordination and then the right to appeal—rights that disobedient policeman of Kate's had been given as an individual. But where hierarchical law, pure and simple, always prevails is when government pulls its superior rank vis-à-vis all the rest of society—"

"Begging your pardon, Hortense," said Armbruster. "I know what you have to say is valuable but I must own that long digressions on the law try my patience. Can you condense it?"

"I'll just say that in bankruptcy cases the tax man gets first crack at the assets instead of taking his place and proportion as an equal of the other creditors. Legislators in parliamentary sessions can safely make remarks for which they would otherwise be liable to slander or defamation suits. Under right of eminent domain, governments can take property for public purposes whether or not the owner prefers to sell, and the taking cancels the contractual rights of lessees. Eminent-domain powers also reflect hierarchical ranking among governments. Under our arrangements, a municipality can't block the taking of even its own property by its state or the federal government, and a state can't block taking by the federal government. Rule of rank. Also, consider impositions of martial law, military drafts, and the fact that in some jurisdictions where capital punishment has been abolished, an exception is made when a policeman is murdered while trying to carry out his duties. A cashier murdered while trying to carry out her duties isn't legally equal, as a victim, to the policeman, the guardian."

"What it amounts to then," said Kate, "is that hierarchical law reinforces prowess."

Opening a new folder and picking up a fresh sheet of notes, Jasper said, "If any single precept can be called key or central in guardian morality, it is *Be loyal.* Governments regard treason as the most wicked crime, bar none. Now I am quoting: 'The heinousness of the crime is worse than an individual murder. . . . It is the worst act that can be imagined.' That was the U.S. secretary of the navy, commenting in 1985 on a spy ring that sold navy secrets to the Soviet Union.

"During the reign of China's last imperial dynasty, conviction for treason meant that the offender was beheaded, and so were his male relatives over the age of fifteen, including sons, brothers, father, grandfather, paternal uncles and nephews, no matter where they lived or how little contact they had with the traitor. All other male relatives were beheaded too, no matter how remotely related, if they lived in his household. Female relatives were liable to slavery. Extreme stuff. If one wanted to research the most gruesome punishments devised—drawing and quartering, dragging on the ground behind horses, impaling, and so on—the task would be much simplified by concentrating upon penalties for treason.

"On the other hand, many stupidities and mistakes have been forgiven guardians whose loyalty is unimpeachable."

"That's how loyalty is looked at in political parties," said Hortense.

"Yes, political parties are guardian entities. So are organized religions, and of course they lay stress on unconditional loyalty to the faith. Political separatist movements are guardian outfits too. They are disloyal to the rule they want to cast off; but that is because of adherence to a rival loyalty.

"Machiavelli's famous advice to the Prince seems to cover many topics, and its ostensible theme is prowess, but its gist is loyalty: its indispensability to a successful prince. He dwells on it from every angle. How to deserve loyalty. How to win it, buy it, inculcate it, cultivate it, terrorize people into it. How to subvert loyalty to rival princes or states. How to sniff out disloyalty and deal with it. All his digressions lead back to loyalty. He is wistful about the loyalty of those free to withhold or bestow it. He sees that, uncynically, as the truly admirable but rare form of this virtue.

"Of course loyalty reinforces obedience, and vice versa, as Kate would remind you if I did not say it first. But obedience is a one-way street, while loyalty works in both directions. A superior is morally obliged to reciprocate the loyalty of underlings, at sacrifice to himself if necessary. The old precept for cavalry officers was: first see to the well-being of your horses, then your men, and only last to yourself. Furthermore, loyalty embodies a mystique transcending obedience— the mystique of unbreakable fraternity, unconditional comradeship. Bonds of loyalty thrive on shared adventure and success, but they also make fear and risk tolerable, and disappointment and tragedy endurable. Loyalty is a powerful comfort; it evens out differences in individual luck, strength, and competence because it makes pride in any individual the pride of all, instead of a source of envy and disruption.

"But here we confront another puzzle. Unbreakable loyalty does not seem to come naturally to us. It is like honesty in the commercial syndrome. Both are key virtues. Yet neither can be depended upon without constant inculcation and watchfulness. Children everywhere are indoctrinated with the righteousness and worthiness of their nation or empire, at considerable expense of truth. In our country, as you know from experience, kids recite a pledge of allegiance to the nation every school morning for years. In my school we began this in grade two and did it to grade eight. Stood up and said those same words more than a thousand times. If you are elected to office you take a loyalty oath. If you go into the armed forces you take a loyalty oath.

"Question: If loyalty must be so drummed in, how did this virtue arise within cultures in the first place? Kate gave me the clues I needed. Tell them, Kate."

"But I didn't know what to make of them," said Kate. "See if you can figure it out before Jasper gives you his answer. The first thing to notice is that armed men are dangerous to each other. As my grandmother used to say, 'When a boy gets a stick in his hands, his brains run out the other end of it.' To escape mayhem from each other, armed men need bonds so strong, so highly valued, so mystical that they aren't broken under pressure of greed, envy, jealousy, revenge, boredom, contempt for a commander's competence, or any other temptation to do in a brother-in-arms."

"You're talking about male bonding," said Armbruster. "The answer lies in what you've just said. Male bonding flourished during thousands and thousands, or rather hundreds of thousands, of years of hunting. Through natural selection it likely became both a deeply rooted resource and a profound emotional need of the human male psyche."

"Activities based on male bonding also afforded a way of escaping from women," said Hortense. "They still do."

"The hunting hypothesis is a nice try," said Jasper. "But it will not do. Brushes off contrary evidence. Go on, Kate."

"Offhand, it does seem plausible that men facing the perils of the hunt and depending on each other to win through would have every reason to develop and value a loyalty mystique. It's also plausible that this would be a useful survival trait for hunters. The same can be said, of course, about firefighters and policemen. I'm not disputing that people spontaneously rally round each other in times of peril, nor that they feel an exhilarating unity when they do exciting and important things together. That goes for men, women, and children. Ancient hunters probably felt so too.

"But loyalty has to extend further. It has to endure in humdrum periods and during intervals when cooperation makes few stirring demands, and it has to be strong enough to withstand contradictory pressures. Here's where the male bonding of hunters falls short. Hunter bonding seems to be fragile off duty. Take the !Kung people of the Kalahari desert. There aren't many of them, but the rate at which the men in !Kung hunting-and-gathering bands kill each other from rage or for other reasons of their own is nearly three times the homicide rate in the United States, and I don't need to remind you that the U.S. rate I'm comparing it with is likely the highest national rate in the world. The murder rate among Canadian Inuit—Eskimos—much exceeds the overall rate in Canada, and I'm not referring to the former necessity of leaving old people out on the ice when they couldn't hack it any longer. That wasn't murder; it was a consequence of the physical vigor that survival in the Arctic demanded in the old days. Inuit murders are now often blamed on alcohol, yet the rates were high when Europeans first came in contact with them and rage was the only befuddler.

"This is a pattern that runs through other hunting-and-gathering societies too," Kate continued. "Probably the most appalling is the small Gebusi society in a New Guinea rain forest. Their murder rate between 1940 and 1982 was almost ten times as high as the current Detroit homicide rate and more than fifty times as high as the current overall U.S. rate. Homicides of adult men and women, always by males, accounted for nearly one third of Gebusi deaths from all causes combined, which is remarkable considering that this is a population badly afflicted by fatal parasites and infections. Among Gebusi, a leading cause of murder is belief in sorcery. In four out of five cases, the victim was branded a sorcerer by the murderer. Superstition—or whatever rage or fear lies behind an accusation—has been far, far stronger than male bonding among Gebusi hunters."

"I can hardly believe what you're saying," said Ben. "It's well known that Bushmen and Inuit are peaceful, sharing, and egalitarian. They aren't corrupted by competition and power trips. They don't make war. So-called civilized people would do well to take them as models. Why are you slandering them?"

"The murderous Gebusi, too," said Kate. "Anthropologists characterized them as strikingly gentle, routinely sharing food among all, and reveling in togetherness and good humor. That was before anthropologists compiled and analyzed the forty-two-year span of homicides. Short anthropological field trips didn't show the homicide pattern. If you're shocked by what I report, Ben, you should see how shocked our students in cultural anthropology are at murder frequencies among hunters.

"But those admirable traits you mention—they're true also. The Kalahari !Kung are called 'the harmless people.' I don't know how many times I've seen television documentaries stressing that quality with never one word about murder. A feature film, *The Gods Must Be Crazy,* depicted them as gentle to a fault. These fictions, and I'm including the documentaries among the fictions, tell more about our own longings for Eden than they do about !Kung hunters.

"How did they get a reputation for gentleness and harmlessness?" Kate went on. "Partly, of course, because they're harmless to us. But largely because they are unaggressive in any organized ways, unlike us. The !Kung and other groups I mentioned are totally unwarlike, and they lack hierarchies, along with cults of discipline and obedience. Those very lacks are among the qualities anthropologists and audiences have found so attractive."

"Now you have the clues," said Jasper. "What do you make of them?"

"I hate to say it," said Hortense, "but does this mean that if men aren't killing each other in warfare, they're programmed to kill each other anyhow, for other reasons?"

"No, no, no," said Jasper. "You are proposing a law of inverse ratios between warfare and homicide. There is no evidence of such a relationship that I know of, and much evidence to the contrary. For instance, Denmark and Switzerland are not warlike nations, but their homicide rates are remarkably low.

"We'll dispense with more bad guesses. Notice, as Kate said, that the !Kung, the Inuit, and the Gebusi are not aggressive in an organized fashion, apart from hunting, on which they've managed to survive for a long, long time. If it is correct that male bonding and unbreakable loyalty derive from the perils of the hunt, just such hunting peoples should display those traits par excellence. But they do not, so we must ask the source and the nature of loyalty as soldiers understand it, other citizens, too.

"To me, it seems a good guess that the same organizations that gave us hierarchies, obedience, discipline, and centralized authority—all of which the !Kung and the others conspicuously lack—also gave us unbreakable loyalty as an ideal moral quality.

"Look at the question from a practical viewpoint. When organized warfare developed, commanders must have learned pretty rapidly that they had to suppress murders and assaults among their own troops. And do not forget that random personal motives and superstitions are not the only reasons for murders by armed men. Family blood feuds and vendettas, too, still common in some rural and village societies. But no successful military force can countenance feuds among men recruited from different families, clans, villages. Willy-nilly, they must become a band of brothers. The bonding and loyalty cult was most necessary where it was hardest to come by—but also where discipline could be most iron, and indoctrination could best prevail.

"I propose that the virtue of loyalty within armed forces extended thereafter to other guardian concerns associated with conquest or protection of territory, and to all derivatives of guardian work taken generally. As Machiavelli understood so well, the indispensability of loyalty infuses all the work of ruling and its derivatives. It is a moral buttress against all manner of guardian betrayals, military or not. It is not for nothing that officials swear fealty to a constitution or a crown."

"Don't forget we're dealing with a syndrome," said Kate. "If other guardian precepts in the syndrome break down, then loyalty converts from virtue to vice. I mean that when a police force goes corrupt, takes bribes, or when a guardian cabal is bent on subverting a constitution, the ranks close against outsiders, loyally protecting wrongdoers and stonewalling honest men. Without direction from the rest of the syndrome, loyalty corrupts. It is a two-edged sword."

Jasper picked up from Kate again. "*Take vengeance.* The drive to retaliate packs enormous emotional power. It seems to come naturally to us, unlike loyalty and honesty. No need to inculcate it in children; on the contrary, it has to be tamed in them. It is forever ready to erupt. Whole populations cry out for vengeance for injuries, or even insults, to individuals they do not know but with whom they identify emotionally. If we want to be gloomy about this, we can call ourselves the vengeful animals. We put a nicer light on it by saying we are the animals that love justice.

"Privately exacted vengeance has an old tradition—witness the blood feuds I mentioned. In some cultures, specific penalties in fines or blood have been prescribed for specific private injuries, yet enforcement has been left to the injured parties. So the question is: How and why did guardians monopolize vengeance? Another puzzle."

"Oh, Jasper, you're so roundabout," said Hortense. "It's the social contract. Citizens surrender their use of force, including vengeance, for the benefits of civil peace."

"Really?" asked Jasper. "And when and by whom was this social contract made?"

"We have constitutions. They're social contracts."

"Constitutions already take for granted the state's monopoly of force, including vengeance," Jasper replied. "They take it so much for granted they typically try to hedge the state in so it doesn't abuse its monopoly."

"Well, in some medieval cities—I should think you'd have run across this, Kate—the commune, the municipality, made every new immigrant agree to surrender personal use of force, leave it to the commune. If he wouldn't agree or broke the contract he was expelled from the city. Sometimes the medieval church made analogous agreements with parishioners in the interests of what was called the Peace of God. Of course there are social contracts, covering just the point you're laboring."

"In all those cases, the monopoly was already assumed or established. Live by it, or be expelled or excommunicated, people were told. G. N. Clark, an English historian, puts the situation well. He calls the idea of a social contract intellectually attractive because it seems to reconcile the need for obedience to government with the desirable condition that government should rest on consent of the governed. But he points out that any such contract, if it existed, could not be between equals, and dismisses what he calls the halfhearted efforts of some old writers to find an ancient historical origin for a social contract. Halfhearted because no evidence exists. He calls the social contract symbolic fiction. You should understand that, Hortense, after explaining that natural rights are symbolic fiction."

"The social contract is an excellent metaphor," Armbruster interjected.

"But I am not dealing in metaphors," said Jasper loftily. "The vengeance monopoly is fact. I look for a factual origin. I could not dig one up and neither could Kate."

"So you and Clark and his ilk are resolved to deprive us of our metaphor, but supply nothing in its place. Disappointing," said Armbruster.

"No answers are better than false answers," said Jasper. "At least they do not contribute obfuscation. But cheer up, Armbruster. I have a deduction for you, built on my prior deduction concerning loyalty in armed forces.

"First point: remember that monopolizing vengeance also means taking responsibility for doing justice. Second point: among armed troops forbidden to wreak private vengeance, some substitute is necessary to deal with soldiers who do, in fact, inflict injuries on brother soldiers."

"You mean," asked Hortense, "a court-martial works better than a soldier and his buddies seeking their revenge on another soldier or officer? But that contradicts dueling."

"Not really. Rulers have typically come down hard on dueling, outlawed it over and over. Even in the short and infrequent periods when they have countenanced it, permission extended only to officers and gentlemen and was usually a privilege of aristocrats—guardians themselves. Of course some men dueled illegally regardless, the same as some vengefully engaged in lynchings. All the more reason to suppose that a vengeance monopoly could originate only in a context of iron discipline, obedience, and hierarchy.

"So I am proposing as a hypothesis that the monopoly originated as a necessity in organized military units and extended, no doubt in fits and starts, into a generalized guardian monopoly. Partly to impose order among contentious subjects, but also to suppress threats to rulers' powers to rule.

"Here is a modern example of just such a threat. A witness to a murder here in New York identified the killer and was scheduled to give his testimony in court. But before the trial took place, he was slain by an unknown gunman. The accused murderer was acquitted for lack of identification. A deputy chief in the district attorney's office said that, next thing, hundreds of witnesses scheduled to testify in other criminal trials 'walked into our office asking what we could do to protect them from such a fate. How many witnesses we lost that way, it is impossible to estimate.' "

"That problem is why the FBI has devised its elaborate witness-protection program," put in Hortense. "It's especially necessary for witnesses in organized-crime cases."

"My point here is that such measures are not only for protection of witnesses," said Jasper. "They are, at bottom, protection of guardian rule—to prevent authority from becoming a sick joke. I will give the last word on this subject to Francis Bacon. He said, 'Revenge is a kind of wild justice, which the more man's nature runs to, the more ought law to weed it out.' ''

Closing his vengeance folder and selecting another, Jasper said, ''Now here is a precept that really can be traced back to hunting life: *Deceive for the sake of the task.* Hunters, both animal and human, try to deceive prey; in the most rudimentary forms of deception they lurk in wait, well hidden, or stalk silently. Add to these the human ingenuities of hidden snares, baited traps, decoys, noise calculated to create panic, and so on.

''On the high prairie in the Canadian province of Alberta is a museum called Smashed-in-the-Head Buffalo Jump. A visitor stands at the foot of a natural rock ledge running through the building, and confronts, above his head, a cluster of huge beasts, frozen at the instant they are about to plunge over the brink. Terrifying. Frantic, doomed, magnificent, pitiful. Other exhibits stir awe for the Indian buffalo hunters, so cunning, so courageous. They would mark out lanes on the plateau behind the ledge, as if with dotted lines, using clumps of buffalo dung, stones, and brush. When the moment to start the death drive arrived, boys wearing coyote pelts howled at the fringes of dispersed groups of grazing buffalo, impelling the groups to draw closer together so the 'coyotes' could herd them into a lane. In the meantime, other boys wearing buffalo-calf pelts bleated near the 'jump' end of the lane. That impelled the deluded mass of animals to rush forward to protect them. With the prairie-wolf howls at their rear and flanks and the calf bleats to their fore, the herd stampeded to its doom.

''Coyote and calf skins are skimpy. Buffalo do not have good eyesight, but even so, these were masquerades for boys, not grown men. This particular jump, Smashed-in-the-Head, memorializes a boy in calf dress who was caught in the onrush and swept over.''

''Which did you identify with?'' asked Kate curiously. ''The buffalo or the hunters?''

''At the time, alternately both. But in retrospect, to be honest, I suppose I identify with the museum's designers and with the descendants of those hunters who staff the museum.

''Hunters' tricks, this one or others, were not meant to fool one another. They were deceptions for the sake of the joint task. It is the same with warriors. They use ambushes, decoys, inducements to panic, all the hunting tricks and more, to supplement brute prowess, but not to fool comrades. It is the same with police, stalking criminals.

''Here is an odd little modern example of hunters becoming the hunted. I like it, although as a good citizen, I suppose I should not. Thieves had set traps to steal money from three or four street phone booths in a well-heeled section of Manhattan—very close to this apartment, Armbruster. They might well have victimized you. Customers complained to police that they could not retrieve returned coins because the chute was filled with 'something disgusting.' The police, camouflaged in plain clothes, of course, staked out the phone booths and caught a gang of little boys. They had filled their money-traps with egg white. One explained to police, 'The thing is, I know what's in the chute and the customer doesn't.' "

"The kids should've kept moving their traps," said Ben enthusiastically, then looked embarrassed.

"The principles of virtuous guardian deception are these," Jasper went on. "It must not be aimed at other members of the organization. That is disloyalty. And unlike the phone-booth trick, it must be for the sake of carrying out a guardian task, the way the plainclothes police in that instance were using deception. If those two conditions are met, guardian deception is esteemed.

"Eavesdropping, reading other people's mail without their permission, double-crossing them after you have cultivated their trust, taking advantage of their weaknesses—this is shameful behavior in the ordinary course. But for spies, this behavior is virtuous, even heroic. An ability to prevaricate cunningly is no disgrace in a diplomat. It is a job qualification. A blatant lie by a head of state in the national interest is customarily considered justifiable, and if it is successful, he is likely to be admired for it."

"If it flops, he's criticized or derided for lying," said Kate.

"I accept your point about the police and spies and military affairs," Ben put in, "but how about bureaucrats, who have no business being deceptive? It's the very devil to get them to admit to abuses, or even plain honest mistakes. They hide what goes on. They give phony explanations."

"Most guardian tasks in modern democratic societies carry no legitimate reasons for deception," said Jasper. "The job of most bureaucracies is to serve the public openly and aboveboard. Deceiving it is thus disloyal. Those people you speak of, Ben, are loyal, but they have narrowed their loyalty to an agency, a department, even a coterie or clique, at the expense of the loyalty they owe the body politic.

"Basically the same trouble intrudes whenever a head of state takes to deceiving his own people. That is disloyalty to them, in favor of narrower loyalties to party, coteries, or his own interests. Illegitimate lies by a ruler to his own people, Kate, are the lies that earn derision and contempt.

"Keeping guardian deception in hand has much in common with keeping commercial dishonesty in hand, although illegitimate guardian deception is, if anything, harder to suppress than commercial dishonesty. Even legitimate deception can so easily ooze into gulling those one has no right to deceive, and into self-deception, too. Guardians entrusted with deceptive tasks ought rightly to have a nicer moral sense than the common run, and be more than commonly clearheaded about their responsibilities and themselves. But the work does not necessarily attract sterling characters."

Armbruster sighed and looked at his copy of the guardian syndrome. "Good. Something more cheerful now, I see."

"*Make rich use of leisure.* I'm doing this one," said Kate. "It's another precept that can be traced back to hunting life. Hunting isn't a continuous, unremitting activity like most commercial work. It's sporadic, demanding intense and energetic bursts of concentration and energy. Men in contemporary hunting-and-gathering bands have enormous leisure by our standards. So do the women foragers. In a !Kung band studied, for instance, adults hunted or gathered only during three days a week on average, and the children didn't work at all, though they do in some bands.

"What do hunters and gatherers do with their abundant leisure? Laurens van der Post and Jane Taylor dug into this question years ago, while studying a group of southern African Bushmen. Van der Post had the advantage of having known some of the band from the time he was a small child, although the group still remained almost untouched by outside influences at the time he and Taylor studied it. Band members were spending extravagant blocks of time etching and then coloring intricate designs on ostrich-egg shells and making gorgeous, complicated necklaces from bits of shell. They told and retold stories endlessly. They played games, dressed up in costumes, and chanted. They drummed and clapped out elaborate rhythms. Their forefathers had decorated cliffs with myriad drawings and paintings of the preferred local prey, the eland. The band had lost this leisure activity because it had lost the territory containing the cliffs. However, one elder was still able to demonstrate how the difficult rock art had been done.

"These people weren't engaging in any of these activities to make their livings, the way designers, craftsmen, artists, artisans, or performers in trade do. Nor were they receiving patronage—even from one another. This was art for art's sake in the purest form.

"But only for art's sake? Glenn Gray, in his book *The Warriors,* comments on soldiers who become killers for sheer pleasure. He says this infinitely dangerous impulse is ordinarily countered not only by other impulses in the soldier's nature but also by the fact that combat is episodic. In that respect it's like hunting life.

"Let's suppose for a moment that back in prehistoric times some hunting bands didn't keep their work sporadic—or, to use Gray's word, episodic. Suppose they went in for unremitting killing for the gratification of it or because they didn't know what else to do with themselves. A poor policy for survival, since they'd have exterminated their food supplies to no economic purpose. By definition, successful hunting bands have a conservation ethic. They confine their activities to their needs."

"I like that," said Ben.

"But sensible as this approach is," Kate went on, "a hazard is built into it. People with time on their hands can molder in sloth and boredom; an unpleasant way to live, also guaranteed to let capabilities and energies deteriorate. A way of getting around this is to take on demanding noneconomic activities. Maybe the first string music came from the twanged bow of an idle hunter. Maybe the first bit of oral literature or drama was the tale, told at leisure, of yesterday's chase. We owe to extremely ancient forebears the very ideas of painting and decoration, the very concept of games, sports, and performances as recreation, and the practice of serious religious rituals, too."

"This is novel," said Armbruster. "You seem to argue that angels find work for idle hands. It goes against the folk wisdom."

"The folk wisdom's correct that as a species, we seem to have low tolerance for boredom," said Kate. "But the sour doctrine that idleness is a playground for the devil belongs to the commercial syndrome with its esteem for industriousness. Often enough, of course, the sour doctrine is true. As Benjamin Franklin observed of a construction work crew he was supervising on the Pennsylvania frontier in 1755, when the 'men are employ'd they are best contented. For on the days they worked they were good natur'd but on idle days they were mutinous and quarrelsome, finding fault . . . and in continual ill-humour.'

"The contradictory guardian syndrome welcomes frolic and esteems the Muses. Think about the flowering of arts and sports among the knightly and noble classes in the heyday of European chivalry: the tournaments, the brilliantly colored tents and pavilions, the fanciful heraldic blazonings, the pageantry, the splendid cathedrals and the splendor of the rites that brought holiness into their soaring spaces; the resounding genealogical recitals, the heroic epics and sagas, the tapestries worked by nobly born women, the costumes, the jesters, the love of secular and sacred songs and instrumental music. All this was savored by people who despised commercial occupations and ways.

"Think also about the long aristocratic tradition of the amateur with time on his hands exerting himself strenuously for sheer love of a sport, an art, or a field of learning—not for economic gain. Think about royal and aristocratic patronage of artists, musicians, writers, opera, and theater, continued by many democratic governments today. And even today, most team sports and board games playfully formalize struggles for territory, the great preoccupation of warriors and other guardians.

"Heralds had the duty of keeping score sheets of blows given and received during knightly tournaments and inspecting the arms of those who took part, like modern umpires. But they also had the duty of verifying from genealogical records that each contestant was sufficiently genteel, without taint of trading. This cult of the amateur, this suspicion of the professional athlete who sells his skill, has only very recently broken down. And we still do make distinctions between amateur and professional teams. We also make distinctions, or try to, between unsullied fine and folk art and the inferior versions implied in the terms 'commercial art' and 'commercialized art.'

"Although I've been speaking of European tradition, much the same has been true in the Orient. Chinese and Japanese warriors and rulers cultivated their leisure and appreciated recreations and refined arts even more wholeheartedly, if anything, than their European counterparts."

"This is a mite farfetched," said Armbruster. "I grant the truth of what you say with respect to historic times, but your argument that the arts originate in the conservation ethic of primitive hunters is a bit hard to swallow."

"Let me give you an analogy," said Kate. "Physical evolution presents us with what Stephen Jay Gould calls 'co-opted epiphenomena.' That mouthful means that many physical organs had early uses different from those of their evolved derivatives. That may be true of most organs. Examples would be fish fins co-opted into reptilian legs; reptilian jawbones co-opted into mammalian inner-ear bones; toenails co-opted into hoofs. Gould suggests that incipient wings, which couldn't yet power flight, may have had earlier usefulness for regulating body heat in the fashion that elephants' big flappy ears do now. Elephants aren't going to fly, because any given co-opted epiphenomenon must have other appropriate physical developments working along with it, such as the light, hollow bones flying birds possess and their weight-saving treatment of body wastes.

"Another thing about surprising potentialities: Gould points out that our brains weren't being used to do higher mathematics at the time they were developing. Yet they did have that potentiality.

"Co-opting occurs culturally, too. For instance, radio, used for urgent messages, has been co-opted for entertainment and filling time; walls, devised for shelter, have been co-opted into also giving views of the outdoors, courtesy of glass, which in turn has been co-opted from beads and vials. Wheels for moving loads have been co-opted into running clocks. Surprising potentialities—culture is rife with them. I'm arguing that in the case of art itself, a phenomenon exploited for one purpose contained other potentialities.

"But please notice, because this is important, the old hunters' morality of sporadic hunting still remains vital for human survival. Think what happens when armed forces like the Khmer Rouge in Cambodia go in for unremitting killing, whether for pleasure, ideology, or because they don't know what else to do with themselves. Or think how Nazi Germany organized its death camps, making an efficient, industrious, factorylike business of murder and genocide. We wonder and shudder at a work ethic of producing and storing nerve gas sufficient to obliterate life many times over. These are examples of behavior that conforms neither to the intact guardian syndrome nor the intact commercial syndrome. This is behavior that picks and chooses precepts from both syndromes, creating monstrous moral hybrids. Now, next—"

"Wait!" Armbruster exclaimed. "Don't go so fast, Kate. What you've just said sounds crucial to me. War is hell, we all know that, but you're telling us that when warriors pick up industriousness from the commercial syndrome, they plumb still-deeper circles of hell. By monstrous moral hybrids, do you mean organizations that, instead of sticking to their own syndrome, take whatever they choose from either—mixing the two moral systems together? Would the same apply to other kinds of organizations and institutions besides armed forces?"

"Bound to," said Kate. "You can't mix up such contradictory moral syndromes without opening up moral abysses and producing all kinds of functional messes. Now, a point about technologies—"

"Wait, wait!" exclaimed Armbruster again. "Wouldn't you call guardians who go in for trading and therefore succumb to conflicts of interest moral hybrids too? And commercial oligarchies that set up military dictators to suppress writers and editors who tell nasty truths about the oligarchies, and that persecute and kill protestors against them? Or commercial people who resort to force in other ways, for other reasons? Those are only a few of the wretched possibilities open to syndrome hybridizing. I think we should follow this up, Kate. It's crucial."

"I agree," said Kate. "It needs following up. But please, let's not just flail around, as you once said. I'm paying attention to your rule about thinking systematically. For now, I want to make a point about cross-use of technologies, as distinguished from cross-use of morals. The difference is important.

"Commercial technologies are continually being absorbed into the arts—maybe always have been for as long as there were commercial technologies. Look how artists took to decorating utilitarian pots long ago, for instance. Look how the arts make use of printing, electronics, film. And in turn, commerce assimilates technologies from art, like plating with precious metals, and from amateur hobbies, like solar heating and organic farming and model making. But in principle this is no different from restaurants putting doormen into eye-catching shakos, or government offices being equipped with electric lights and copying machines. If the shako-wearing doorman is there to advertise the place and amuse customers, that's one thing. If he's there to intimidate or rough up unwelcome customers, that's quite another. In other words, cross-uses of technologies or their products, per se, don't strike at the moral nature of activities; but cross-uses of moral precepts do."

"But if the arts derive from guardian life, where does artistic originality come into culture?" asked Armbruster. "You've left originality out of the guardian syndrome, and put in its opposite, tradition."

"Not I," said Kate. "I mean it wasn't I who made the decision. I recorded what I found to be esteemed. But to respond to your question: both the fine and the folk arts are infused with tradition. Competitive games are too. Originality diffuses gradually into the arts as a rule, small bits at a time. Artists of great originality customarily work within a matrix or context of tradition. To pull out an exalted example, Shake-

speare, for one. They discern new potentialities within familiar phenomena. Even in politically revolutionary regimes, art remains astonishingly
traditional; the art and other design that followed American separation
from the British Empire, and the French Revolution, too, harked all the
way back to classical times for inspiration. Marxist revolutions have been
death on artistic originality. Even modern painting took much of its
inspiration from traditional arts, especially exotic primitives. Originality
in the most radical sense, meaning art that deliberately rejects and
jettisons tradition, is rare and usually transitory—paradoxically, quickly
dated, like so much of modern architecture.

"When originality within a matrix of tradition does speed up, it
seems usually to be associated, like science, with prior notable development of commercial life. Late Greek sculpture is different in sensibility
from archaic Greek works; connoisseurs today, with no stake in fashion
after the passage of so many centuries, regard the later, less traditional,
sculpture as inferior.

"In Renaissance Holland, when commercial subject matter emerged
in painting—burghers, comfortable bourgeois interiors, markets, city
and town street scenes—this was very radical. Prosperous commercial
people had become patrons of art themselves. But it's interesting that
many of these radical painters still turned their hands to the traditional
religious, mythological, and classical subjects as well.

"But I'm no art critic, these are snippets I've noticed in passing, and
I want to get back to my point—the usefulness of rich appreciation of
leisure in the guardian syndrome. Even when the leisure affords nothing
more glorious than a policemen's ball or the roistering of soldiers and
sailors on leave, it reinforces loyalty. And of course arts and recreations
of all kinds—literature, dance, music, painting, sculpture, tragedy,
comedy, slapstick, holiday feasts and customs, monumental architecture, rituals of celebration, supplication, mourning, and victory—they
all give body, give human and cultural meaning, to territorial loyalties,
meanings that geography alone, no matter how dear the geography,
can't satisfy.

"This leads me into *Be ostentatious*." She looked apprehensively at
Ben, who did not disappoint her.

"Gross! You're going too far now. Nobody esteems braggarts.
You've confused esteem with envy, which is well known to be a sin."

Before Kate could reply, Armbruster broke in. "Let me field this
one. I'm getting the hang of your distinctions, Kate. Ben's thinking of
personal boasting. You're thinking of impersonal guardian display."

Kate nodded. "Virtuous guardian ostentation isn't self-indulgent, like ostentation on the part of individual consumers or rich commercial companies that go overboard throwing their money around. To be sure, when it's divorced from other moral purposes, even guardians reduce ostentation to sheer silliness—witness Mrs. Marcos's shoe wardrobe.

"Ostentation at its most naked, as in military shows, parades prowess and is calculated to evoke awe, fear, or reassurance. But in most guises, guardian ostentation is somewhat subtler. It expresses pride, tradition, continuity, stability. Think of the rich paneling and high ceilings of important courtrooms, approached by wide flights of marble stairs—"

"Where the quality of justice dispensed may or may not be miserable and in any case isn't produced by the marble," said Ben.

"To be sure, trappings aren't substance. But those trappings reinforce respect for law and government, as the ostentation of churches or temples does for spiritual traditions and worship. Modern capitols, much like old royal or ducal palaces, or like cathedrals, make statements about hierarchy as well—how firmly established authority is, how dignified, how impregnable, how worthy of obedience and loyalty. Governments also use ostentation to impress other governments—for instance, the pomp trotted out for state visits and the ostentatious parties embassies throw. Self-constituted guardians, exposing or protesting acts of official guardians, or seeking to swell their memberships, muster what ostentation they can with posters, parades, and eye-catching gimmicks.

"Official guardian ostentation links back tightly with tradition, which I said I'd return to. Ostentatious tradition is highly visible continuity with the past; it thus also implies continuity with the future, therefore stability and security. Guardians treasure symbols of tradition to the point of adoring them—flags, anthems, solemn days of remembrance—and tirelessly cultivate veneration for the symbols throughout their territories. They're also devoted to traditional procedures, such as elaborate diplomatic protocol, fixed and ancient courtroom practices, archives, forms prescribed for memoranda, hearings, approvals. And of course the procedures help substitute for individual conscience, as I mentioned."

"Substitute for wisdom!" said Ben bitterly.

"There are no substitutes for wisdom, either in commerce or guardianship," said Kate. "Without wisdom everything limps along or breaks down. But wisdom is a complex quality, a combination of common sense, foresight, judgment, awareness, and moral courage. Paragons of these combined virtues, even when they exist, aren't necessarily in the right places at the right times. Most societies have learned from experience to pool individuals with the object of contriving group wisdom: elders, councils, boards, cabinets, juries, appeal tribunals, parliaments. That's a wise tradition in itself, especially for guardians, considering how stupid, vicious, and even insane rulers can be when they consult only their own conceptions of wisdom.''

"It would now be wise for us to have lunch," said Armbruster. "I order it unilaterally, without advice or vote." The centerpiece he whisked in and unveiled with the air of a conjuror was a large and dazzling platter of sushi. He augmented it with sake and mineral water, a salad with sprouts, a bowl of yogurt salad dressing, and a plate of peanut butter cookies.

"You paid attention to all of us!" Kate giggled.

"Shall we continue while we eat?" asked Jasper. "Appropriately, the moment has come for *Dispense largesse.*"

"Are you using that as a quaint term for charity?" asked Ben.

"By no means," Jasper replied. "True charity has only the well-being of its recipients as its aim, like this splendid lunch. Largesse often masquerades as charity, but it's not the same.

"Largesse is the guardian form of investment: specifically, investment in power, influence, and control. Back when Henry Kissinger was secretary of state, he announced a policy of cutting back aid to poor nations if they voted against positions taken by the United States in the United Nations Assembly. He made it clear that the cutbacks would include food and other humanitarian relief. He was so openly ruthless in this instance because he wanted the mere threat of withdrawing largesse to accomplish his political purpose.

"The art of dispensing serious largesse," Jasper went on, "is the art of calculating just who in a domestic population or a client state needs persuading, placating, or threatening at a given time. Largesse can win elections. Even the promise of it can win elections.

"In days of chivalry, when largesse was deemed one among the four greatest knightly virtues, feudal commanders and dignitaries had control of vast wealth, for their times, but they had entirely different uses for it than as productive investment for the commerce they thought so contemptible. Commercially productive investment was not then, and is not now, the object of guardian largesse. To be sure, it sometimes masquerades as productive investment. Projects we call pork barrels are largesse in commercial masquerade.''

"Goodness, you make it sound so mean and manipulative," said Hortense. "After all, welfare—"

"Largesse manipulates," said Jasper. "That is its object. However, the consequences are not always ugly. Nor does it always represent waste of capital, according to a broad view of waste and gain. Largesse, when used astutely, can not only buy loyalty, as Machiavelli understood so well; it can buy a measure of contentment and tranquility—territorial aims not to be sneered at. Commercial criteria of productive investment are irrelevant for much territorial well-being: for instance, the health of a population, or help when disasters like floods, earthquakes, or unemployment strike. Largesse can finance desirable territorial amenities, such as preservation of historical treasures, say, or natural wonders; and it upsets many of us if we sense that traditional objects of largesse, like those, are being commercialized.

"Even if we were to discount all power-driven uses of largesse— although in reality we cannot—it is impossible to imagine governing a territory either badly or well without falling back on largesse. It is a powerful instrument for shaping the world, well or badly. All funds in guardian hands tend to be dictated by exigencies of largesse, even when their initial goals are intended to serve development of commerce. That is why government 'economic development' projects so quickly convert to pork-barrel projects for political purposes, the world over. That is why government insurance schemes—unlike commercial insurance, which must be supported by premiums or else go broke—sooner or later tend to become largesse and draw upon general tax yields or government borrowing.

"But of course largesse, unlike commercial productive investment, is not a primary means of enlarging material wealth. Rather it is distributive. What it distributes depends upon guardian extraction of taxes, tribute, or plunder—in our scheme of things, taxes."

"I associate the word with Robin Hood's good works," said Hortense.

"Sure, if Robin Hood and his bandits had merely taken and taken and had not distributed some of the take as largesse, he would not have enjoyed enthusiastic local protection for long, we may be sure. In Sherwood Forest and its environs the rich involuntarily provided Robin Hood's wherewithal. The poor got the largesse. This is such a popular and appealing arrangement, it has been the policy of innumerable Robin Hoods, down to our own day. Even the most flagrant robbers of the poor for the benefit of the rich—like the Marcos regime in the Philippines—typically make a show of their largesse to the needy.''

"Robin Hood may not have been a real person,'' said Armbruster. "Some scholars trace him into pagan Saxon myth and say that his story, as we have it, may have symbolized English guerrilla resistance to the Norman conquerors and their collaborators.''

"Symbolic fiction or not,'' said Hortense, "we seem to need him. Other cultures have their Robin Hoods. I've read that Japan does. One of them, Benzuiin Chobei, a seventeenth-century figure, was famed for defending the weak and standing up to the powerful, and he's been adopted as patron saint and namesake of a Japanese gang of organized criminals. They point out that he recruited his band from social outcasts, with whom the modern gang identifies.''

"One last point about largesse distributed by established authority,'' said Jasper, consulting his notes. "It creates dependency, as both Machiavelli and Kissinger understood well. But a historian of Ireland has made this comment about the use of largesse by English overlords there: 'Dependency enjoined at once conformity and defiance. Conformity was necessary for survival; defiance was necessary for self-regard.' That last is something Kissinger may not have understood.''

"Is there a connection between largesse and religious bans against usury, do you think?'' asked Hortense.

"The task of state religions is to protect their territories spiritually,'' Jasper answered. "That is guardian work. The traditional sources of religious income are donations and taxes or taxlike levies such as tithes. Even though many religious institutions nowadays do go in for business or investments that yield interest, the tradition persists. You have surely noticed that small items like candles, postcards, or pamphlets are not for sale in churches. Instead, a 'donation' is requested. I once had the deuce of a time getting an Irish sexton who had offered me a tour of a Dublin cathedral to name what he thought was a reasonable fee for the trouble he had taken. He obviously wanted something, because he spoke repeatedly of the cathedral's need for funds, but he would not name a tour charge. He would say only that a 'donation' would be welcome.''

"I had exactly that trouble with the Presbyterian clergyman who officiated at my wedding,'' said Armbruster with a reminiscent smile. "My bride told me that supplying the wedding ring and paying the clergyman were my responsibilities. Her family was assuming other wedding expenses. After the ceremony, which took place in my bride's family home, I took the minister aside and asked what I owed him. No fee, he said, adding that a donation was customary. How much? He wouldn't give me a clue.''

"What did you do?'' asked Hortense.

"Mental arithmetic. I calculated, from my weekly pay rate at the time, what I was earning per day, guessed a half day's pay would be reasonable, a full day's generous, and decided to be grand. Since my gaucherie was embarrassing, I never went further into the subject and still don't know whether I paid him too much or too little. He was gracious.''

"Church incomes pay operating expenses,'' said Jasper, "but surpluses have traditionally been used for charity, ostentation, and propagation of the faith. It would follow from this that lending was perverse. I deduce that religious establishments, sticking by the guardian syndrome, rationalized that what was right for them was right for all. The wonder is that Calvinism dissented from that. Notice that Calvinist clergy retained the guardian traditions for themselves; they continued to solicit donations and use surpluses for charity, moderate ostentation, and missions to spread the faith, but until recent times seldom for commercial investment.''

"Their modern sorties into commerce are usually justified as ways of augmenting funds for charity,'' said Armbruster. "Even so they often plunge clergy and congregations into controversy.''

"This is a notion, and a wild one,'' Kate put in, "since we know so little about the dim, ancient origins of territorial religions. Perhaps largesse originated as a religious practice, patronage, too, and was imitated by other guardian institutions. That might explain why largesse achieved its high reputation for virtuousness.''

"It's refreshing to hear you speculate that largesse wasn't invented by the military,'' said Armbruster.

"But of course military commanders, especially in occupying forces, do have largesse at their disposal,'' said Jasper. "Police, too, for persuading and rewarding informers.''

"Rich commercial companies consider largesse virtuous,'' said Hortense. "They preen themselves on sponsoring sports events, public service television programs, foundations, and the arts.''

"The line between commercial largesse and commercial advertising is blurry,'' said Armbruster.

"You can say that again,'' exclaimed Ben. "It slays me when I see some notorious polluter or oil-spiller taking credit for a documentary on the environment. Look how cigarette companies sponsor athletics so health will rub off on them. Hypocrisy! Camouflage!''

"That's too sweeping, Ben," said Armbruster. "But it's true, commercial companies aren't shy about advertising their good works."

"Distributing largesse is alien to Japanese commercial culture. There is no word for 'philanthropy' in Japanese," said Jasper. "It seems to have mystified Japanese companies when they found it was expected of them in America, also Europe. Lately they've taken it up. A Mitsubishi executive with experience running a factory in North Carolina has explained to his countrymen what he makes of the practice, and I doubt American or European executives would disagree. I'll quote him. 'Philanthropic activities are important to the corporate identity, and from a long-term perspective they are linked with enhancing the corporate image.' Of course guardian largesse is an old story in Japan."

"Why don't they lower prices instead?" Ben grumbled. "Why don't they leave customers with more money, to make donations of their own? And leave taxpayers with more too? Make it easier to fight logging companies and support other movements."

"I take it the next precept, *Be exclusive,* contradicts the commercial ideal of collaborating easily with strangers and aliens," said Armbruster.

"So it does," said Jasper. "It has links with loyalty and with deception for the sake of the task. Remember Fawn Hall, Oliver North's secretary, during the televised congressional investigation of the Iran-contra affair? She claimed that when she shredded documents or hurriedly made off with them tucked in her brassiere, she was protecting 'the initiative.' Protecting it from whom? one of her questioners asked, pointing out that the FBI wanted the documents, not the KGB. Our guys, not their guys. She seemed baffled, but finally blurted out, 'Everybody.'

"That is exclusiveness taken to its extreme. Exclusiveness likely originated in the armed forces."

"It might have come out of older cults, Jasper," said Kate. "Like hunters' initiations of boys into manhood."

"Maybe, but what we do know is that organized military forces set their members conspicuously apart from the rest of society with uniforms, special insignia, special manners such as salutes, special traditions—in all of which no one else is permitted to share. Citizen armies take these on like professional armies. Of course guerrillas and terrorists do not, since they want to move through society like fish in the water, as Mao put it. But they are superexclusive about those they admit to their secrets and organizations. They have to be, for survival.

"Clergy often use special garbs and customs and styles of life, setting them exclusively apart. Present-day Catholic nuns have abandoned their archaic habits precisely so they can collaborate more easily and naturally with lay people."

He selected a clipping. "An American reporter in Poland, while it was still under Communist rule, interviewed a former aristocrat, bred to guardianship but now excluded from guardian circles. The reporter asked if he recognized others like himself. Yes, said the former aristocrat. 'We all have exactly the same habits, starting with the way we eat.' "

"Sounds like the British upper-class old-boy network," said Armbruster. "The answer, in that case, might have been 'starting with the way we speak.' That galled George Bernard Shaw, you may remember, who attacked this as a mark of exclusiveness in *Pygmalion*."

"In the time of chivalry," Jasper went on, "exclusiveness was so well recognized a guardian virtue that 'courtesie' was deemed indispensable for knights and other members of the guardian classes. It meant knowing what is done and what is not done in court, that is, in ruling circles. Seems such a triviality until you think, in terms of power, about the distinction between 'us' and 'them.' The ostentation of top power-holders has often emphasized exclusiveness, expressed it in establishments like Buckingham Palace, the Kremlin, the old Forbidden City of Peking, or, for that matter, the White House.

"Now that governments have taken on so much mundane work, and their functionaries have become intimately involved with fishermen and their problems, the unemployed, trade commissions, and so on, and their bureaucracies have such vast numbers of employees, and now that the most exalted positions are open to folk of humble origins, we might suppose guardian exclusiveness to be worn thin. In some ways it is. But as Fawn Hall informed us, it keeps surfacing. Nowadays fears of terrorists and assassinations encourage it. Guardian exclusiveness is likely on the rise in our times, after a period of decline."

"Yes, it's incredible now to recall that the public was permitted to traipse through the White House on weekday mornings for a look at the state reception rooms and the exhibits of presidential china and first ladies' clothing in the basement," said Armbruster. "I was taken there as a boy by a schoolteacher. A holiday junket. You just lined up, no questions asked about who you were or where you were from. It's equally incredible to think of a president leading a group of diplomats on an impromptu hike through a public city park, the way Theodore Roosevelt did in Rock Creek Park—a jaunt that culminated in a spur-of-the-moment skinny-dip in the creek after they outdistanced the Secret Service contingent plodding behind.''

"Exclusiveness is another two-edged sword," said Jasper. "Those old Bourbons, Ben, became so insular and culturally inbred they got out of touch. That was their trouble, more than their love for tradition.

"Now for *Show fortitude.* Accept hardship with uncomplaining stoicism.''

"Wait a minute," said Hortense. "Isn't that at odds with guardian exclusiveness? I'm thinking about the exclusive shops for Soviet guardians where they could get luxuries, comforts, and quick service."

"Those perks of guardian power were kept inconspicuous," said Jasper, "because they conflicted so blatantly with the fortitude being demanded of everyone else. That's why the comparatively rich and easy official life became such a scandal with *glasnost.* Exclusiveness of officials was expected and acceptable. But disregard of fortitude was not.

"Fortitude has obvious roots in military life. It is greatly esteemed in police forces, and for clergy, too."

"And for people running in elections," said Hortense. "So grueling. And they can't whine or show weakness. Remember that Maine candidate for the presidential nomination? I was a young girl at the time. When opponents cast aspersions on his wife, he wept in public. I thought it endearing of him. But it put him out of the running."

"Heroes are esteemed, among other things, for fortitude," said Kate. "National heroes, mythical heroes, religious heroes; they aren't diverted from heroic duty by the easy life. Or if they are, they swiftly mend their ways and redeem themselves."

"*Be fatalistic* links with fortitude," said Jasper. "Fatalism is useful, and maybe necessary, for people in highly chancy pursuits like warfare, police work, and even running for election. Incidentally, fatalism often encourages superstition. That may be another reason why science makes little headway in noncommercial cultures."

"Superstitions aren't always so dumb," said Ben. "Hunting people who throw the bones before a hunt to tell them which direction to go—they have better luck than hunters who choose a direction because it was successful last time. Somebody made a comparison. Random choices—which is what the bones give—prevent overhunting in some parts of the territory and give better results over the long run.''

"Sports players are great ones for lucky charms, gestures, garments, and so on,'' said Hortense. "They really believe in them. My own sons—one had a horseshoe he touched before games and the other kept an old red sock in his pocket. I think they still do it. I always laughed at them but I could see it helped; it gave them self-confidence.''

"Whoever compared the hunters was employing scientific curiosity and scientific methods,'' said Kate. "So were psychologists who saw a rational connection, the way you did, Hortense, between charms and confidence, rather than charms and luck. Science is interested in superstition. But superstition isn't interested in science.

"Jasper's left *Treasure honor* to me,'' Kate continued. "I put it last in the syndrome because it's such a catchall. What does 'honor' mean? It's not honesty, with which it's often vulgarly confused. 'On my word of honor' can solemnize almost anything, including a promise to cover up the truth, or to lie if pressed. Even children know that. 'Honor among thieves' is not an oxymoron.

"Traditionally, when applied to a woman, it meant chastity, including the appearance of chastity. Appearance was as important as the fact, if not more so. When it was applied to a gentleman it could mean, among other things, that he paid his gambling debts promptly at all costs. Now consider what, if anything, the following have in common: the members of a monarch's annual honors list; students in a high school honors course; recipients of honorable discharges, honoraria, honorary degrees, and honorable mentions in competitions; bearers of honorifics such as the Honorable Member, the Honorable Penelope So-and-so, daughter of a titled aristocrat; an honorary chairman; and His Honor, the mayor?

"It comes clear once we recognize what dictionaries themselves tell us. Honor is recognition of status and the respect owed to status. It's much the same as 'face' in China.

"Here is the crux, for either honor or face. The respect is owed, and the self-respect earned, because honor implies moral obligations, and its possession certifies that the obligations attached to a position—whatever they may be—are admirably fulfilled.

"The concept of honor arose in the guardian life and has always been taken most seriously there. When the guardian life is lived honorably and responsibly, constant sacrifices are expected in service to duty. That's especially true in the higher ranks of guardians. I'm not thinking now of passing up opportunities to make money. That's obvious. I'm thinking of forfeiting freedom to associate with whomever one pleases, freedom to air personal opinions openly if they conflict with policy, and, often enough, freedom to speak the simple truth; also forfeiting easy and casual privacy except through the difficult stratagem of being incognito.''

Hortense stared at Kate openmouthed, then sputtered, ''But you're putting things backward, Kate! Those are fetters authoritarian and totalitarian rulers fasten on other people! Deny them freedom of association, speech, truth telling! Invade their privacy!''

''It's analogous, in a way, to the medieval church's forbidding lending at interest,'' said Kate. ''Obliviousness to the other syndrome. Authoritarian and totalitarian rulers don't recognize what I've been harping on from the beginning. They act on the premise that what's right for guardians is right for everybody. Such a mistake.''

''As great a mistake,'' said Jasper, ''as the one commercial people make when they suppose governments should be run like businesses. That ends our joint report.'' He and Kate gathered up their notes. ''I trust you did not find it a disjointed report, Armbruster?''

''No, and I'm curious why not.''

CHAPTER SIX

Trading, Taking, and Monstrous Hybrids

Aᴿᴹᴮᴿᵁˢᵀᴱᴿ clinked his ice for attention as they settled down after a late-afternoon break. "Jasper, what happened to your skepticism? How come you've embraced a syndromal pair? Second, you're our expert on crime but we're getting no enlightenment from your expertise. For instance, how does organized crime fit into this scheme? Or doesn't it?"

"I will take up your last question first. Organized crime fits in as one of those monstrous hybrids of the two syndromes, to use Kate's phrase. The Mafia will stand as my illustration because it is the form of organized crime I know most about. But whether by imitation of the Mafia or by independent invention, other durable and successful organized-crime outfits share the Mafia's moral—or I should say, immoral—structure. This includes the Colombian drug lords, the Neapolitan Camorra, the Hong Kong crime associations now preying on North American Chinatowns, the internationally operating Corsican gangs, or, for that matter, the fearsome, well-established street and housing-project gangs in Chicago and Los Angeles, the two cities where indigenous American youth gangs seem best rooted.

"According to the Mafia's own lore of its origins, the organization began an unspecified number of centuries ago in Sicily as a grass-roots defense against alien conquerors. That may be a romantic tale to boost self-regard. The Mafia could as plausibly have started as auxiliaries in the service of overlords. It became that—often hand in glove with oppressive Sicilian landowners. In World War Two, following determined campaigns against it by Italian police under Mussolini, it got a new lease on life in Sicily by ably and willingly serving the U.S. occupation army.

"In any case, the Mafia bears ample marks of guardian moral provenance: Prowess—the Mafia's reliance on physical force, or threat of it, to get its way. That's why it is so dangerous to cross. Respect for hierarchy—the Mafia 'families' have their soldiers, their capos, or captains, their consiglieres, or councillors, their dons, and in alliances among families, their dons of all dons. The families know as much about loyalty as Machiavelli himself—how to deserve it, buy it, subvert it, terrorize people into it, sniff out disloyalty, penalize it. Execution is the penalty for treason. *Omerta,* the law of silence, is the law of unconditional loyal mutual support against outsiders. The Mafia venerates tradition and rituals. It is exclusive and inbred. It dispenses largesse; that is the 'godfather' side of dons. It thrives on deceit for the sake of its operations. It makes a cult of fortitude. It employs ostentation—shows of conspicuous force or wealth to impress henchmen, rivals, and people it seeks to subvert.

"To the Mafia, the drudgery and industriousness of honest work is for poor slobs. Its members richly enjoy galas and go in for a lot of them. I was once witness to a Mafia convention of two families in an expensive Caribbean resort. The most interesting feature was how they carried on business in the midst of their play. The two dons, after conferring at a beachside table, stationed themselves separately out in chest-deep ocean water. There each summoned subordinates, one at a time, and conversed with them. In the ocean waves they could not be bugged.

"Like other crime groups, the Mafia has not surrendered its right to vengeance. When members cannot escape jail they accept it fatalistically, like the possibility of violent death. Honor is very important. The higher a member, the touchier his honor. Affront to a don's honor is unforgivable. From away back, they have called their outfit the Honored Society, and their 'made men,' their ritually inducted inner circles, are Men of Honor.

"They are preoccupied with control of territory and its exploitation. Their rivalries and internal wars concern rights to territories; so do their alliances.

"Where the Mafia most resembles legitimate guardians and differs from other crime groups is in its protection of city or suburban neigh-borhoods where important members live. No random robberies by outsiders occur in tight Mafia neighborhoods; no purse snatchings, even; and no neighborhood robberies or other rough stuff by the Mafia either. No drug sales to young people in those neighborhoods. The penalty for transgressions is quick execution. Paradoxically, a tight Mafia neighbor-hood is a wonderfully safe place to live as long as you remain incurious why.

"But that is all that can be said for the Mafia as guardians. Otherwise, they use their guardian morals only for self-aggrandizement and self-protection, nothing else. They use prowess for those purposes, unfet-tered by law or even decent humanity. A friend of mine, a photographer, prepared a portfolio on life in Little Italy here in Manhat-tan at a time when artists were moving into the neighborhood—at-tracted by its safety and low rents. Among the scenes he photographed was a Mafia clubhouse that used the cover of a storefront. That night he received an anonymous phone call demanding he destroy the films of that location and the sidewalks near it. He brushed this off by saying he alone exercised control over his work."

"The Mafia didn't want the location of the clubhouse revealed?" asked Hortense.

"It just looked like any nondescript, down-at-the-heel store, and my friend had not realized himself it was a clubhouse. That he found out later. Apparently the objection was about certain people his camera had picked up. Evidently two men in particular, according to his caller. The Mafia tries to keep pictures of certain personnel out of all records.

"The following day, my friend received another call in the early morning and a second one in the evening, each more menacing, to which he responded with indignation. Then about a week later came the call in the middle of the night. Same voice, but this time no allusion to the pictures. Instead, an expressionless recitation of the daily schedules of my friend's three children: at what time in the morning, on which corner, his little daughter waited for her school bus; the route by which she came home; the playground where his two boys played softball, on which days; the store where they bought candy and chewing gum, and so on. At the end of a long, thorough account, the voice said, 'You understand,' and the phone went dead. My friend understood. He destroyed the negatives and prints. Telling me about it even a year later, he sounded chilled and shaken."

"Why didn't he go to the police?" asked Ben.

"He had no confidence the police could protect his children. For how long? And from any sort of contrived 'accident'? He was also afraid that the first people to know he had gone to the police might be his hounders. How did he know they had not infiltrated the police—as they probably had? The Mafia gets its way by illegal and corrupt uses of prowess.

"The Mafia picks and chooses as it pleases from the commercial syndrome. While its basic framework is the guardian syndrome, it adds trading in the form of giving bribes and also by engaging in a lot of commerce in its own behalf. A monstrous moral hybrid indeed.

"In America, the nineteenth-century Mafia of poor Sicilian immigrants made its living by extorting small sums of protection money from other poor Sicilian immigrants. The protection bought was protection from the Mafia itself. Pay up or your bakery will be bombed, your pushcart smashed, your windows broken. Go to the police and your kneecaps will be broken or worse. That was plunder; or you can think of it as the Mafia's scheme of business taxation backed by prowess.

"Then came Mafia commerce. Plunder was lent to people who had no access to credit from other sources. Extortionate interest rates were backed up by physical violence to defaulters, or seizures of their businesses if they had any. Profits and seized businesses went into further commerce, frequently illegal, like pimping, gambling, bootlegging, acceptance of murder contracts for fees, smuggling, drug importing and dealing, eventually money-laundering services. Legitimate activities were adopted too: construction trades, restaurants and nightclubs, work of unloading ships, vegetable wholesaling, trucking, waste handling, to mention some favorites. But when the Mafia infiltrates legitimate commercial activities, it converts them into local monopolies when possible—which it can do through use of prowess against competitors—or cartelizes them through alliances, or combines them with labor racketeering by corrupted unions. Sometimes businesses become dens for robbery, as in that case in the garment district. Garages are converted to havens for disguising and shipping stolen automobiles, warehouses to havens for the loot of truck hijackers, political clubs to machines for electing corrupt officials. Mafia waste handlers, who began modestly by monopolizing or cartelizing restaurant garbage collection, branched into accepting troublesome toxic wastes from supposedly responsible chemical companies, factories, and hospitals, then irresponsibly dumped the wastes; very profitable.

"The Mafia does not conduct commerce in accord with the commercial syndrome, with the exception that it does value enterprise. Voluntary mutual agreement means nothing to the Mafia. It practices commerce in accord with guardian precepts.''

''But I've heard rumors of businesses financed by organized crime that are not only legitimate but upright and honest,'' said Hortense. ''Is that true?''

''Those are rare exceptions, usually set up for Mafia offspring who want no part of the criminal life. When they are obdurately set against it, they are not pressured into it. Would only make trouble. They are given good professional educations if that is what they choose. Some get a start, usually, I understand, a generous start, as business people if they want that. And employment in non-Mafia businesses is found for still others. Even the Mafia has its misfits.

''Individual criminals,'' Jasper continued, ''like free-lance embezzlers, murderers, or robbers, are personal misfits within contexts supposed to be ethical. Essentially banal subjects, to my mind, except as idiosyncracies, local color, suspense, and the circumstances of bringing them to book make them interesting. These are what I supply in my novels.

''But what if the context itself is criminal? The Mafia is an instance. So is a corrupt, discriminatory, or brutal police department, a dishonest appliance-repair shop, a valve-manufacturing company that cheats on specifications, a military-equipment producer that falsifies costs or wins contracts with bribes. Or even, in its prissy way, that genteel nest of pirated-software customers you turned up, Armbruster.

''Then it is the scrupulous and moral man or woman who becomes the misfit. I find that less banal and more tragic than criminal misfits in morally strong contexts. Enough on crime to suit you?

''You also asked me, Armbruster, how I had come to agree with Kate that we have two moral syndromes, no more, no less. I will answer that now. At the same time—how is this for thrift of means?—I will address Ben's belief that we are given a third syndrome along with the ideal that each person should contribute to society according to his ability and receive according to his needs.''

''It stands to reason that this gives us a different, third kind of morality,'' said Ben. ''It does away with competition for property and prestige and dominance. Just because the possibility and opportunities haven't been used intelligently so far by rulers doesn't mean this third syndrome couldn't be used well.''

"That Marxist vision is booby-trapped from the word go," said Jasper. "To show you why, let me take you through the fate of our two familiar syndromes in the Soviet Union, beginning with how the guardian precepts fared.

"First, shun trading. That stood firm in the sense that guardians were not to profit personally by trading on their positions and power. In fact, the same applied to everybody, whether guardians or commercial people.

"However, that same precept, to shun trading, was massively breached in another way. The guardians took responsibility for commerce and production. They had to, given public ownership of the facilities. Right there, a moral hybrid was contrived.

"No need to labor how prowess fared. It backed up state plans, decisions, and edicts concerning commerce and production, along with the customary guardian jurisdictions over territory.

"Respect for obedience and hierarchy: that applied not only to guardians but to everybody. Tradition was accorded such extravagant respect that individuals who so much as questioned the state ideology, which had now taken the place of a state religion, were reviled as traitors or branded as mentally diseased. The hardest-line Communists were accurately understood as conservatives, odd as that seems to us in light of our differing traditions. Oh, another point about hierarchy. In practice, rights were attached to duties, and duties to status. Individual rights got lip service but not the practical force of access to contractual law.

"The state's monopoly of vengeance was taken as seriously as in any regime. No need to labor deceptiveness. Its excesses made *glasnost* electrifying.

"Largesse was ruinously extravagant. Besides income redistributions, food and rent subsidies, largesse to client states, and so on, investments ostensibly intended for productive purposes were dictated instead by political aims."

"The Soviet Union tried hard to promote productive investments," protested Ben. "That's why they had their five-year economic plans."

"Consider that decade after decade the state poured capital into state and collective farms. That was investment less in agriculture than in an ideology about agriculture. Even the vaunted heavy industry, excuse for so many sacrifices, became obsolete, rickety, and backward for lack of genuinely productive investment. For one thing, the locations of industries were chosen to produce maximum dependence of republics on the centralized economic structure. Single-factory monopolies of items like detergents made customers dependent on huge suppliers, sometimes thousands of miles away. A breakdown in one spot translated into universal shortage of an item."

"You're harping on bad planning," said Ben. "That doesn't prove it had to be bad."

"It was not necessarily all that bad from a political point of view," said Jasper. "It did expunge private property. It did locate factories where there was no work otherwise. It did make republics outrageously dependent on each other and the central structure. If you put economic planning into guardian hands, you get planning for guardian priorities. The planning apparatus that presided over these investments became, in itself, a pork barrel providing millions upon millions of desirable jobs, increasingly for their own sake, not because they were pulling their weight by creating viable production and commerce.

"Now a brighter spot," he continued. "Make rich use of leisure. The state established halls of culture in even the dreariest towns and funded them with largesse. Athletics and competitive games flourished, from hockey down—or up—to chess. Museums were well maintained and the scholarship of many Soviet curators was first-class. The state fostered music, dance, and theater of high standards, also folk and regional versions of the arts, again to high standards. Book publishing burgeoned within its permitted limits, with stress on inexpensive editions of Russian and international classics. The state supported literary journals and made celebrities of approved novelists and poets. It also supported plentiful and inexpensive newspapers, dull and dishonest until *glasnost;* same with radio and television. The state took literacy very seriously, for practical, cultural, and also recreational purposes."

"Censorship and persecution of authors and artists who got out of line weren't respectful of the arts," put in Hortense.

"That is because loyalty and obedience took precedence. And of course artists and writers lacked the great loophole of independent commercial support and unofficial patronage.

"Ostentation was so excessive that Gorbachev complained of it in one of his early speeches. I will quote him. He said 'serious shortcomings' were being 'disguised with ostentatious activities and campaigns and celebrations of numerous jubilees in the center and in the provinces. The world of day-to-day realities and that of make-believe well-being were increasingly parting ways.' Add to this, normal ostentation, of which he did not complain: awesome official architecture, monuments, military parades, lavish embassy parties.

"Exclusiveness was expressed in the Party with its carefully chosen membership and monopoly of political life, also in the insularity so long imposed on almost all citizens.

"Honor produced another complaint from Gorbachev. He said 'real concern' for people was 'often replaced with the mass distribution of awards, titles and prizes.' He could have added the state's reliance on dishonor, stripping honor from those in disfavor. In sum—"

"You forgot fortitude and fatalism," said Kate.

"As everywhere, fortitude was esteemed in heroes and military life and, besides that, for model workers. Fatalism—was that the spirit in which all this was accepted? I would think hope, at first, followed by resignation, and then—"

"Fatalism was a bulwark, surely," said Armbruster. "After all, the ideology had it that communism was scientifically and historically fated to triumph. Hardships along the way must be accepted."

"So much for the guardian syndrome," Jasper resumed. "It did not yield—except that the precept to shun trading was breached when guardians assumed responsibility for managing and running commerce. But it was a massive breach. So with guardians handling commerce, let's take a look now at how the commercial syndrome fared, precept by precept.

"I have already mentioned that investment for productive purposes was crippled in favor of guardian priorities. I do not refer to the enormous costs of military production, although they conventionally get the blame for starving other production. Military costs could possibly have been supported—as they have been in so many regimes for longer than in the Soviet Union—had largesse actually resulted in productive investment in industry, trade, agriculture, and transport."

"Let me try this game too," said Hortense. "Voluntary agreement succumbed to government edicts and plans, and competition succumbed to state monopolies. There is not much use for contractual law without private property and private commercial plans."

"Anybody else?" asked Jasper.

"Without competition, individual enterprise and innovation and ef-ficiency couldn't flourish," said Kate. "Commercial dissent was squeezed out as decisively as political dissent."

"Easy collaboration with strangers and aliens went by the board," said Armbruster. "Nobody's mentioned honesty."

"Dishonesty was institutionally forced on commercial managers," said Jasper. "Many factories turned out goods so shoddy they were a fraud on consumers. That was to fill unrealistic output quotas; those five-year economic plans, Ben. Shortages led to networks of favor exchanging that amounted to bribery, and to black markets. Honest accounting was so little respected, or even understood, that from top to bottom nobody knew the costs of production. But this did not much matter, since the guardians set prices politically, without regard to costs. Your turn, Ben."

"At least they were industrious and thrifty. You have to give them that."

"Don't be so sure. Ideological requirements for full employment, along with inefficiencies, led to overstaffing and goofing off. Hence the joke 'We pretend to work and they pretend to pay us.' Gorbachev, early on, identified lackadaisical work habits as a weakness obstructing reform. Thrift, yes. That was the pretend-to-pay-us part. But in the commercial syndrome, as Kate explained, the point of thrift is not scrimping for its own sake. Nor is it having money left only because there are not worthwhile goods and services to spend it on. Like to think about 'Promote comfort and convenience'?"

"That was for the future, after basic needs got top priority," said Ben glumly.

"You forget this is a syndrome," said Kate impatiently. "Loss or destruction of any part impairs the integrity of the whole. Attention to comfort and convenience can't be put on hold; it's a source of energy—a major source—driving commercial life."

"Pondering all this, Armbruster, I came to this conclusion," said Jasper. "The fanfare blew, the curtain rose to display a new form of social morality—and the stage was empty. Lurking behind the scenes were merely the same old guardian syndrome and a disastrously crippled commercial syndrome. That was all. Marx himself despised bourgeois values and ways, wanted them to disappear. So in a sense, his program was a success.

"Reluctant as I was to believe in two syndromes, no more, no less, I am impressed with the obduracy of these two and the nonappearance of a third. When the commercial syndrome fell into ruins, all that remained was reliance on the guardian syndrome.

"Here, we can see Castro in this same ridiculous fix. He explained it all to a mesmerized crowd of half a million in a long, charismatic speech in 1970. His subject was how to develop Cuba's economy. It was a battle, he said, that could be won only 'by the people's will aimed at a given goal, marching down a single road, united in a single spirit!' He spoke wholly in terms of combat—battles against the past, against limitations, against what he called 'objective factors.' All, he explained, was to be successfully coordinated from the top. The vision he invoked, at length and repeatedly, was of a well-oiled, popular, conquering army. But what in the world was he talking about? By his own account, manufacturing shoes, repairing machinery, attracting tourists, and mobilizing construction materials and transport—challenges that could be overcome, he preached, with discipline, loyalty, fortitude, and prowess!''

"He was trained as an economist," said Armbruster.

"It does not matter. He may have learned some appropriate mentifacts but he did not absorb appropriate ethifacts. And he was unable to invent others to serve in their place. He had to fall back on guardian morality—flawed by a great breach of the precept to shun trading."

"Goodness, you make Marxism sound like a gigantic case of organized crime," said Hortense.

"Structurally, they do much resemble each other; in both cases, into an otherwise strong guardian syndrome comes the same massive breach of the guardian precept to shun trading. Since the guardian syndrome is neither morally nor functionally suited to carrying on production and trade, the commerce involved is corrupted and its moral foundations ruined. This is the structural similarity between Marxism and organized crime. But of course there are important differences between the two: different motives, types of commerce, and power bases. Today's organized crime gangs are still not the state, but rather nests within states.

"But to return to my point about the two syndromes and lack of a third even when it was expected and sorely needed: it follows that I am no longer skeptical of the idea that our working-life morality is based on only two ways of getting a living."

"I wish you wouldn't say 'only,' " said Kate.

"Yes, I know, the other animals. But I do have a point of disagreement with you, Kate. You said the prototype of the trading approach would be a simple village market—"

"Yes, where people set out their wares in confidence they won't be seized and then haggle until they reach voluntary mutual agreement,'' said Kate.

"That tame little village market does not ring true to me. Not as an origin of trading. Try imagining, instead, two distinct and separate parties of hunters meeting up at the border between two distinct hunting-and-gathering territories and trading off to each other some of their naturally differing territorial booty.''

"That's really good,'' said Kate.''More plausible than the market I thoughtlessly pulled from the top of my head. And what you say checks with early evidence of prehistoric trading: territorial resource goods turning up outside their places of origin, things like amber, shells, copper, obsidian.''

"One annoying thing about archeological evidence,'' said Armbruster. "It depends on imperishable materials. The more ancient the evidence, the more this is so. It leads one to picture our remote ancestors interminably chipping stones until they took to interminably making pots. Most things traded now are perishable, and no doubt they always were.''

"That checks with trade in territorial resources among hunters and gatherers in historic times,'' said Kate. She dug through an envelope of battered file folders and extracted some photocopied pages. "Listen to this about the Gitkasan and Wet'suwet'en American Indians in British Columbia. This is from a legal brief they submitted in court in the course of an interminable battle with the province about their territorial claims. From time immemorial, it says, these peoples occupied neighboring territories with distinctly different coastal and interior ecosystems. They already enjoyed a heavy import-export trade between these two territories, and some trade with other territories, before the arrival of Europeans—long before.

"Some trade was in durable goods, such as obsidian, imported from far distant places, and toothed shells exported far and wide from the coastal territory. But a lot of their trade goods were perishable, Armbruster. Dried berries, dried seaweed, dried salmon, and edible candlefish grease—that was a big item—exported from the coast to the interior. Caribou meat and moose hides—another very big item— exported from the interior to the coast. A web of trade routes, it says here, by river and land both, laced many, many communities into the system. Geographic isolation of groups didn't mean economic isolation.

"When Europeans reached the region, the Indians easily and quickly incorporated trade with them into their existing network. They sold skins to Hudson's Bay Company traders, fish and timber to railway construction crews, and salmon to settlers in return for farm produce.

"Now here's an interesting point. At the time Europeans encountered them, the territories of the trading Indians were supporting higher concentrations of population than the territories of simpler foraging bands. And that wasn't because the trading Indians practiced agriculture. They didn't. This suggests that, from away back, before the invention of agriculture, trading territories were more productive and richer than others—the same as commercial economies are today."

"Maybe that's because they were more industrious than plain hunters and gatherers," said Hortense. "They'd have had to be—building those freight canoes for the rivers and carrying those skins and bags and baskets of stuff back and forth over the land, besides getting the goods in the first place and preparing them. It sounds like a lot of work."

"In what's now Peru," said Kate, "there was a city about thirty-five hundred years ago where they did practice agriculture—but not for food, for trade. The people lived on seafood, wild plants, and some land animals, not agricultural produce. What they grew instead was cotton, and what they traded was cotton nets and twine and cotton clothing. They were rich and productive enough to have an impressive city of huge stone structures, but as far as the archeologists can figure out, they belonged to no centralized political structure."

"You are not negating my point," said Jasper, "but you are getting me off it. Pretend with me that we are back at the first instance of trading anywhere, ever. A hunter exchanges bright-colored bird feathers from his territory for a gourd of wild honey from the territory next door."

"So one fellow robs a bird of its life and then its feathers," said Ben. "Half an hour later he exchanges his plunder with a fellow who robbed the bees. It all comes down to taking."

"No, no, it does not," said Jasper. "Something new has been added. The bird man did not rob the honey man or vice versa. And it was not a case of simple sharing either, even though it was close to it."

"The giant difference lies in that innocuous phrase I used when I first talked about trading and taking: 'depending on what's available,' " said Kate. "I'm going to add to your bird-feather man foragers with reeds to trade."

"I can see that bright feathers and honey are tempting," said Hortense. "But reeds?"

"Oh, reeds are desirable," said Kate. "In clever fingers they can be transformed into everything from roofing and mats to baskets and musical whistles. Now, here's a reed forager talking. 'Hey, boys and girls, gather a lot more reeds so we can get more honey at the big trading rock. And while you're at the shore, keep your eyes out for shells. Maybe we can tempt the honey people into letting us have one of those big-noise horns they carry.' That's the trading approach to multiplying things available. Traders add more things to trade as they go along. As a by-product of the increasing diversity of things traded, volume of trade expands too.

"In contrast, hunters and gatherers working a territory only for themselves, much as other animals do, can multiply things available only by expanding their territory or abandoning a poor one for a better one.

"That approach was bound, sooner or later, to lead to raiding and then to warfare. Pretend with me that we're back with foragers who know nothing of trading. They've overhunted their territory, or the rains haven't come, and they're desperate. So they raid the adjoining territory, taking anything they find and killing off anyone barring their way. Then they retreat back to home base. I'm leaving out the possibility of cannibalism. It's too iffy and anyhow doesn't change the principle. There's no way of knowing when hunters started raiding territories of other hunters, but without trading, that would be their only way of multiplying things available.

"If a raided group had any sense of self-preservation, its own hunters would convert to ad hoc warriors, either for retaliation or for defense when they feared another foray from the neighbors. Now the fat is in the fire.

"The next stage, we must logically suppose, would be border jockeying; that is, both sides would try to enlarge their territorial defense buffers, each at the expense of the other. However that started, start it most certainly did, likely in many parts of the world. It has persisted through history. One example is the interminable Scottish-English raiding, which was the normal way of life in the border country as late as the seventeenth century. Each side kept swooping in on the other, making off with cattle.

"Border jockeying is so usual that it wasn't until 1718 that maps of Europe first fixed borders between states as lines. Previously the borders had been understood and located as zones of contention, called marches, fluctuating back and forth with the fortunes of war.

"Let's flash back to prehistoric border jockeying and raiding. In themselves, those are only temporary means of taking territory or seizing what a territory yields.

"Making territorial conquests stick is more difficult and complex. Conquest demands more discipline than raiding. It requires sophisticated military organizations of the kind Jasper referred to when he talked about loyalty, vengeance, courts-martial, hierarchies, obedience, and shunning trading to keep treachery in hand. Any more ideas about armies of conquest, Jasper?"

"Sure, to make conquests stick it would be necessary either to wipe out the prior inhabitants or else to treat them, too, as resources for the taking: enslave them, assimilate them by forced concubinage, force them to yield tribute. Gods might be expunged or trivialized, to bring the territory under the spiritual protection of the conquerors' gods. You will have no trouble thinking of endless historical instances of all those sequels to conquest."

"So a further point," said Kate. "Conquest that sticks demands more than military force. It requires calculated physical and psychological techniques to impose internal peace in the territory as far as that is possible. It also requires deliberate protection of the territory from outside rivals. In short, exactly the two big guardian duties Plato recognized, and along with those duties, a regularized method of ensuring guardians' upkeep, by levying tribute and taxes in kind and eventually in money.

"All these complications of governing, right down to this day, can be traced back into the taking way of getting a living, just as surely as quantitative and qualitative increases in trade can be traced back to the trading way of getting a living. Taking and trading are themselves fundamentally different from each other. The derivatives from each approach also remain fundamentally different. The derivatives incorporate their own moral marks, their contradictions to the other syndrome, right down to this day. It's bootless to try to harmonize commerce and guardianship into one joint system of morality. Trying to do it can't produce harmony—quite the opposite. The contradictions are innate. We have no way to escape them.

"To seek harmony in the sense of oneness is a profoundly false lead. But harmony can be sought by seeking to maintain each syndrome's own identity and integrity. Then the two can support and complement each other, as I tried to show when I explained why commerce needs the support and help of guardians and why guardians need the support and help of commerce. Symbiosis: from the Greek for 'together' and 'living.' As the dictionary tells us, it means 'the living together of two dissimilar organisms, especially when the association is mutually beneficial.' "

"You are digressing, Kate," said Jasper. "And if you do not mind my saying so, you have a bit of a tendency to preach. Come on back with me to conquest of territory and the guardian function of maintaining internal peace. In cases of conquest, that task requires, among other things, trying to get people in a conquered territory to see things from the conquerors' point of view—see things their way. Another thing Machiavelli understood. This can be easy, of course, if the conquered territory is repopulated with the conquerors' own people. Otherwise it is very difficult. We did not have much success during the Vietnam War 'winning the hearts and minds of the people.' Even after the passage of centuries, dim and long-lost sovereignties or allegiances retain an underground life in the memories of the conquered."

"Don't religious conversions largely overcome that?" asked Hortense. "And teaching a new language and introducing new law and customs?"

"Very difficult," Jasper repeated. "Conversions did not prevent the successful rebellions of Spain's territories in Latin America, nor a shared ideology prevent the dissolution of the Soviet Union. Isaiah Berlin, speaking of conquered ethnic groups, says that sooner or later they ask themselves the questions: 'Why do we have to obey them?' 'What right have they . . . ?' 'What about us?' 'Why can't we . . . ?' He likens them to bent twigs, forced down so severely that when they are released they lash back with 'fury' and 'irrepressible force.' "

"If you stand back and look," said Hortense, "you can see that demands for new sovereignties are getting to be a big historical theme."

"Getting to be?" broke in Armbruster. "Where have you been, Hortense? In 1904 there were only fifty sovereignties in the world. Starting with Norway's secession from Sweden in 1905, the number of sovereignties has now more than tripled and is well along toward quadrupling. Granted, most of those have been results of the breakup of empires. But now it's becoming the turn of nations.

"Existing nations, with few exceptions, embrace conquered territories—ethnic groups or old sovereignties, taken by force. Sowing the wind; at length comes the whirlwind in the form of demands for territorial take-backs. Separatist cults build up into separatist movements, demands for take-backs.

"We know this has been a terrible century. As Berlin says, the next one may be worse: blood feuds on a giant scale. Perhaps we're getting a foretaste with the violence between Serbs and Croats, Serbs, Croats, and Bosnians, Iraqis and Kurds, Jews and Palestinians, Catholics and Protestants in Ulster, Azerbaijanis and Armenians, Spaniards and Basques, Punjabi Sikhs and Hindus.

"On the other hand," Armbruster continued, "suppose secessions and separations were to follow the civilized example of Sweden in letting Norway go, and Bohemia—the Czechs—in letting Slovakia go, or the civilized expulsion of Singapore by Malaysia. Then the world might have, say, three hundred or so reasonably stable sovereignties, more comfortable internally with their loyalties than many an existing state today. Perhaps more than three hundred—God knows how many take-backs of territory could emerge within those behemoths China and India."

"You're contrasting the possibility of territorial give-backs with territorial take-backs won by prowess," said Jasper. "It's almost unheard-of for guardians to give back conquered territories to the people conquered. If what was taken by force is eventually given or sold, guardians generally have given or sold to each other. After the Napoleonic Wars, for instance, the victorious powers took Norway from Denmark and gave it to Sweden. That was to punish Denmark. The American Virgin Islands in the Caribbean used to belong to England, which gave them as a royal wedding present to Denmark. Then Denmark sold them to our government. That miffed the English; they thought it unbecoming to profit by selling off a gift, but they let the transaction stand."

"Here's an idea," said Hortense. "There could be an international organization called Friends of the Kurds, say, that gives benefits and solicits donations to buy up the Kurdish territories in Iraq, Iran, and Turkey and give them back to the Kurds. Then there could be the Friends of the Basques, and so on. Why not? It would be better than war, terrorism, or supplying guns. Jasper said it was honorable, from away back, for guardians to accept ransoms for prisoners of war. This would be ransom on a big scale."

"Ransom for people, yes," said Jasper. "It is still done. In the old days, cities sometimes paid out ransoms for themselves, in lieu of being sacked by the enemy. But ransoms for long-conquered territories incorporated into nations? I doubt it, Hortense."

"Well, getting back to trading," said Hortense, "I have a complaint for you and Kate to consider. 'Honey man.' 'Bird-feather man.' You were visualizing the very first traders as men. I don't see why. Logically, women would be the first people to trade goods across territorial boundaries. For one thing, they likely wouldn't have been as leery of each other as armed men. And I think it'd come more naturally to women to try peaceable mutual agreement in place of taking by force. Then, when men got a look at what was going on at the big trading rock and saw how it worked, they'd get in on it too.

"Furthermore," she went on, "think about new kinds of things put into trade. Mostly it amounts to the traditional work of women, with men getting into it when it enters trade. Look at spinning, textile manufacturing, food processing, garment industries, cosmetics, pharmaceuticals, obstetrics, geriatrics, hospital administration—why, only a couple of generations ago hospital administrators were all nurses—and kitchen equipment, baking, leather tanning. Give me time and I'd think of more. You could make a good case that the history of economic development is the history of men taking up women's work. Where they don't, economic life is poor and stunted, like life in Muslim countries unless they have oil."

"The transfers of traditional men's and women's work cut both ways," said Jasper. "Look at you, Hortense, working in the law. Look at Kate, working in the university. Women work in armament factories."

"Whatever the divisions or collaborations between the sexes, early takers and traders both were likely youthful by our standards," said Kate. "Adolescent soldiers and officers. Child hagglers. Average life expectancies of people in the wild today tend to be short. Through most of history that's been true; until modern times, whoever you were, highborn or low, if you survived infancy and continued lucky, you got an adolescence and a young adulthood, and then you'd likely had it, unless you were the rare exception. You know those very ancient little statuettes of females that male prehistorians named Venuses? They like to suppose those were fertility-cult objects. Well, I've handled some replicas and examined photographs of others, and I know enough about the female body to see these are accurate representations of fat old women. Drooping breasts, pendulous bellies, lumpy buttocks. Dispose of corsets and that's what you'd see. Those look like statuettes of fat, prosperous survivors. Why not survivor cults? Extraordinary individuals to celebrate, hoping their magic would rub off?"

"In that case, you would expect to find some telltale marks of the cult in historic times," said Jasper.

"You do. Many societies venerate aged people, for no reason whatever except that they're aged. Anyhow, to get back to my point, it astonishes me to think how much of the moral foundation of our working life must have been laid down by youngsters."

"Listen to this," said Armbruster over his shoulder as he dipped into a bookshelf. "This is John Holt writing about his elementary-school pupils in Boston. 'Ten is a heroic age for most kids. They remind me in many ways of the Homeric Greeks. They are quarrelsome and combative; they have a strong and touchy sense of honor; they believe that every affront must be repaid, and with interest; they are fiercely loyal to their friends, even though they may change friends often; they have little sense of fair play, and greatly admire cunning and trickery; they are both highly possessive and very generous—no smallest trifle may be taken from them, but they are likely to give anything away if they feel so disposed.' "

"Why go back to the Homeric Greeks?" asked Ben. "Sounds like our own government leaders."

"If John Holt had been watching those same ten-year-olds helping out at a yard sale or neighborhood fair, he'd have been struck with another set of traits and been reminded of 'market mamas' in Ghana or stall keepers in Guadalajara," said Hortense. "Boys and girls both. Such salesmanship. Much enjoyment of meticulous change-making. Wonderful memories for what's on sale in this higgledy-piggledy pile of goods or that one, and what isn't there because it's already been bought and by whom."

"I think we're badly mistaken," said Kate, "if we assume that grandfatherly types—or grandmotherly types, Hortense—constructed the moral syndromes. To repeat myself, what starts in function becomes principle. What becomes principle is eventually codified by solemn old geezers.

"Every normal person the world over," she went on, "is inherently capable of both trading and taking. We're born with those abilities, much as every normal person the world over is capable of using language and grammar. But knowing when it's appropriate to use the one or the other approach, trading or taking, and how to do it properly—those things are culturally learned, mostly by imitation and practice."

"Also by precepts and law," said Armbruster, looking up from his notepad. "In the absence of imitation and practice, precepts and law are weak and artificial. But if imitation and practice are lost—what an appalling cultural loss—precepts and law have to fill the gap, or try to." He returned to scrutinizing his notepad.

CHAPTER SEVEN

Anomalies

Y ou two have tied up most of the loose ends I noted," said
Armbruster. "But early on, Kate, you spoke of anomalies. You
specifically mentioned law and agriculture."

"We've already dealt with the law," said Hortense. "How a lawyer
in government works under the guardian syndrome but in private
practice under the commercial syndrome."

"It's not that simple," said Kate. "That's no anomaly. The law has
that in common with many other professions. Medicine, for instance. A
public health officer or military doctor is in the service of the state, a
guardian. He doesn't depend on voluntary mutual agreement; he can
call upon prowess if necessary to put people in quarantine, to make
them accept mandated vaccinations, to close contaminated wells or
beaches.

"Not so with a physician in private practice, even if a state medical
care system is paying the bills. Now voluntary agreement on the part of
the patient—the doctor's customer—takes over. The doctor is morally
bound to be honest with his patients about the treatment they're getting
and its possible side effects and to put the interests of his patients ahead
of conflicting interests, including those of the state.

"That's not like a doctor in a military field hospital, for instance, who has to consider guardian priorities, perhaps with the object of returning as many of the wounded to battle as possible, if necessary at the expense of quick attention to those unlikely to survive or to be permanently disabled if they do. Just the opposite of what happens in the emergency department of a civilian hospital. Another consideration could be the value of the training a given soldier has received, or the current need for his skills. Stewart Perry, a writer about community organization, says that as a trainee in the Army Medical Corps during the Korean War he was 'instructed that medical assistance should go first to officers, then to enlisted men.' He adds that he has been informed by a nurse who served in the Vietnam War that helicopter pilots were 'a priority category for medical care.' "

"Sorting, or triage, as it's called, was a grim rule back in the Civil War," put in Armbruster. "A strange story about that has come down in my family. My great-grandfather was lying in pain and despair with a severe saber wound. He'd been more or less ignored in favor of men with lighter wounds. Late that night the supervising doctor came through with an aide, totting up how many beds would be freed to receive heavy battle casualties expected the next day. The doctor pointed to my great-grandfather's bed and told the aide, 'This will be available.' Then they moved on.

"That doctor, it so happened, was my great-grandfather's own father. His callousness and coldness so enraged my great-grandfather that he resolved with all his will not to die and release the bed, just to prove his father wrong. He did manage to hang on through the night, was nursed and treated in the morning, and even returned to battle in due course."

"Did the doctor realize he was pointing at his own son?" asked Hortense.

"That was left unclear in the story as it came down to me. Maybe the son was just another anonymous torn body to the desperately overworked, tired doctor. Maybe he'd steeled himself to his guardian duties, regardless of his own feelings. But who knows? Maybe he was shrewdly counting on the shock value of his words. We can hope so."

"That is a pretty nasty story," said Jasper.

"Yes, isn't it? I take it, Kate, you're making a basic distinction between a physician in service to the state for its purposes and a physician in service to patients in their own right."

"Yes, and that story is not as nasty, Jasper, as the monstrous moral hybrids of medical care when physicians pretend to be at the service of patients but are actually serving the state. Criminal Nazi physicians practiced experiments on patients without their knowledge or consent, or let patients die deliberately, or even killed them, if they were deemed worthless by the state. Soviet psychiatrists incarcerated and drugged political dissidents at the behest of the state. Stalin, it's said, became paranoid about doctors during his last days, as well he might, knowing the kinds of things they'd done under his policies. Back in the 1950s, a CIA-corrupted psychiatric clinic in Montreal performed disastrous and wicked brainwashing experiments on patients while deceiving them and their families into believing the treatment was in their interests.

"There are many fine points to medical ethics, and some difficult puzzles, but the most rudimentary morality is the line between the guardian and commercial syndromes. It's as crucial that physicians understand it as it is that lawyers recognize that when they go into guardian service they can't morally also be in service to clients seeking to influence legislation or regulatory decisions.

"A different kind of problem, Hortense, is built into private practice of the law. It's a genuine anomaly. Lawyers in private practice often have to switch back and forth between the two syndromes. I'm thinking about defending a client against criminal charges. In our legal system that's an adversarial proceeding and the defending lawyer is duty bound to give the accused client the best possible defense short of perjury, right? Let damaging facts lie under the rug if the prosecution doesn't bring them up? Battle of wits and cunning? Keep alert for any chink in the prosecution's armor? Make the most of any weakness you spot in the evidence and magnify it?"

"You've been watching TV courtroom dramas," said Hortense. "But yes, it's true. Private law practice does demand use of both syndromes, and not only when defending criminals. Suits and their defenses and countersuits heard in the civil courts are adversarial too, although you're ethically expected in that case to bring all material facts into the open beforehand, during what's called the discovery part of the process, so the other side knows them too and neither of you springs factual surprises later. But they're battles, no doubt about that.

"English lawyers get around the anomaly," Hortense went on. "They're divided into solicitors and barristers, keeping battle distinct from commercial work. The barristers do battle in court. The solicitors handle deeds, tax puzzles, contracts, papers of incorporation, wills, that sort of thing. They also give routine legal advice. If a client has to sue or be defended in court, the solicitor briefs the barrister with the facts.''

"That's simple division of labor," said Armbruster.

"No, it isn't a single occupation, merely divided into two for convenience," said Hortense, excited now. "Listen to this. The barrister carries moral marks that show his work has a different origin from the solicitor's work. Solicitors, you must understand, don't disdain trading. Besides being in trade themselves, they deal all the time with its paper tools.

"Of course barristers get paid for their services, and more handsomely, as a rule, than solicitors. But to this day they aren't paid matter-of-factly. Arm's length! A barrister himself can never discuss his payment. His clerk discusses it with the client's solicitor or the legal-aid office. If a barrister isn't paid his fee he isn't permitted to sue for it. So sometimes he has to wait years, or he never receives it. He has a quaint little black bag unobtrusively attached to the back of his court gown. It's a vestige, a vestigial moral mark. In olden days the fee in coins was dropped in the bag and the barrister sat down when the weight satisfied him. But his honor remained intact because he didn't see the base and shameful transaction occurring, the money materializing. This was pretense, like Santa Claus or the tooth fairy. This morning I'd have said sheer snobbery to all this. But now I see an intellectual knight, morally constrained from selling out, fighting as a champion for the sorely beset.''

"Do you think our system of having the same person serve the two different kinds of legal functions is a good idea?" asked Kate.

"Usually, provided the lawyer has the skills and temperament for both, and many do. Good lawyers understand the distinctions. Of course, just as some guardian lawyers take bribes or other private benefits—like promises of lucrative future private employment—so do some lawyers in private practice use adversarial tricks and cunning in what ought to be straightforward commercial arrangements. That always makes trouble. It also makes people distrust and hate lawyers.''

"Here's the anomaly built into agriculture," said Kate. "It's entirely different. Please notice, first, that agriculture can be operated under either guardian or commercial ways.

"Take the guardian form: big landholdings worked by slaves, serfs, peons, or some form of captive tenants, like sharecroppers kept in debt or peasants imprisoned by class. In the case of landholding aristocrats or hereditary gentry, it's obvious the duke, the count, or the squire is a member of a guardian class and lives by the guardian syndrome. But the same is true of slaveholders even if they aren't hereditary grandees and never were.

"For instance, slaveholding planters in our South before the Civil War were self-made men or the progeny of self-made men, not aristocrats or hereditary rulers. But their slaves had been taken by force in the first place and were retained by force. The arrangement demanded unquestioning obedience from slaves. It also required ironclad hierarchy, with planters and their families at the top, overseers, if any, in between, and slaves at the bottom. If the plantation was large, even the slaves took on hierarchy: house servants at the top, other slaves with special skills or training next, and field hands at the bottom. No, really at the bottom would be fugitives in hiding, if any.

"Given this much of the guardian syndrome as the planters' survival system, the remainder of the syndrome followed. Planter society venerated tradition and harked all the way back to the Old Testament to justify the tradition of slavery. Planters took vengeance into their own hands or delegated it to overseers or sheriffs who were given the planters' side of the story and subscribed to the system. Planters were ostentatious and thriftless in their style of life, the richer, the more so. Much grander life-styles than northern farmers. They made rich use of leisure: sports like cockfighting, balls and formal dances, hunting, open-handed hospitality. Some among them were scholars, writers, and even excellent amateur architects, like Thomas Jefferson, who was all three, as well as a politician and student of politics.

"For a picture of a much humbler slaveholding family, see *Huckleberry Finn.* Mark Twain got the whole guardian syndrome into the doings of the family that sheltered Huck for a while, including the vengeance of a blood feud and a leisured lady of the household, who painted and embroidered ghastly memorial pictures, kind of a pale reflection of the noble Norman ladies who created the Bayeux tapestry.

"But to continue, the southern slaveholders, who set moral patterns for even small planters holding on economically by the skin of their teeth, set great store by their honor. They were exclusive. They revered the virtue of loyalty for themselves and also conned themselves into a sentimental fiction of slave loyalty and gratitude, until emancipation stripped away that veneer, to the shock and disbelief of many a planter family. Pretended undying loyalty was part of the slaves' own survival system within this guardian world.

"The planters were perfectly conscious of the syndrome they lived by. Romantically, and for the most part accurately, they identified it with chivalry. They contrasted their moral superiority with the base, inferior, hateful commercial spirit of the North.

"Guardian-operated agriculture in one form or another has been common. Wherever in the world a clamor arises for land to be divided and given to its workers, the system being attacked is the guardian type of agriculture. New forms of it are always possible, it seems. The Soviet and East Bloc collective and state farms were a recent variation."

"Then do you think agriculture is basically a guardian activity, derived from the taking approach to getting a living?" asked Hortense.

"No, the opposite. I'm convinced it's basically a commercial activity and I've three reasons for thinking so. The most important is that when agriculture is operated in accordance with commercial precepts, placing value on voluntary agreement, thrift, productive investment, efficiency, and openness to innovations, it is much more productive than guardian-run agriculture. Worker for worker, it supports its people better. Guardian ways are a drag on agriculture.

"My second reason is the work's natural demands, so to speak, for commercial morality. It innately requires thrift: the farmer must deliberately set seeds and breeding stock aside, even if it means going on short rations. It also requires industriousness, much unremitting drudgery day after day after day, especially before machines lightened the work. How it could ever have arisen straight out of foraging, as prehistorians have liked to think, is hard or impossible to understand. Apart from the contrasting moral demands built into simple taking versus agriculture, subsistence farming is far harder work, for poorer and chancier returns, than hunting and gathering in the wild.

"My third reason is that trading or bartering is almost invariably associated with agriculture and animal breeding. Farm households everywhere struggle to get something to market if they possibly can. This is true even when members of the household spin, weave, and practice other crafts. For a household to produce food and fibers for itself and for nobody else, and therefore by definition also supply itself with all its other needs, too—since it isn't buying or bartering—is so impractical it's uncommon. So impractical it's a guaranteed recipe for poverty. We have no records from the early millennia of agriculture and animal husbandry to inform us whether the work arose in close association with prior trading and its moral inducements. But the earliest hints we do have imply the association. Those ancient Egyptian Books of the Dead

I mentioned—the letters of recommendation to the gods—even imply that farmland itself was a commercial commodity, let alone agricultural produce. They also associate honesty, as a major virtue, with dealings in land and grain. In Latin, the very word for money, *peculas,* is derived from the word for cattle. The word 'fee' similarly derives from an ancient Teutonic word for cattle. What could speak more loudly of ancient commerce in the products of animal husbandry?

"Yet we have this anomaly of guardian agriculture. To understand why, consider that farmers and stock raisers need land as their major raw material. Basically, this is no different from saying that writers need paper as their raw material, or that paper makers need papyrus, parchment, rags, or pulp. In that one sense only, the raw material necessary, farming is territorial work.

"However, that has been enough to make agriculture irresistible to guardians. What would a duke, a count, a conqueror, have been without landholdings? They were of the essence to his status, which derived from taking and holding territory. And given the existence of agriculture and pastoralism, how make use of landholdings without including tillage and pasturage—alongside such clear and direct derivatives of the taking approach as deer parks, grouse hunts, and boar chases?

"In other words, an economic activity that is functionally and morally commercial has historically been skewed to conform to the contradictory values and morals of guardian landowners. That anomalous situation has been to the detriment of agricultural workers, agricultural prosperity, and often enough agricultural land and its fertility, for long spans of time, throughout much of the world."

"But even where slavery, serfdom, and fiefdoms are gone," said Hortense, "governments don't keep their hands out of agriculture."

"How right you are," said Armbruster. "Governments that would hoot at the idea of sponsoring boot-and-shoe boards or subsidizing the manufacturing of glass bottles—necessities though these are—maintain egg boards and wheat boards and subsidize producers of wine, rice, sugar beets, butter . . ."

"Pressure by farm blocs," said Ben, who up to this point had seemed bored by the discussion. "So they can buy more poisonous pesticides and weed killers and artificial fertilizers and get on faster with poisoning the planet."

"I wonder if the farm blocs really explain it," said Jasper. "Farm subsidies have increased stupendously, regardless of the fact that the farm vote has become very small, both absolutely and proportionately."

"The reasons keep changing," said Armbruster. "Government pre-occupations with agriculture used to be justified on grounds of combating food scarcity, or the threat that war would cut off trade. But then came an opposite problem, overabundance of agricultural production, and that became quite as powerful a reason for subsidies and other meddling."

"Here's what I suggest," said Kate. "Rulers long ago became preoccupied with agriculture because it meshed with their preoccupations with territory. Tradition has perpetuated the fixation. Any ostensible reason for maintaining the tradition will do."

"But you have to recognize that once guardian largesse and controls are in place, any attempt to abandon them becomes disruptive," said Jasper.

"Indeed," said Armbruster, "but don't overlook the reality that the largesse and controls are disruptive themselves. Some examples: They stoke trade wars. They foster absurd stockpiles of food and drink—witness the European Community's wine lakes and butter mountains. They require ever-rising taxes to support agricultural programs. In some countries, including ours, they squeeze out family-sized farms because disproportionate subsidies go to the biggest farms. They foster quasi monopolies of cheese making and egg producing in some countries, Canada for one. And when the guardian-mandated disruptions become too knotty, the response is to tinker further with largesse and controls, make them still more elaborate. Meanwhile, from the viewpoint of farmers, one crisis comes on top of another, and another and another."

"By now," said Kate, "nobody knows what agriculture would be like if it were restored fully and truly to the commercial syndrome and its workings, and everybody is afraid to find out."

"Wouldn't art be another anomaly?" asked Armbruster. "You have it in the guardian syndrome under the precept 'Make rich use of leisure.' You say this syndrome is derived from the taking approach to getting a living—picking up what's available in a territory without a by-your-leave, fundamentally as other animals do, and then later taking territories themselves and the tribute or labor their inhabitants yield. That approach to economic life is the less creative of our two ways of getting a living, and yet you're associating it with the zenith of creativity: art. Isn't that an anomaly—a glitch in your guardian syndrome?"

"Art did arise in hunting-and-gathering life," said Kate. "Of that there can be no doubt. And historically it has flourished in the ambience of guardian life. Of that there can be no doubt either. However, if my hypothesis is correct, it was associated with the necessary conservation ethic of hunters and the leisure that ethic imposed.

"So although art came out of the taking life, it didn't arise from taking itself but from the idle periods: the not-taking aspect of foraging. Neither did it originate with trading. A decorated cliff or a cave is not trade goods, for instance. Like sports, games, music, dance, and story-telling, painting, costumes, and other decoration didn't come into human life and activities as a way of making a living at all. In that respect, art is economically sui generis.

"To be sure, artists in our own time, and historically, who have lacked incomes from jobs or inheritances have had to depend on patron-age or commercial support of their art, or mixtures of the two. Artists make out as best they can. In an extreme case, a poet may live like a wraith in her family's upstairs rooms, or a painter at his wits' end may cut off part of his ear and be productive in an asylum. Then we cluck our tongues, shake our heads, and murmur banalities about how well off they'd be on their posthumous earnings.

"Lewis Hyde, a New England poet, argues at book length in *The Gift* against the artist's need to beg patronage or peddle his work. His thesis is that the artist has been blessed with special gifts, with talents. He bestows these on the community as gifts. He should receive, in turn, pure gifts. Root and branch, the whole phenomenon is a gift transaction and properly ought to be recognized as such.

"So far so good. But then he extends his argument into a diatribe against all commercial transactions, not distinguishing among trading, taking, and activities that lie outside them. The subtitle of his book is illuminating: *Imagination and the Erotic Life of Property*."

"How is that illuminating?" asked Hortense. "It sounds to me obfuscating. A commercial entrepreneur, thinking up how to grind drill bits at lower cost than the competition, uses imagination too but isn't asking for gifts. And contracts don't rest on erotic qualities in property. I don't get it."

"He might better have said '. . . the Erotic Life of Artists' Prop-erty,'" said Kate. "Maybe the entrepreneur loves his work too; if he's good at it, he probably does, but not to the point of disregarding economic realities. On the contrary—he concentrates hard on them. In the sense of extreme economic disregard, artists often are special, just as Hyde says. The artist's love for the art is the energy that drives artistic creation. Other forces, drives, and energies of commercial and guardian work are beside the point as far as the artist can disregard them.''

''Aha, you're talking about a third syndrome after all,'' said Ben.

''No, I'm drawing your attention to the infinitely important fact that not everything we do, or everything we are, can be bracketed within trading and taking. Let me put it this way. Rape or marriage without a bride's consent is sexual taking. Prostitution or marrying for money is sexual trading. But sex for mutual love is outside taking and trading both. In fact, it's often subversive of the syndromes; they're beside the point. Love versus loyalty, that's one of the great human themes. Romeo and Juliet were not being loyal to the Capulets and Montagues. Love versus money, that's another. Also, when a love is forbidden, love versus honesty. Maybe personal love in all its aspects—friendship, love among family members, sexual love, the intensely personal love of the artist for the art or the scholar for the subject—is too profoundly important to us to be governed by something so extraneous to love as the strictures of commerce and guardianship.''

''I withdraw my suggestion that art is an anomaly within the syndromes, like law or agriculture,'' said Armbruster. ''Its independent provenance from both taking and trading does seem to make it sui generis, and its difficulties different from those of commerce and guardianship.'' He looked at his notes again. ''At some point, I didn't jot down who, but I think you, Jasper, referred to 'casts of mind.' What did you mean by that? Can you elucidate it?''

''I can but I won't,'' said Jasper. ''It is an important subject but now is not the time for it. I am tired. When I contracted to indulge your obsession I did not contract to go without dinner.''

Armbruster looked stricken. ''I've been thoughtless. Sorry, sorry. Let me send out for food. Pizza? Chinese? What would you people like?''

''I'm tired too,'' said Kate. ''I agree casts of mind are important but let's put it off until next time. If the rest of you want a next time?''

Armbruster said hastily, ''I'm planning myself to make the next report. Systematic corruption of morals. It won't take me that long to work it up, you've already, among you, laid so much groundwork. Two weeks from today?''

"I can't come then," said Ben. "But don't let that interfere. You go ahead without me. I told you, I hate both these nasty syndromes."

"Oh, let's wait for Ben!" exclaimed Hortense. "You add so much, Ben!"

"Four weeks, then?" asked Armbruster.

As the door closed behind Ben, Hortense said anxiously, "Do you think Ben'll be back?"

"I doubt it," said Kate.

❖

CHAPTER EIGHT

Casts of Mind

To Armbruster's surprise and gratification, Ben was the first to arrive at the next session, brandishing a printed newsletter as he seated himself. "Wait till Kate hears this," he said. "She'll flip."

"Something to refute her?" asked Armbruster as he started the coffee and set out muffins and fruit.

"No, as a matter of fact, the opposite. From an unexpected source. A good source that I respect."

As soon as the others arrived, Armbruster gave Ben the floor. "This is a newsletter from an international ecological research organization based in England," Ben began. "It tells about important insights and breakthroughs made by Dr. Steve Cousins, a researcher on their staff. Wait till you hear! Ecologically speaking, we're part of the biosphere, like geology and climate.

"To understand this, you need a little background. The definition of an ecosystem says that it is 'composed of physical-chemical-biological processes active within a space-time unit of any magnitude.' All serious students of ecology consider that definition basic. But this newsletter points out that ecology still remains more a concept than a solid scientific discipline. So much research leads only into blind alleys. Cousins thinks 'of any magnitude' is too vague and that this fuzziness in the definition is a handicap.

"An objective way of delineating concrete ecosystem units and setting boundaries to them is missing. He's proposed that ecosystem units should be identified by their food webs, sometimes called food chains. However, that's just another concept unless there's a technique for identifying them and setting boundaries. So he proposes using the range of a locality's top predator group, the animal at the top of the local food web. For instance, polar bears' presence would identify and bound some units. Kodiak bears' ranges would identify and bound others; timber wolves' ranges others, and so on."

"I am not sure I understand this," said Jasper. "I would think human beings would be the top predator species everywhere. Take those polar bears. Eskimos kill and eat them. Where does that get you? It gets you one single ecosystem unit all the way from the Arctic to the tropics."

"Wait, there's more," said Ben. "When Cousins and his colleagues were first weighing the pros and cons of possible ecosystem unit definitions, before they hit on the food web as key, they puzzled over whether nonbiological factors like climate and geology could be paramount markers: rainfall, sunlight, temperature, wind forces, elevation, that sort of thing. They decided not, on the good grounds that they're already reflected in the food webs. So those factors were separated out. They're the biosphere environments in which biological ecosystem units sit.

"That reasoning led Cousins to another big breakthrough. He conceded that isolated human bands using primitive weapons to hunt could qualify as top predators. But he also pointed out that including human beings is unsatisfactory and that this must have been true even in olden times. For instance, ancient peoples came into wooded ecosystems and replaced the forests with field-and-hedgerow agriculture. Nothing else—this is important—except a radical change in climate would convert woodlands to grasslands and shrubs. So it follows that the effects of our species must be lumped in with effects of the biosphere.

"In short, he recognized that we're qualitatively different from other animals as ecological presences. But why? He puzzled over this until he came up with the answer. Trade! Trade pays no attention to ecosystem unit boundaries. It skips over them as it pleases, transferring surplus energy from this and that ecosystem unit into other ecosystem units. That's why we're unique, Cousins says. I thought you'd get a bang out of that, Kate. Fits right in with what you've been saying."

"Well, well," said Armbruster. "So the ecologists have rediscovered economy. That's ironic because, as I understand it, the early ecologists explained their preoccupation as 'the economy of nature,' to distinguish it from zoology, botany, or plain old-fashioned natural history.''

"I received that same newsletter, Ben," said Kate. "A different point struck me. Look again at the basic definition, 'physical-chemical-biological processes active within a space-time unit of any magnitude.' The definition has two parts. A scientist latches onto 'physical-chemical-biological processes' as its core, the knowledge to pursue. That's what Rachel Carson did in *Silent Spring,* for instance. This approach has given us all the good, hard information that we do have about ecology so far. In fact, that's even where the concept of food webs themselves came from, along with the understanding that they are incredibly intricate and vulnerable.

"But if one is guardian-minded instead of science-minded, the seductive part of the definition is its dependent clause, 'within a space-time unit of any magnitude.' Territory! And then it's logical for guardian-minded people to identify a given territorial unit by the range of its top predator—its prince. However, in the real ecosystems of the real world, obscure creatures can identify ecological units more tellingly than animals at the top of the food chain.''

"Why is that?" asked Jasper. "Explain what you mean."

Kate furrowed her forehead and said aloud to herself, "How shall I get into this? Ah, truffles!

"Here's an example," she went on. "In old-growth forests of the Pacific Northwest, vital types of organisms are certain kinds of fungi, called mycorrhizae. Some of them live underground. Their familiar name is truffles. They infect tree roots, because they depend on getting their nourishment from the trees. Infected trees grow tiny hair roots that spread across the forest floor and find phosphorus and nitrogen that is unavailable to the deeper roots. All the conifers in Pacific Northwest forests require truffle infections or they die. One experiment with Douglas fir seedlings showed that they died within two years of planting if they didn't become infected with mycorrhizae—truffles. Does this bore you?"

"No, no," said Armbruster. "Go on."

"Well, for the infections to maintain themselves, truffle spores must repeatedly come into direct contact with tree roots. The spores are dispersed in the droppings of mice, squirrels, chipmunks, and voles. They eat truffles. These little creatures form the food supply of the little northern spotted owl. If the owl population in such a forest declines, it can indicate that the truffle incidence has fallen too low to support good populations of the owls' prey, or it can mean that the healthy part of the forest has shrunk—the ecosystem unit is contracting its borders—so that it doesn't any longer afford a large enough range for owls. So the owls are a sensitive, useful indicator—"

"Like a canary bird in a coal mine, keeling over first if the air has gone bad?" asked Jasper.

"Sort of like that," said Kate. "Therefore the owl has been designated by foresters as an 'indicator species.' It defines this type of ecosystem unit more tellingly than top predators, which in this case would probably be black bears or bobcats. Those animals are more adaptable and wider ranging than the owls. So those territorial princes neither identify this type of unit nor indicate its boundaries with any accuracy, the services Cousins is looking for.

"His proposal to get more scientific by mapping out top-predator ranges is another blind alley. Instead, it's a rote, arbitrary, bureaucratic way of trying to impose order on reality. And he's wrong in thinking that science is retarded because 'a space-time unit of any magnitude' is too vague. It's not too vague. It's a plain statement that the magnitude is identifiable only by addressing chemical-physical-biological processes—in the case I just gave you, chemical reactions between fungi and trees, physical consequences to growth of tree roots, and necessary biological interventions of little creatures scampering on the ground. Cousins's bureaucratic predator mapping can't successfully shortcut the different kinds of investigation really needed, and could even be obfuscating. He's putting the cart before the horse."

"Whoa, Kate," said Armbruster. "Your fixation on science is blinding you to this institute's probable reason for being. Why have you jumped to the conclusion that its purpose is to slake scientific curiosity? Or that if it isn't, it should be?"

"Well, it does call itself a research institute. And I hate to see effort wasted on top-predator mapping—that takes a lot of fieldwork—when work and resources could be spent better learning about chemical-physical-biological processes. We need to know so much more about those than we do."

"Surely this outfit Cousins belongs to was formed because of anxiety about the natural environment, and with an intent to protect it," said Armbruster. "Indeed, help rescue it from great peril. Information is useful weaponry in that guardian cause, hence the yearning for research. You must recognize that protection of territories is of the essence in this cause. The primary aim. Therefore, a certain speed in identifying territorial units is desirable—even if the method adopted doesn't meet your criteria of the most important tasks.

"Furthermore," he continued, "we have here an interesting case of symbiosis between our two syndromes. You ask where ecology would be as a science if primary attention was not devoted to physical-chemical-biological processes. But we must also ask where ecology would be as a movement if primary attention was not paid to territories and their protection. The human impulse toward territorial protection and alarm at tidings of territorial peril are drives that are making what you scientists learn about physical-chemical-biological processes influential on our behavior. If you care about putting scientific learning to constructive use—and I know you do—then you need guardian-minded ecologists too. And you have to take them with their habits—fixation on territories and territorial princes, bureaucratic ways of bringing order to reality, and all. You went off half-cocked this time when you spoke of wasted effort. I applaud Cousins and his institute for understanding their guardian mission and researching ways to further it expeditiously."

Hortense, who had borrowed the newsletter from Ben, suddenly whooped. "There's no doubt, Armbruster, about this organization's thoroughly guardian point of view! Listen to this, apropos Cousins's insight into human uniqueness. They say, 'The depressing aspect of this perception is that human beings should be characterized by "trade." . . . The benefits are that we are part of something else, the biosphere.' "

"Nature worship is old, attractive, and tenacious," said Jasper. "So is the heady philosophical subject of mankind's puzzling place in the great overall scheme of things. This is theo-ecology, or maybe eco-theology—"

"You're ridiculing this," said Ben indignantly, then looked hurt and deflated.

"If something is a large, important truth, many entirely different avenues should lead to it," said Hortense thoughtfully. "Kate began with contradictory precepts and values. Cousins began with grasslands and shrubs. And look, they arrived at the same conclusion: trade makes us unique among animals. I think we owe Ben thanks for recognizing the significance of that." Ben smiled gratefully at Hortense.

"Casts of mind," said Jasper. "We postponed that from last time, remember? We are already into them. What I notice is that Cousins and his colleagues seem to have taken their guardian cast of mind for granted. They give no indication of recognizing that it differs from a scientific outlook like Kate's."

"But they probably have fine scientific educations and credentials," Ben protested. "Cousins, too, probably; his title is Dr. Cousins."

"So? Castro has credentials as an economist," said Jasper. "Education does not guarantee a cast of mind appropriate to the training. At the institute, Cousins and the others no doubt sincerely thought they were engaging in free intellectual inquiry. Yet their guardian assumptions, their guardian cast of mind, governed the root questions they were putting to themselves."

"You make casts of mind sound like fetters," said Hortense.

"That they can be, the more so, the less aware of them we are. Suppose we play a game, Kate. I will be Mr. Guardian and you be Ms. Commerce. I am saying, 'The love of money is the root of all evil.' "

"The love of power is the root of all evil," replied Kate.

"History tells of dynasties and the fates of nations and empires."

"History explains how material and social conditions have changed," said Kate.

"The most valuable archeological findings are works of art, tombs of royalty or chieftains, and evidences of palaces and religions," said Jasper.

"The most valuable archeological findings are evidences of how people made their livings, the tools and materials they had, the absence or presence of trade, and its components and extent," said Kate.

"War and preparations for war are normal in human life and peace is a chancy hiatus."

"No, peace is normal. War is an aberration and interruption."

"Man is the weapon-using animal. I have lifted that from Ardrey, one of the guardian-minded ethologists."

"Human beings are the tool-using animals. That's from Leakey and other science-minded scholars of human fossils," said Kate.

"Man is a territorial animal."

"People are city-building animals."

"Knowledge is a weapon, also an adornment," said Jasper.

"Knowledge is a tool," said Kate.

"Intelligence signifies knowledge of the enemy and his plans."

"Intelligence is deftness at picking up skills and reasoning well. The heck with the enemy. Look for intelligence among your friends and the people you work with."

"Natural resources are fundamental wealth," said Jasper.

"No, fundamental wealth is the knowledge and skills possessed by a population. Jasper, we make a vaudeville team of sorts, but we're sounding too frivolous." Kate searched in her rat's nest of frayed folders. "Here, Francis Bacon said this: 'The increase of any state must be upon the foreigner (for whatever is somewhere gained is somewhere lost).' Zero-sum thinking. It makes sense with regard to seizures and losses of territory, and gambling wins and losses, but otherwise not. People with guardian casts of mind tend to carry zero-sum thinking with them into their attempts to understand all kinds of gains and losses. When Cousins tried to explain trade in that newsletter, he called it transfer of 'surplus energy' from some ecosystems to others. Zero-sum thinking; more evidence of his guardian cast of mind. Marx analyzed gains of commercial wealth by some people as all but inescapably at the expense of others."

"I want my piece of the pie. Fair distribution is social justice," said Jasper.

"I want to make pies. Fair opportunity is social justice," said Kate.

"Taxes and public borrowing should be governed by public need, because well-being and success in everything depend on the public good."

"Taxes and public borrowing should be governed by what business can reasonably bear. Don't kill the geese that lay the golden eggs," said Kate.

"The declining economies in the former Soviet Union need to be brought under control," said Jasper.

"The declining economies in the former Soviet Union need to be decontrolled," said Kate.

"Japan is prosperous at our expense."

"Japan's prosperity enlarges total prosperity—which is open-ended, not zero-sum," said Kate.

"Ask not what your country can do for you, but what you can do for your country. That was President Kennedy."

"The state exists for the sake of its people. That's the supposed social contract," said Kate.

"Well, have we made a point, Armbruster?" asked Jasper. "That guardian and commercial casts of mind exist?"

"Indeed," said Armbruster, "and that they can have practical consequences. Bewildering, isn't it, how different the same subject matter can look? Now I'm going to report on why crazy things happen systematically when either moral syndrome—guardian or commercial—embraces functions inappropriate to it."

CHAPTER NINE

Armbruster on Systemic Moral Corruption

Aʀᴍʙʀᴜsᴛᴇʀ pushed aside his coffee cup to make room for his notes and asked, "Remember Quincy? When he dropped in the first night we met, he told us that foreign loan defaults had put his bank in a pickle? I've had lunch with him since I saw you last."

"I remember his seeming very down," said Hortense, "and saying he didn't think dwelling on morality could throw any light on his troubles. Why didn't you invite him here today?"

"He declined. He's more than preoccupied, which is how I'd figured him. You're perceptive, Hortense. Quincy's deeply pessimistic and depressed. But I bullied him into talking more, and you'll have to put up with my secondhand account.

"I put it to him that those foreign loans hadn't been for productive investments, because if they had been, then by definition they would have been able to support interest and repayments of principal. He agreed. Ergo, they must have been something else."

"Couldn't they have been bad judgments about investments?" asked Ben. "Never underestimate the stupidity of bankers."

Armbruster smiled. "In some ways you and he think alike; he tried to sell me that bill of goods about honest mistakes all over again. 'Come on,' I told him. 'At that scale, and that consistently, and by so many banks simultaneously?' He finally agreed that ordinary investment mis-judgments didn't seem to cover the situation adequately. Ergo, I said, that 'something else' must have been largesse.

"Upon reflection, he agreed more quickly than I expected, although he said that was less evident at the time than in hindsight. The gist of what the banks did, as he described it to me, was to cooperate with the World Bank by financing the pork-barrel projects it worked up, gigantic ones. The World Bank, in spite of its name, is a thoroughly political outfit, not a commercial enterprise. The banks were also egged on by our own government to make loans that bolstered anticommunist regimes and influenced iffy regimes that might otherwise lean toward the Soviets. Some loans were calculated to undercut popular unrest. In sum, he now views the bad loans as fallout from the Cold War. In the receiving countries, he conceded, a lot of loan money went into ostenta-tion on the part of rulers and largesse to their own henchmen, also domestic subsidies to keep things calm. Of course all of these are classic uses of largesse, including the big pork-barrel projects.

"I pointed out to him that unless his bank was blind, the nonproduc-tive uses to which borrowed money was put must have become evident fairly early on. 'How did you people get in so deep,' I asked, 'and why did you keep on with this charade so long?'

"In sum, his answer was 'competition.' His own bank, he admitted ruefully, set up offices in poor foreign capitals, in competition with other banks doing the same, and flew in hustlers to press and persuade poor governments to go deeper and deeper into debt.

"In other words—pay attention to this, now—the normal commer-cial virtues of competitiveness, industriousness, and efficiency made matters worse. Under the circumstances, those normal virtues automat-ically converted to vices."

"Like loyalty automatically converting to a vice when bribe taking occurs in a guardian organization," said Kate.

"It's the same dynamic," said Armbruster. "And Quincy told you himself about the next stage—the expedient of resorting to false ac-counting—with the expedient collusion of the guardians, to be sure.

"Using this as my first example, I give you my Law of Intractable Systemic Corruption. It's this: Any significant breach of a syndrome's integrity—usually by adopting an inappropriate function—causes some normal virtues to convert automatically to vices, and still others to bend and break for necessary expedience. *Voilà!* A systemic process of intrac-table corruption."

He consulted a note. "Here's what Sir Lewis Namier said. He was an English historian of the behavior of members of Parliament. He commented, 'In groups and when in office men frequently act out of character'—he was speaking of moral character—'as though driven by an extraneous force . . . a power hidden behind the circumstances.'

"If my Law of Intractable Corruption is a true description of the results of a significant syndrome breach, then the 'extraneous force' and hidden power that puzzled Namier is the automatic sequel to the breach. It wasn't in Quincy's character, for instance, to resort to false accounting, dishonesty, with or without guardian collusion. Regardless, he and others like him were driven to it as a sequel to their moral mistake of dispensing largesse.

"As Kate and Jasper explained them, these syndromes fall into the great category of self-organizing systems. They arose existentially as events and activities required them and tested them. I'm now arguing that when integrity is significantly breached, these self-organizing systems become self-disorganizing. Again, existentially."

"You sound so profound, but this is so superficial," said Ben. "A mess like Quincy's comes from the mania for growth, growth, growth. If we'd get back to simpler and saner ways of life, you'd see moral messes automatically disappearing."

"Simplicity is no protection against the Law of Intractable Systemic Corruption," said Armbruster. "Let me tell you what happened to the Ik."

"The what?"

"Ik. Here's a simple life for you. The Ik are a group of brown-skinned Africans, ethnically typed as Nilotics; possibly they're descendants of an outlying branch of ancient Egyptians. But for as long as is known, by them or by others, they'd been roaming about in the wild mountains where the southern Sudan, Kenya, and Uganda meet."

"Remember your telling me to ignore exotic information about tribesmen?" Kate asked mischievously.

"Indeed. That was before you and Jasper persuaded me it could be germane. To continue—there they were, making their livings by spearing antelope and leopards, rifling ants' nests for edible larvae, setting fires in gorges to smoke out birds and then netting them, digging up wild roots, and the like, not bothering anybody else and not being bothered. You'll be interested to know that in their abundant leisure they made sculptures, which they hid in almost inaccessible caves in the faces of high and dangerous cliffs. As hunters they were masters of deception, and a chief recreation seems to have been contriving deceptive practical jokes, which they thought hilarious.

"That was Ik life until the 1950s, when Kenya established a vast game preserve incorporating much of the Ik territory. The Ik were rounded up and relocated on tracts too small to accommodate foraging livelihoods. The idea was to convert them to subsistence farming. They were shown how to plant, weed, harvest, and construct granaries. They were given supplies of seeds and tools. They were presented with sites for villages, along with gifts of field watchtowers so the children could shoo off marauding animals and birds. They weren't saddled with a mania for growth, Ben. They had no obligation to produce surpluses for export or any other purpose, even taxes.

"But the Ik already had a different way of getting a living and a simple but appropriate moral syndrome for it. They had the hunting-and-gathering conservation practice of exerting themselves only as they needed for current requirements. I've already mentioned that as hunters they were masters of deception. They had no need for centralized organization nor for hierarchy and obedience since neither aggressive nor defensive warfare was part of their experience.

"The moment a new way of getting a living was imposed on them, it proved to be not only a significant breach of their old morality but a fatal breach. Their former virtues automatically converted to vices. Instead of drudging away industriously during seasons of good rainfall and piling up currently unneeded supplies for lean seasons ahead, they did only the minimum of work to get by at the moment. Instead of saving seed for the next planting, they ate it. Their hunters' virtue of deceptiveness, combined with the practice of picking up whatever was available, turned ugly. People who ran short of food raided neighbors' fields and granaries. Those who'd been raided did the same. Takers all.

"Colin Turnbull, an anthropologist who first studied them when they were about ten years into their new life, said: 'Every Ik knew that trying to store anything was a waste of time.' It would only be seized. Hungry and idle adults had taken to snatching food out of the very hands of foraging toddlers.

"When Turnbull was first among them they were famished because of drought and because the able-bodied young men monopolized relief food entrusted to them for the women, children, and the infirm. Turnbull excused the rapacity and brutality he saw as the results of near-starvation. But when times got better, nothing improved socially or morally. Turnbull returned at a time of good rainfall and gluts of food in neglected fields. He observed, 'If they had been mean and greedy and selfish before with nothing to be mean and greedy and selfish over, now that they had something they really excelled themselves in what would be an insult to animals to call bestiality.' Anyone injured or otherwise at a disadvantage was cold-bloodedly robbed, then taunted or worse. The brutality to children was more appalling than anything except the brutality of children to each other and anyone else they could victimize.

"But don't think these were stupid people. For purposes of picking up whatever was available, they were clever as could be. The young men had now made a permanent racket of coaxing relief food and monopolizing it for themselves. An elder who was a supreme master of deception deliberately fomented cattle raids among Masai herdsmen wandering into the vicinity. He cunningly set herdsmen against herdsmen and then got payoffs from them all by serving as informer and double agent. The police were at their wits' end trying to control the mystifying outbreaks of Masai raiding and fighting. The Ik found an advantage in this police activity, too. In return for payoffs from all sides in the cattle raiding, they set up a well-organized service for concealing stolen cattle from the police, complete with a warning system of horns sounded from village to village. Intractably corrupted themselves, the Ik were now corrupting everything they touched.

"Family life had broken down. The population, which seems to have been about three thousand when the game preserve was established, was declining drastically, mainly because of horrible treatment of one another. Might and cunning make right, the law of the jungle, isn't conducive to human survival even when the locale is wilderness. Apart from a few exceptions—"

"Aha, so there were exceptions!" said Hortense.

"As far as Turnbull tells, two misfits: a woman who managed to make crude pottery and tried to trade it with neighbors, and a young man who tried to be a good father and became an enthusiastic builder in wood for Turnbull. He became a tradesman, in the sense of learning a trade and getting a livelihood in exchange for his work. It's sad about them. Both were soon dead of misfortunes and brutalities from the others. I suppose you could say some young women—hardly more than children, really—went into trade too because they traded sex to the police for trinkets and food.

"Turnbull went from shock to deep despair. Like so many anthropologists who've studied intact hunting-and-gathering groups—as he'd previously done in another region of Africa—he admired these societies for their egalitarianism, harmony with nature, humor, and hospitality, and their lack of attachment to private property. He cherished a faith that human nature was innocent and good before it fell afoul of hierarchies and profit making. But now, to his horror, he thought he was seeing human nature naked. It undermined his confidence in the whole human enterprise.''

''Do you think he really was seeing naked human nature?'' asked Hortense.

''Who knows? All we encounter are human beings dressed in cultures and values of some kind. But as Kate drummed into us, you have to have the right values and morals for the job at hand, not contradictory ones. Farming didn't fail the Ik because they were physically incapable of the work, nor because they didn't have the material equipment for it, nor because they didn't know how to use the equipment, nor because they were unintelligent. They'd been given the artifacts and taught the mentifacts but they had the wrong ethifacts. To return to your happy supposition about simplicity of life as a shield against corruption, Ben— if anything, simple societies are most vulnerable to corruption. They have so little cushion.''

''The authorities were to blame for this,'' said Ben. ''It was their mania for profit and growth. They probably made the game preserve to bring in rich tourists—''

''Agreed,'' said Armbruster. ''Turnbull was describing an extreme form of the intractable degeneration that often follows when authorities, intent on their own territorial schemes, displace those who stand in the way of their plans.''

''Maybe the Ik should have been included in the preserve,'' said Kate. ''They needed protection as much as zebras or leopards and they were a normal part of the ecosystem.''

''Or maybe they could have been hired on to combat poachers and encroachments by pasturing,'' said Hortense. ''They must have known the territory better than anybody. Think of the traps and ambushes and warning systems they could have set up!''

''We can't undo what was done to them,'' said Armbruster, ''and neither can anyone else. Turnbull's proposed solution was to take all Ik children away, kidnap them, in effect, and disperse them among other tribes and cultures. Whether that was done he doesn't tell, nor do we know how the displaced children might have fared. It sounds reasonable, perhaps, but so did making the Ik into farmers evidently sound reasonable. Turnbull himself was anguished by his recommendation because when he came among the Ik and solicited their forbearance and cooperation—such as it was—he promised them no harm would befall them as a result of his presence. His own morality—in this case, holding to a solemn promise—broke under the press of expedience. That was another element in his despair.''

"In comparison, one can almost view Quincy's problems lightheartedly and see how neat and easy a way out could have been found for the banks," said Jasper.

"In a sense, his problems are connected with what I've just been telling you. Not connected with the Ik, but with displacements and pauperizations of hundreds and hundreds of other simple communities, mostly peasant, by the inane megaprojects of the World Bank—unproductive dams were the worst—that Quincy's bank helped finance. The environmental degradation, the plight of the displaced victims, and their helplessness in face of the alliances among the World Bank, the commercial banks, corrupt and uncaring rulers, and North American manufacturers, engineering firms, and consultants who benefited from contracts for the pork-barrel projects—all this has been documented and described by Patricia Adams in her books *Odious Debts* and *In the Name of Progress*. She also describes further big schemes in the works, promising more of the same. Add to this that when the large-scale defaults hit the banks, the International Monetary Fund, a sister institution of the World Bank, imposed austerity programs on defaulting countries as a condition for receiving further loans.''

"Quincy didn't tell us about that," said Hortense.

"No, but I discussed it with him. This was the first line of defense tried, to evade debt write-downs. The stratagem was to mandate expanded export work in poor countries to earn hard cash for interest payments; cut imports; and cut or cancel domestic subsidies for food and other necessities. Poor people with low living standards, who'd been promised development and better times, found their living standards were dropping still further. Following riots in some poor cities and threat of more, the IMF had to pull back. What's the easy, neat solution you had in mind, Jasper?''

"I did not mean a solution for the harm done by largesse masked as loans. As you said of the Ik, what has been done to victims cannot be undone. I referred to a neat, easy solution for banks like Quincy's. The just thing would have been for our government to assume their losses, because largesse is a government function.''

"No, Jasper, think what you're saying," Hortense interrupted. "You're proposing that banks lend on their own responsibility and then, after the fact, extract compensation for defaults from taxpayers. That isn't control of the public purse by elected representatives of the people. It's subversive of democratic government itself.''

"But the taxpayers are on the hook for salvaging bank failures caused by the savings-and-loan scandals," said Jasper. "Largesse seems a more legitimate taxpayer responsibility than savings-and-loan frauds, bad loans to cronies of bankers, embezzlements, incompetence, and money laundering.''

"The taxpayers are legitimately on the hook there," said Armbruster. "Our elected representatives, for whatever reasons, crooked or well meant, obligated the government to insure deposits in those banks. They also laid a long series of legislated financial minefields, which led to scandals and failures. To be sure, the taxpayers didn't realize what they were in for. Insurance is a commercial device, supported by premiums, but sooner or later insurance in guardian hands converts to largesse instead, as it has in this instance.''

Armbruster now rose to his feet and waved a new sheet of notes. "Listen carefully to this," he demanded, "and then tell me what you suppose these phrases refer to:

"Hired guns. Impending carnage. Circles vulturelike. Commandos. A stark clash of cultures. Fear of becoming a scalp on someone's belt. Ferocious opposition. Protect the castle. Breathing time to mount a defense. Hysteria. War chest. Scorched earth. Unsuspecting prey. Rival predators. Defense turned offense. Larger fiefdoms. Hit list of targets. Sharing the prey. An army on a sprawling battleground. A donnybrook. Throwing roundhouse punches. Epic struggle. Going for the jugular. Conquerors. Blood money. Pull the trigger. Well?''

"A week's worth of television violence," said Kate.

"Sounds like the war in Lebanon," said Hortense.

"An amateur's attempt at a historical novel," said Jasper.

"Cards for some new game," said Ben. "Something for people bored with Monopoly.''

"Pretty close, Ben," said Armbruster. "But it's for real. I copied all those phrases out of ordinary, factual news stories in *The Wall Street*

Journal. They were reporting doings of investment bankers and their corporate clients in the mid-1980s.''

"Bizarre," said Jasper. "Do you have any more such lists?"

"I stopped only when I got tired of making them. Here's one drawn from phrases in a single article featured in the business section of another staid newspaper. It composes itself into a gruesome little poem:

"Frog-marched off to the barren lands
Toppled from the throne
Axed with primitive savagery
Shot down in a dog fight triggered by a poisonous letter
Blown away by a time bomb ticking since his loss of a murderous battle
Stripped of the swords and epaulettes of power.

"That was to bring business readers up to date on corporate presidents and chairmen who'd recently lost their jobs."

"Reporters always indulge themselves if you let them," said Jasper. "I know, I was one myself; my first job. But I don't know what's happened to editing."

"This is war reporting," said Armbruster. "No guns and axes, to be sure. But to find words for the aggression, conquest, mayhem, and defenses being reported it was necessary to resort to war imagery. Commercial imagery can't supply them. The protagonists themselves were thinking and talking in these terms. They themselves invented and named such weaponry as poison pills, white knights, and greenmail."

" 'Green' is a good word," said Ben. "But that sounds like black-mail."

"Indeed. The 'green' in this case is money, and the word's an analogue to 'blackmail.' Extortion of high prices for stock held by the extortioner, backed by threat to use the stock in a takeover battle if payment demands aren't met. 'Camomail,' a variant, is camouflaged greenmail."

"That was the eighties," said Hortense. "It's passé."

"Not as passé as the Ik. I'm not giving you a class in current events, Hortense. I'm reporting on the principle of intractable systemic corruption. The eighties were very educational.

"In this case, the key system corrupted was investment banking. That's the banking, you may already know, that organizes and under-writes issues of stocks and bonds for corporations and bonds for governments and puts them on the market. These specialized banking houses also sometimes arrange loans to corporations from their own bank capital or help arrange financing from other institutions. A logical addition to these services has been advice to clients on mergers and acquisitions and negotiations to arrange them. For instance, a company with a good product but weak marketing and distribution might merge with another having complementary strengths. One with extreme seasonal fluctuations in its work might merge with another that evens out the ups and downs. A corporation might buy up a range of other companies as practical production footholds for new products its own researchers had been developing. A failing company might seek a merger that could resuscitate it.''

''Why wouldn't the failing company just hire some resuscitation whizzes?'' asked Ben.

''Could happen, but the failing company might lack other resources, too, like a good credit line or cash flow for investment in its operations.

''All this is quite in harmony with the commercial syndrome. But the line between mergers and acquisitions ruled by commercial criteria and those responding to sheer aggrandizement is subtle and insidiously easy to cross. All the same, it's a portentous line—nothing less than the basic line between trading and taking.

''Let me take you through a little history. The types of mergers most obviously at odds with the commercial syndrome are contrived to dispose of competition—create monopolies. About a century ago in this country aggrandizers were rigging regional and even national monopolies for themselves at a great rate. These were called trusts, an inappropriate word if there ever was one. There was even an ice trust victimizing the big cities of the Northeast—this was in the days before artificial refrigeration. In all kinds of fields the trusts were squeezing out or gobbling up competitors and exploiting captive customers and suppliers. This was in such blatant contradiction to ethical commercial practice that early this century the guardians—in this case, Congress— passed antitrust laws making monopolistic mergers and acquisitions illegal. Those already contrived were prosecuted by the Department of Justice. When trusts lost those suits, they were broken up into separate parts by court order.''

''Why wouldn't the parts still work like monopolies behind the scenes?'' asked Ben.

''Those stratagems—say, joint price fixing or colluding on bids—

were practices in restraint of trade,'' put in Hortense. ''They were illegal and could be prosecuted too.''

''Were investment bankers involved in building trusts?'' asked Ben.

''Indeed, although some corporations managed sufficiently on their own. Now we come to a different stage of mergers that cross over into taking: conglomerate building. Conglomerates aren't illegal as long as they don't monopolize any given field. They're contrived by picking up diverse collections of enterprises with little or no working relationship to one another—just conglomerations, hence the name. All that the parts have in common, really, is their consolidated ownership by a holding company or a corporation.

''Even though the line between the commercial and the taking approaches was being crossed by organizations picking up whatever was available, ready at hand, at least voluntary mutual agreement between buyers and sellers of companies was still being respected.

''But in due course along came bolder and more ruthless acquisitors. They cared nothing about voluntary mutual agreement. Their aim was to take what they coveted, regardless. That's when the pages of the business press began to read like parodies of barbarian sagas and Old West shoot-outs.''

''When do you date that?'' asked Kate.

''The great decade of conglomerate building was the 1960s, although the practice had been increasing rapidly through the fifties and it continued later. Hostile takeovers began sporadically in the 1970s. By 1983—and especially in the six years through 1988—they were ordinary, everyday occurrences. They grew steadily larger, too, to the point that huge conglomerates were hostilely taking over other huge conglomerates, sometimes only to be taken over by yet another.

''Investment banking houses were in the thick of this. They searched out enterprises to be picked off for the picking, stalked them, and drew them to the attention of aggrandizing clients. They helped plot aggressions for some clients and defenses for others. They made enormous fees in both services. And as ingenious workaholics they found ways of financing raiders and aggrandizers hitherto unknown, and ways of defense also hitherto unknown—in fact hitherto unneeded.''

''It sounds rather like the Ik setting herdsmen against herdsmen,'' said Kate.

''Mind you,'' Armbruster continued, ''all this was legal. And I'm not describing cases of individual commercial misfits in ethical contexts.

Entire organizations, in the end an entire system composed of many organizations, had slid by degrees across the commercial syndrome barriers, into taking. They prided themselves on it.'' He waved a newspaper sheet. ''Here's a full-page advertisement for the investment-bank arm of the country's largest bank holding company. In its entirety, this is its message in large black letters: 'Investment banking should be defined only by customer needs and our imagination in meeting those needs.' It used to be defined by much else, specifically commercial morality.''

''What kinds of tricks did the bankers think up?'' asked Ben.

''The most far-reaching in its consequences was the leveraged buy-out.''

''Stop right there,'' said Ben. ''I've heard about leveraged buy-outs—who hasn't—but I don't understand them.''

''It's a way of making a corporation pay for its own change in ownership and control, pay for its own taking. First, there's likely a bidding war for a controlling share of its voting stock. The winner, who puts in some money of his own but also borrows heavily for stock or stock options—''

''Wouldn't it be risky to lend money on that?'' Kate asked.

''Not really, because the stock and stock options are collateral for the loan, and the bidding war in itself drives up their price. No, the amazing part is that whoever wins control in this contest can use that lever to commit the corporation he's taken over to buying the stock he ac-cumulated for the takeover. The corporation takes on debt—a big debt burden—to do just that. If it can't get enough financing at regular bank rates for the purpose, it arranges with an investment banking house specializing in this problem to float an issue of what are called junk bonds and sell them to investors willing to take more than a usual risk in return for more than usual interest, say fifty percent higher. In short, the corporation whose control has just been purchased borrows to pay for its own purchase.''

''You mean the guy who got the corporation is getting it free, for nothing?'' demanded Ben. ''You mean he uses what he took to pay for taking it? What a racket!''

''That's what guardians taking territory by military conquest have often done,'' said Kate. ''Invested in the prowess for taking the terri-tory, or borrowed to pay for the campaign; then the conquered territory paid in plunder, tribute, taxes, or natural resources for its own sei-zure.''

"But how does this corporation that paid for its change in control pay back the debt it had to take on?" asked Ben. "Seize another corporation?"

"Sometimes, but there are other ways. Payments come due at different times. For the most pressing, the new people in control may sell off divisions or subsidiaries as going concerns. They usually try to bargain off the least profitable. If there aren't takers, the divisions or subsidiaries can be closed down and their assets sold off—inventories, equipment, real estate. That means employees are out of jobs. But in any case there are job losses. To carry the interest and eventually the repayment of principal, other costs are pared, a painful process known as becoming lean and mean.

"All sorts of bystanders get entangled in these thorns," Armbruster went on. "Some innocent, some, in the end, not so innocent. Corporations taking on a lot of debt need to assure lenders they'll be able to handle the burden. Satisfactory assurance can be a 'solvency letter' from a certified accounting firm that's audited the books and investigated what's behind them. It's satisfactory only because accounting firms are trusted. Normally they hew strictly to the commercial syndrome and put honesty first and foremost. That's their function in commercial life—to deliver and certify honest accounting. But as of 1987, according to *The Wall Street Journal,* the going price being offered for solvency letters by corporations desperate for unjustifiable financing was five hundred thousand dollars. The letters became newsworthy because one was an issue in a bankruptcy case involving a corporation that didn't prove solvent."

"Half a million's a lot for a letter," said Hortense. "But I'm surprised a respected accounting firm would think of jeopardizing its reputation for the money, to say nothing of possibly opening itself to suits by falsely lulled creditors."

"Accountants told the *Journal* that corporate clients threaten to change auditors, take their accounting business elsewhere, when the solvency letters they want aren't forthcoming."

"Competition converting to vice," said Kate.

"Yes, and other virtues breaking under pressure. The *Journal* also reported that accounting firms were pressed to find new sources of income because mergers had so severely reduced the ranks of corporate clients. As for the junk bond gambles on leveraged buy-out debt, the whole society, more or less, was implicated. Maybe you, Ben, if you have an insurance policy or money in a pension fund." Armbruster

consulted a pie-shaped diagram. "At the end of 1987, insurance companies held thirty percent of junk bonds. Mutual funds and money managers, including managers of institutional funds like university
endowments, held another thirty percent. Pension funds, fifteen percent; savings-and-loan banks, eight percent. Junk bonds have been a
very American thing. All foreign investors combined held only five
percent.

"Economists say low rates of saving on the part of Americans have
put this country at a disadvantage compared with Japan, Switzerland,
Denmark, Norway, West Germany, and others. But what do savings go
into? It could be argued that if Americans saved more, nonproductive
uses of money would only soak up more.

"I've been giving you a somewhat slanted account so far. I've omitted
the logic that said conglomerate building, leveraged buy-outs, and hostile takeovers were harmless or even beneficial. In the interests of
fairness, we must take such views into account. Buying and selling
corporations is essentially no different from buying and selling anything.
Borrowing on a corporation's assets and future earnings to pay for its
own control is essentially no different from borrowing on assets and
future earnings to buy new machinery—"

"It's totally different!" said Hortense. "Productive investment—"

Armbruster held up his hand. "Let me continue. Even in the case of
hostile takeovers, success depends on getting hold of sufficient stock,
and this is accomplished through voluntary agreement, as the result of
bargaining with sellers of stock. Plants closed up and dismantled, even
in cases where they'd been paying their way as producers, weren't
pulling their proportionate weight as corporate profit makers, which is
why they got the ax. This argument has it that the common economic
good is the winner, the beneficiary, if equipment and other assets fall
into the hands of enterprises more successful at producing profits. The
weak are being weeded out to enhance survival of the fittest."

"Poor Darwin," said Kate. "Intellectual recourse of the ruthless!
The Ik who grabbed food from children could have used that argument
just as wrongheadedly if they'd known it."

"The lean-and-mean part of which I spoke has been widely extolled
as the discipline required to improve efficiency and thus competitiveness."

"But Armbruster, there's something illogical here," said Hortense.
"If a corporation takes on a lot of debt to change control, the debt costs

have to be added to whatever it sells—where else can it get them over the long run? So doesn't that harm its competitive pricing?"

"Certainly," said Armbruster. "But the new management hopes leanness and meanness will compensate."

"That's different from improved efficiency arising out of inventiveness requiring productive investment," said Kate.

"There isn't much scope for commercial inventiveness in this turmoil and battle and survival of the fittest," said Armbruster. "Hostile takeovers and leveraged buy-outs have drained away management time and attention. So have defenses mounted to try to defeat them, even if successful. Other business was shunted aside until crises were resolved one way or the other. For a given corporation, threats and then battles could continue a year or more. Then there were results of mismatched mergers, not infrequent. They're called clashes of corporate cultures. The internal frictions, misunderstandings, and rivalries these create also tend to go on for years. During all these events the morale of employees typically plummets while stress and anxieties soar. Beginning with the first rumors of threatened takeover, there could be, and often was, an exodus of capable people hoping to find more secure berths.

"But to take the part of devil's advocate again, I must mention the argument that hostile takeovers replace old, tired management with energetic, aggressive new blood."

"Do you believe that?" Hortense asked.

"Sometimes it may be true. But old, tired, declining companies aren't what takeover virtuosos really want. They're drawn to successful companies for obvious reasons. So it's quite as probable, or more so, that a hostile purchaser who knows nothing about the business except how to get hold of it replaces capable and conscientious management. Or mediocre management may be replacing mediocre management.

"Now I'll argue a mitigating result," Armbruster went on. "I got this from Quincy at lunch. I think he was trying to cheer himself up. You may remember he mentioned that defaulted buy-out loans, along with bad real estate loans—largely for unsalable condominiums and half-empty office towers and shopping malls—had piled themselves on top of the foreign-loan loss allowances. At least, he told me, leveraged buy-outs came pretty much to a halt immediately after a few cases of big bankruptcies and threats of others. Self-correction of the economy, he said. The frenzy ran itself into the ground—for the time being, that is. Of course waste inevitably does, eventually.

"But water over the dam carries debris, I told him. Between 1960 or, say, 1955 and 1990, American industry has been restructured, as economists put it. Much has come under the control of people with a taking cast of mind, conquerors as unfit for guiding commercial life as Castro. Great gratuitous debt burdens remain. Maybe most seriously, much time has been wasted while practical problems were piling up unsolved and constructive opportunities slipped away along with the water gone over the dam. All that isn't inconsequential debris. How deeply our economic life has been wounded, and how permanently it may be handicapped by this grand exercise in restructuring, we have yet to see.

"Now that I've become aware of the susceptibility of our syndromes to significant breaches of their precepts and subsequent self-disorganization, I'm alarmed at the lack of general understanding of working-life morality. Such confusion! People who ought to know better don't seem to."

"I seem to remember," said Jasper, "that your own publishing company, before your retirement, put out a book counseling business managers to study Machiavelli's advice to the Prince and apply it to their work. So you, too, are implicated in this confusion, right?"

"Yes, our mistake. Machiavelli was the managerial fashion that year unfortunately. At least we turned down another, based upon Clausewitz on war, and passed up the Sun Tzu fad."

"Never heard of it—what's that?" asked Ben.

"A two-thousand-year-old Chinese book on the art of war. The advertising come-on for American businessmen tells them Japanese businessmen are on to it; describes the book as meant for managers 'who look upon the marketplace as the equivalent of a battleground.'

"Apropos managerial advice books, here's another list I compiled for you. Thank God we had no responsibility for this one. It's by Antony Jay, an English author who bills himself as a successful manager—which he was in the British Broadcasting Corporation, where he wrote and helped produce two marvelously comic television series on the machinations of English civil servants and politicians. Then, by his own account, he turned business consultant at the service of corporations. He draws his precepts for managers—mind you, he's serious about this even though insufferably arch—from prisoner-of-war camps, sports, boys' schools, conspiracies, tribal hunting bands—he's big on hunting bands—baronies, duchies, principalities, empires, the Roman legions, the army of Genghis Khan, the British army, the U.S. Army, wolf packs, and troops of baboons. The picture on the jacket shows a bisected man, half of him dressed in a suit and holding an attaché case, the other half with a fur loincloth and a stone-tipped spear.''

"He sounds like an individual with a guardian cast of mind who has strayed into business," said Jasper.

"Indeed. He's a more-clever-than-usual example of a type: the Englishman well furnished by education and interests to take his place in the affairs of empire. With the empire gone, these chaps condescend to help business shape up.

"But we can't blame this sort of confusion on the playing fields of Eton. Here's *The Wall Street Journal* again, speaking for itself, not quoting anybody. It calls 'middle management' the junior officers and top sergeants 'of the American business army.' Let's break for lunch.''

Hortense had organized lunch: yogurt in five flavors and, to Ben's delight, a salad of bean sprouts, alfalfa sprouts, raw mushrooms, and cooked chickpeas. Dessert was fruit, fresh and dried. Armbruster, dismayed, was mollified by the addition of a cheese board.

Polishing off his Gruyère and an apple, Armbruster took up his discourse again. "So vulnerable are syndromes to systematic corruption, systemic self-disorganization, that in some cases the only breach necessary is an operational method drawn from the inappropriate syndrome. For example, some years ago the management of the transit police—the special police for our subway system—hired a consultant to study the force and suggest improvements. He seems to have had a commercial cast of mind. At any rate, he emphasized industriousness and proposed encouraging it by tracking it statistically. His intellectual model was output of product per man-hour of work, as if policing were a form of factory production—commercial work—instead of guardian work. He needed a quantifiable measurement of output and settled on numbers of arrests per work-hour. Policemen achieving the best productivity records were to be rewarded by better assignments. His expertise impressed the management, who, I must say, appear to have been dim-witted, and they adopted the scheme.''

"Oh, oh, I can see it coming," said Hortense.

"Yes, false arrests. Of course they had to be plausible enough to stick under prosecution. So most of the innocent victims were Hispanic or black men, who are typically given little credence in court against the word of police. They were easily persuaded to plead guilty in return for reduced charges.''

"How were the busy beavers unmasked?" asked Jasper.

"Bad luck. They made the mistake of falsely arresting a regular New York City policeman who's black and was off duty in civilian clothes. He was suspended from his job and had a terrible time proving his innocence. But he refused to plea-bargain or stop struggling, and finally his own detective work and tenacity yielded confessions from false witnesses brought against him. There followed an investigation in the district attorney's office which uncovered the extensive pattern."

"What about the cast of mind of the crooked policemen?" asked Ben. "Would you say it converted to commercial?"

"Oh no. Like most police they were hunters. This virtue converted to vice when their quarry was redefined for them as a statistical record. It reminds one of enemy body counts in Vietnam, which made officers look good to superiors up the line, all the way to the White House. Warfare on a production model. Much commercial thinking has filtered into modern warfare. Cost-benefit analyses of bombing runs; kill ratios.

"Simultaneously, armament factories have picked up unbusinesslike waste, such deceptions as falsified time sheets to conceal idleness, and above all deceptiveness in their cost estimates. A wondrous machine, the military-industrial complex, for churning out intractable systemic corruption.

"Consider the contracts between the Pentagon and producers of highly engineered equipment like tanks, planes, missiles, and other sophisticated weapons. I emphasize 'highly engineered' because of a subsidiary corruption that follows when industrialists breach commercial integrity in contracts they make with the military.

"One such contract is called the buy-in. A manufacturer of military equipment or a prime contractor who organizes the work of many manufacturers submits a deceptive bid for design and production work—a bid deliberately set too low to pay for the work. This is done in collusion with the customer, the Pentagon. If the probable true cost were revealed, Congress might not authorize the undertaking or might reduce its scope and scale. However, once a deceptive contract is let, the manufacturer or prime contractor counts on being paid more later on, as much as several hundred percent more. The appropriations for those increases can be extracted by the Pentagon later, with the argument to Congress that if they aren't forthcoming, the money already granted and spent will have been wasted."

"Congress can't be that dumb not to realize what's happening," said Hortense.

"Certainly some members are well aware, particularly those whose districts are receiving the jobs on a given buy-in. To them, it's largesse, and the prospect of later inflation of cost and jobs is an additional benefit. However, every now and again, when the subsequent added costs become too outrageous, Congress does refuse to play the game. It turns off the money taps and then some companies are trapped by their own false buy-in bids. Lockheed Aircraft was trapped in so many buy-in contracts at one point that it became insolvent. Congress then had to rescue it. Incidentally, one consequence of the rescue operation was a congressional investigation of what Lockheed had been doing with its income, which is how the company's bribery payments to aircraft purchasing officials and other big wheels in foreign governments were publicly uncovered.

"The usual alternative to the buy-in is the cost-plus contract. Sometimes the 'plus' part of the contract is a flat fee; sometimes it's a percentage of costs."

"But that's not deceptive; that's honest in acknowledging that costs are not solid and fixed," said Hortense.

"Yes, but here's where I come to the significance of 'highly engineered' products. Neither type of contract exerts the cost discipline of commercial life. If anything, the cost-plus may be the greater offender; when the profit, the 'plus,' is a percentage of costs, it can be an incentive to increase costs.

"Industrial engineers are the great custodians of productivity in manufacturing—major antagonists of waste and inefficiency, major dissenters to doing things an old way if a better new way can be devised. Their objects are to maximize efficiency and minimize costs. Normally, commercial cost discipline and competitiveness keep them up to snuff.

"Now, consider the observations of Seymour Melman, professor emeritus of industrial engineering at Columbia University. Engineers working in the military-industrial complex are skillful at designing ingenious products but, Melman points out, they fail to combine this skill with thrift of means. He calls the situation 'trained incompetence' and says it has corrupted the abilities of most of the country's best and brightest engineers over the span of the past forty years. In addition, lack of cost discipline—or you can think of it as efficiency and productivity discipline—has side effects outside the military-industrial complex. That's because when costs are of little or no concern to a manufacturer, it becomes slipshod about the costs of its supplies, too, including engineered equipment purchased from others. That carelessness rubs off on people like machine tool designers and producers. Melman thinks the decline in American machine tool manufacturing, accompanying the rise of the military-industrial complex, is no coincidence.''

''I had an idea that we're leaders in machine tools,'' said Hortense.

''Ancient history, that. Just in the years between 1980 and 1988, our share of machine tool world markets dropped from eighteen percent to seven percent.''

''Couldn't that be a result of the great restructuring you ex-pounded?'' Hortense persisted. ''You said people weren't minding the store.''

''Could be, but it is specifically a failure of industrial engineering. Our machine tool industry has become so pathetic we can't supply our own needs now for advanced, affordable machine tools. Melman points out similar backwardness in fields like railway equipment, shipbuilding, and waste-management technologies. Tiny Italian companies nowadays are outdoing us in advanced, affordable textile-making equipment and production methods. The interesting thing, which supports Melman's point, is that American engineers have indeed remained marvelous at inventing in fields that can afford to support such work. But the trouble comes from inability to produce the inventions at affordable costs and with competitive efficiency. Then, even though invention has given us a head start, we lose out to Italians, Germans, Japanese, and others. It's a pattern.

''Pentagon contracts in the aggregate are enormous. Melman says that between 1948 and 1988 they amounted to more than the total 1988 value of the country's industrial plants, equipment, and services, mili-tary and nonmilitary combined. This includes all kinds of military purchases and personnel costs, of course, but within these gigantic costs are so much engineering and so many engineers that, Melman says, they set patterns for the profession. Melman thinks that engineers laid off from military work will have 'a lethal effect' in civilian production because of their lopsided experience in disregarding costs.

''So here's a case of guardian largesse worming its way again into the commercial syndrome. This time the commercial organizations, the manufacturers, along with their engineers, are on the receiving end of military largesse. Oh, to be sure, it's payment for what they do, but being largesse, dispensed by guardians for whom the costs of what they're buying have very low priority, the payments—like the contracts under which they're dispensed—lack cost discipline. In the wake of those contracts, normal commercial virtues wither: thrift, efficiency, competition, and productive investments to achieve thrift of means— that hallmark of good technology. Intractable systemic corruption again.

"Now, please notice two points about the tales I've been telling you. First, in every case the integrity of the appropriate syndrome was lost. I've already explained how lost in each case, and the consequences. So I won't repeat that.

"Second point, which I've touched on but haven't emphasized. Pay attention to it now: there are no decent ways out of these intractable messes. No just solutions exist for setting them right.

"Take the case of the foreign largesse that Quincy's bank and the other banks dispensed. The IMF made a try at one solution: imposing austerity in poor defaulting countries. Bitterly unjust to poor people. The possible alternative—our government assuming the losses—would have been unjust to taxpayers, besides subverting principles of democratic government, as Hortense pointed out. So what remains as a solution? Leaving the banks holding the bag. However, not repaying debts would be unjust to lenders, to the banks' stockholders, and also, likely, to many putative legitimate business borrowers the banks couldn't serve as they would have if they hadn't been constrained by these losses.

"To be sure, there is a seldom-used international doctrine, now known as 'odious debts,' which holds that public debts assumed by corrupt or irresponsible rulers can be justly repudiated. The principle was invoked by our own government to repudiate Cuba's colonial debts after the Spanish-American War at the turn of the century. But of course the doctrine leaves lenders holding the bag. 'Tough luck; those were odious debts; you had it coming to you.'

"Even the 'successful' emergency expedient of false accounting was a sleazy way out—to say nothing of the part it possibly played in helping subvert the moral sensibilities of government bank examiners, who subsequently were so negligent at letting savings-and-loan chicaneries slide by them.

"At the root of all this Point Two trouble—no decent and just solutions—was the Point One trouble—organizations picking and choosing functions and precepts from both syndromes and mingling them together. Making monstrous moral hybrids of themselves.

"Take the case of the transit police who made the false arrests. The false witnesses brought against the wrongfully charged New York City policeman whose ordeal I described—they committed wrongs and should have been charged with perjury. Confession alone can't absolve a wrong like that. Yet no doubt they had little choice, or felt they didn't, fingered and pressured as they were by the transit police.

"What about the many innocent plea-bargainers who were victims of the false arrests? When they untruthfully pled guilty on demand, they too were perjurers. But would it be just to prosecute them for that? After they'd been unjustly accused and told their perjured pleas were their only escape routes? They were taught a profoundly immoral lesson, the kind of lesson that makes people conclude that legally constituted authority is crooked and unjust. Nevertheless, as a generalization, that assumption is also unjust, however understandable.

"Exposure and punishment of the crooked policemen who made the false arrests, and suborned perjury as well, produced a dollop of justice. Good. But what about the consultant and police executives? They assumed they could improve the guardian syndrome by plucking industriousness from the commercial syndrome and disregarding tradition in their guardian syndrome. Their morally obtuse demands set the wicked events in motion. We may be sure the consultant received a fee and harvested an impressive new line for his résumé. The executives? 'Honest misjudgment, discernible only by hindsight,' as Quincy would say; no onus.

"There are no decent or just exits from the imposed syndrome-mingling to which the hapless Ik fell prey. Not even theoretically, by canceling the game preserve and restoring things to the status quo ante. How unjust that would be, now, to those other people who've come to depend on the preserve for their livelihoods—policing it, serving the tourists and scholars it attracts. Turnbull, a good man who wanted to do good, was understandably in despair when he contemplated the two wicked options for the children: leaving them to their deprived and depraved society, or kidnapping them and in effect rendering the Ik extinct. And again, what of the morally obtuse experts who organized this doomed enterprise? Rewards for them! Fees and impressive lines in their résumés; unjust deserts. Kate tells me they can hardly be blamed, since undisputed academic dogma at the time held that subsistence farming emerged naturally from foraging. So what could be more logical than aiding and hastening the process? Learned as they were, those academics hadn't a clue to the evils and wickedness of syndrome mingling.

"I could go on and on with examples to elucidate and reinforce my point that picking and choosing as we please from precepts in the two syndromes and mixing them up together breeds endless chains of injustice: great wickedness, great harm. What do my words remind you of ?"

There was silence for a moment. Then Jasper and Kate exclaimed simultaneously, "Plato!"

"Indeed. We may have the answer to a puzzle that's been hanging about for twenty-five hundred years. What I've just been telling you must be what Plato was driving at when he said mingling kinds of work or meddling with other people's tasks was 'the greatest wickedness,' did the 'most harm' to the community, and was the very incarnation of injustice.

"Remember how his statement that justice 'is to perform one's own task and not to meddle with that of others' bewildered us? How could one interpret what he meant to say? No interpretation is necessary, however: he must have meant precisely what he was saying in so many words if his point was the need to maintain the integrity of the morals and functions associated with the two great classes of work he identified."

"If that's so, then why do you suppose he didn't explain his meaning more clearly?" asked Hortense.

"He seems to have thought that once he'd stated his conclusion, it was self-evident. It's been right in front of your noses all the time, he had Socrates tell his listeners, and they didn't demur or disagree.

"True, he did confuse matters with his ill-chosen cobbler-carpenter example. But that was the usual Socratic trick: starting with an extreme simplicity as his springboard for arguing a complexity. In this case, too simple. But then, nobody's perfect. And from this oversimplification he did immediately move on to the subjects of guardian and commercial work, specifically warning against people in either one meddling with work of the other or mingling its tasks into their own work.

"Once it hit me that he must have been advocating syndrome integrity, I felt rather like you, Kate, when I told you his division of activities into two great classes corresponded with yours. He got there first. I was reinventing the wheel with my Law of Intractable Systemic Corruption. However, I flatter myself that parsing the why's and how's, and tracing them as a dynamic, is a not unworthy addendum to Plato's astuteness and ancient insight."

"You and your law—I do think you could have the modesty to call it a hypothesis,'' said Hortense, ''even if now you're construing Plato to agree with you. You make it sound as if we don't dare tinker with these syndromes and their functions in any shape or form. Or that if we do, we fall into the pit. I don't like that and I don't know that I believe it. It leaves no scope for will and ingenuity, and none for better visions of what might be.''

''Oh, but it leaves plenty of scope for will and ingenuity,'' said Armbruster. ''Provided, that is, the tinkering stays within the morality and functions of the syndrome concerned. How do you think guardians assumed policing of commercial honesty? That was surely an ingenuity in its day, but quite in harmony with the guardian function of supervising a territory's morality and promoting peace and justice. Constitutions, separations of guardian powers, independence of judges from unsuitable pressures, representative governments, guardianship of a population's health, guardianship of territorial environment, assimilating adjudication of contracts—all that ingenuity. Even the income tax was an ingenious idea. But mind you, this was syndrome-friendly tinkering; not syndrome-destroying tinkering.''

''Not like putting the guardians in charge of running trade and production,'' said Jasper.

''Right, a vital distinction. As for commercial people,'' Armbruster went on, ''how do you think they got contracts, insurance, fairs and trade conventions with their product displays—or even forerunners of those, the simple market stalls—bank checks, receipts, stocks and bonds, product research, market research, advertising, and a thousand other things to help along their work? Syndrome-friendly tinkering, ingenuity, and will.

''I see no reason to suppose we've reached the end of the line with respect to what we can make of these two syndromes and what they can do for us. So to end my report on a heartening note, here's a recent example of syndrome-friendly tinkering. It's small but important to me; it ties in with my concern about theft of copyrighted material.

''My information comes from John-Willy Rudolph, a Norwegian book publisher. Besides managing his own commercial company, he is chief of Kopinor, a Norwegian organization of five publishers' associations and seventeen other associations of writers, photographers, translators, dramatists, and composers. The groups set up Kopinor in Oslo in 1980 and gave it the job of combating thefts of their work. Everybody else was getting paid—the manufacturers and distributors of copying machines, the paper suppliers, people who ran or supervised the ma-chines—everybody but the people whose intellectual property was being stolen with the machines.

"At first, the idea was to collect evidence of unauthorized reproduc-tions and pester the police to lay charges. But, Rudolph says, it was a nasty business and didn't really get results. So Kopinor shed its guardian cast of mind and looked at the problem commercially. Instead of regarding the people who were making unauthorized copies as enemies, it now viewed them as eager and welcome customers with whom no convenient way of doing business had been invented.

"The law forbade unauthorized copying. Kopinor got the Norwegian legislature to mitigate the law in 1984; the change permitted copying in institutions where the great bulk of transgressions occurred—universi-ties, schools, libraries, museums—but the institutions were required to report to Kopinor twice a year on the gross amount of material they'd copied and pay for the portion protected.

"All copying machines have meters. This made reporting easy and convenient for the customers. It was a matter of jotting down meter readings on a simple form, like jotting down gas or electricity meter readings, except that Kopinor doesn't need its own meter readers. The users do it."

"What's to prevent them from sending in false reports?" asked Ben.

"Nothing is to prevent it except honesty. The Norwegians have faith in the honesty of their institutions in such matters, and according to Kopinor's surveys of accuracy, it's justified. From other surveys, Kopi-nor established the average percentages of metered materials that enjoy copyright protection. The percentages differ among different kinds of institutions and are updated from time to time. Kopinor makes out bills calculated on this information. In turn, the customers were relying on the honesty and accuracy of Kopinor's surveys. The government itself is a massive copier of protected materials. Based on survey information, it pays Kopinor an annual lump sum and allocates costs and rights among its agencies. Total fees to Kopinor from all customers are equivalent to about two dollars per Norwegian a year, but this is not levied as a tax because it is paid by customers for purchases."

"Do you think individuals who have copying machines would be honest enough to pay?" asked Ben.

"I'm reminded that a few years ago my own company was surprised to receive payment from a college teacher for six copies of a book that was out of stock but that his students urgently needed. He talked it over with them and made six unauthorized copies of his own copy, then collected from them and, deducting the cost of the copying itself, sent us the money. A good teacher, I suspect, and a good incidental lesson to students, in commercial morality. Nothing prevents institutions with Kopinor contracts from charging individuals who make use of their machines, members of the general public, and putting those receipts in its kitty for Kopinor bills.

"Kopinor distributes its income to member associations according to formulas they've worked out together. It's up to each association to distribute its proceeds to members, whether companies or individuals. Or an association can use the income for joint purposes, if that's what its membership decides. The system isn't fair in the sense that each individual or company gets back precisely what its work earned, but it's as fair as can be feasibly figured, and the earnings do go back into the working communities.

"Kopinor is efficient. It began with a staff of four. The full-fledged operation has stabilized at ten, including those who make surveys. Administrative costs come to seven percent of receipts, a good record."

"Doesn't sound like the usual government bureaucracy," said Ben.

"You haven't been listening. This isn't a government bureaucracy. It's a private commercial enterprise, serving its customers and receiving payment, and paying its producers. The government's role was to legalize the system and take normal policing responsibility against corruption, embezzlement, fraud, or the like, should these occur. Kopinor adheres unambiguously to the commercial syndrome: convenience for customers, honesty in its dealings with them, efficiency, enterprise, openness to innovation, shunning of force—and, of course, optimism."

"Has the invention spread?" asked Hortense.

"Rudolph says most Western European countries and Japan, along with a scattering of others, have adopted at least some rudimentary forms of what is now generically known as copyright collective systems, or they are in process of establishing them. Although the Kopinor invention applies only to printed materials, I can imagine it's being adapted for other types of copyrighted materials susceptible to easy theft, like software."

"Have we anything of the kind in the works?" Kate asked.

"Not even a start. It's ironic that Americans, who invented and developed modern copying machines, should be so slow to catch up with their moral and practical implications. Maybe publishing has been too busy with mergers and acquisitions.''

He sighed and looked at his watch. ''I've forgotten how fast time flies when one is pontificating. Let's sum up what we've agreed on and where our trail points next. I take it we're in agreement that societies need both commercial and guardian work. We're also agreed—aren't we?—that each type of work has its appropriate syndrome, contradicting the other. And we're also aware the two types of work are prone to corruption if they stray across either their functional or moral barriers.

''Those are the Whereas's. Now the Therefore.

''Therefore, work organizations need to be protected—or protect themselves—from mutual corruption. The question is how such a feat can be managed. Symbiosis without corruption. We may be confronting an insolubility here: a mess intrinsic to the human duality of ways and means, which has been spared the other animals. But being a commercial sort of person, I'm sufficiently optimistic to feel there's hope. Would anyone care to address this subject?''

''I'll take it on,'' said Hortense. ''Four weeks?''

''Good. And could I ask you all to keep your eyes and ears open for syndrome-friendly inventions and tinkerings? Before we break up, here's a parting gift. It isn't new. It comes from Lao Tzu, a sage who was Keeper of the Imperial Archives of China in the sixth century B.C. He distilled his wisdom into small poems. Here's one on good guardianship:

> ''A leader is best
> When people barely know that he exists,
> Not so good when people obey and acclaim him.
> 'Fail to honor people,
> They fail to honor you';
> But of a good leader, who talks little,
> When his work is done, his aim fulfilled,
> They will all say, 'We did this ourselves.' ''

''Read us some more,'' said Hortense.

''No. I'll lend you the book. Read it yourself. So sane. It should put you in a hopeful frame of mind for your report.''

CHAPTER TEN

Syndrome-Friendly Inventions

I FOUND ONE!" said Ben triumphantly.

"One what?" asked Armbruster. They had assembled again at breakfast.

"Don't you remember? You asked us to keep our eyes open for the right kind of tinkering. You said we hadn't reached the end of the line in what we could make of these syndromes, or what they could do for us, as long as we watched our step and didn't make hash of them. I found a new banking invention. You won't believe this, coming from me, but I like it."

"Me, too," said Kate. "I turned up a pretty splendid example. A new kind of commercial function in harmony with the commercial syndrome. A new way for carrying on business, no less."

"I managed to dredge something up for you," said Jasper.

"Good, this is very gratifying," said Armbruster. "You sound as if you've taken it seriously that these syndromes aren't so rigid as to afford no scope for ingenuity and improvements—as long as the ingenuities stay within moral bounds. Since you're so full of your discoveries along those lines, let's hear them before Hortense's report on managing commercial-guardian symbiosis without mutual corruption. So: syndrome-friendly ingenuities. You first, Ben."

"I ran into this up in western Massachusetts two weeks ago. I was there to give a talk, and I heard about a fellow who's logging with horses for people who don't want roads and machinery tearing up their wood-lots. Everybody's happy with him and he has all the work he can handle. He told me he was able to get established because of a two-thousand-dollar loan from SHARE.

"That stands for Self-Help Association for a Regional Economy. He introduced me to its founders, Susan Witt and Bob Swann. Did you know banks can't afford to make loans of a few thousand dollars? They take about as much work as big loans and they don't bring in enough interest to pay the bank for its work."

Hortense interrupted. "My bank's got a glossy little new leaflet every month begging me to take out a car loan or finance my lovely tropical vacation with their convenient credit card."

"That's different," said Armbruster. "Car loans are standardized, and besides, the bank can routinely sell them off in batches to an acceptance corporation and get its money back. It's much the same, by the way, with loans for standardized chain businesses like franchised fast-food outlets. All that's assembly-line banking. To issue a credit card, the bank merely checks whether you have blots on your credit rating. Even that work's been reduced nowadays. Some of them put you into a computer and check whether you fit a stereotyped profile of who gives trouble and who doesn't. Very unfair, by the way, like all stereo-typed profiles. But Ben's right about unroutinized small businesses. Or medium-sized ones, too. You'll have better luck if you can use a loan of a hundred million than a hundred thousand."

Ben resumed his story. "Bob Swann and Susan Witt, the founders, are New Yorkers who moved out to the country years ago. They noticed farm kids usually had to leave the area when they finished school, whether they wanted to or not. So few jobs. They also noticed neighbors who had skills for going into business, like the horse logger, but no money to launch themselves."

"Why didn't people like that take out credit cards?" asked Hortense. "The logger could have raised two thousand dollars on a credit card."

"The interest rates are too high when every penny counts," Kate put in. "Some manage by juggling half a dozen cards, but for a struggling little business, that's flirting with bankruptcy. Why don't they use credit cards? Hortense, that's like asking why don't they eat cake."

"How come you suddenly know so much about this?" asked Ben.

"You'll see. My discovery's about the same problem. Sorry to interrupt."

"Bob and Susan invented a new way to lend," Ben went on. "They explained it to one bank after another, but they weren't interested because they'd all been merged by bank holding companies in Boston. But finally they found a bank that was still independent, and it agreed to experiment. Here's how it works. The bank keeps a special savings account for SHARE depositors. It pays them its regular savings interest. The depositors agree to leave their money in the account for two years. Anybody who wants to makes a deposit. Most deposits run between one hundred dollars and five hundred dollars, and there aren't any really large ones. At a given time, there's a total of about twenty-five thousand dollars and seventy or so depositors.

"They elect a board of directors from among themselves—volunteers, who don't get paid. The board takes small loan applications. If it approves an application, the bank issues the loan next day, no questions asked. It charges the regular interest rate for good business risks, because the loan is guaranteed by money in the SHARE account. So the bank doesn't do any investigating and doesn't take any risk. It keeps the difference between the interest it's getting and the interest it's paying SHARE depositors. That's about half the take. I'd have thought that was a rip-off but Susan says it's a fair fee for the bank's bookkeeping and collection work. She calls it separating two different bank functions—lending and accounting. That's the invention. SHARE takes over the lending."

"There's still the risk to SHARE," said Armbruster. "What's the record on defaults?"

"Not one yet, and they've been in business since 1982 and made dozens of loans."

"What's the secret?" asked Armbruster. "Hundred percent on business loans is unheard-of."

"SHARE started with good rules and it's kept to them. Rule One: The loan can be used only for producing goods and services for sale. This isn't like a credit union where members can borrow for any kind of thing. Borrowers don't have to be depositors, either. They seldom are. Rule Two: A borrower has to make a good case to the board that probable earnings from local customers can support interest and repayment. Rule Three: The work has to be ecologically and socially responsible; no rip-offs.

"They almost had a default once. A fellow borrowed a thousand dollars for materials and equipment to clean houses for summer people. When fall came he couldn't find customers to replace the vacationers who'd gone away. The day after he missed a payment the bank informed Susan, who was board chairman at the time. They called a board meeting and one member, a teacher, knew of a private school whose janitor had left. The house cleaner got that contract, repaid the loan in full, and since then he combines the two kinds of work—summer and winter."

"He is like a corporation with extreme seasonal fluctuations that merges with a complementary outfit," said Jasper. "But you cannot build much of a regional economy taking in each other's washing, and that is what this sounds like."

"Oh, it goes beyond that. Take the biggest single loan, seven thousand dollars to a woman who makes good goat cheese, with herbs and without. She had a few private customers but she wasn't legally allowed to sell to restaurants and stores unless she got stainless steel equipment and put a new floor in her milking parlor. That's why she needed the loan. Since making a local success, she's worked up a little mail-order business, too. A local printer does her brochures and other local people make the wooden boxes for shipping. There's a woman who had a knitting machine her mother gave her years before. She designed sweaters and children's wear, and local stores stocked them. She got a series of three SHARE loans to buy large bargain lots of yarn coming onto the market as manufacturers' closeouts and to get a couple more knitting machines. With that help, she started selling to stores in New York and employing neighbors, who combine the jobs with farm work and looking after their kids. The bank has accepted her as a regular commercial customer for credit; she doesn't need SHARE any longer. Then there's the kite maker; she's generated jobs and sells her kites far and wide."

"Then I do not see why they have the rule about justifying loans on a basis of local demand," said Jasper. "Why aren't ideas for products meant purely for export eligible too?"

"The board figures that's too chancy. They can make informed judgments about demand from local people and stores. Besides, they've put their minds to improving the local availability of things people seem to want or need. Giving customers convenient access to what they want is part of their notion of improving the regional economy. Susan says the most important advantage of the rule is that when a business is serving the community well, the community wants it to succeed. This support is as valuable as the loans themselves. Even the work you'd call taking in each other's washing, Jasper, amounts to more than that. It saves people money, so they have more disposable income. Take the man who repairs appliances and rebuilds worn-out ones, good as new, but resells them cheaper than new. He needed a two-thousand-dollar loan to buy parts for getting into rebuilding.

"Nobody I've mentioned had good enough collateral to get a bank loan, and besides, their needs were too small. But there are other reasons a borrower can need SHARE. A seventeen-year-old with a desktop printing business wanted a larger printer. The equipment he already owned could have served as collateral, but he was underage. The board especially likes getting young people into business. Two daughters of farm families had jobs as waitresses. They made their own clothes, and customers in the bar where they worked liked these so much that the waitresses started making clothes for sale on the side. After two SHARE loans for silk-screening equipment and materials, they were able to quit their jobs and start a little garment company.

"The bank manager told Susan these are the kinds of loans he should be making, except he can't afford to. Remember, the SHARE board worked on applications, free, for nothing. That's the work the bank couldn't afford."

"You turned up a volunteer do-it-yourself lending circle," said Kate. "I ran into do-it-yourself borrowing circles. They overcome the same gap. But my example is so large by now it's world famous. The Grameen Bank in Bangladesh: it makes only micro-loans to micro-enterprises. It started about the same time you say SHARE did and now it has about seven hundred branches and seven hundred thousand borrowers. It doesn't have quite as good a record as SHARE—defaults run at two percent."

"But a ninety-eight-percent repayment rate on business loans is equally unheard-of," said Armbruster. "That would sound like heaven to Quincy."

"Yes, and one thing it proves, according to the bank's founder, Dr. Muhammad Yunus, is that poor businesspeople can be the best credit risks, which goes against all previous assumptions, and conventional assumptions still. Would you like to know how this got started?"

"How'd you find out about it?" asked Armbruster. "More news clippings?"

"Partly. But last week I got a chance through a friend I was in school with—he works for a foundation now—to hear a talk by Yunus, and afterward he took time to answer my questions. He spends part of his time lecturing on the bank's methods to people like my friend.

"Yunus is an economist, educated here in the United States. He returned to Bangladesh to teach at the University of Chittagong. One afternoon after classes, he says, he was wandering around in the village next to the campus, watching the action, which consisted of very poor people selling to other very poor people. He was like you in Hanover, Armbruster. Suddenly the commonplace struck him as extraordinary. He realized he was seeing the basic and major economic life in his country, and he realized with a shock that what he'd learned in graduate school and was now teaching had nothing to offer this economy. His expertise was beside the point.

"In this mood he fell into conversation with a market vendor of small variety items and learned how little the man had left from his work after he paid the moneylender who financed his stock. The interest rate was seven times the commercial bank rate to businesses. Yunus asked why he didn't take out a bank loan instead. The vendor said he'd been refused, so Yunus offered to accompany him to the bank and help him try again.

"They were politely received and the banker said he'd lend to the vendor if Yunus would guarantee the loan. Yunus thought this over and decided that if he was going to guarantee the loan, he might as well make it himself at the same rate of interest as the bank. He advanced the vendor the equivalent of two hundred dollars, which is like SHARE making a two-thousand-dollar loan, Bangladesh is so much poorer than Massachusetts. He was repaid on time, and the vendor had not only more than doubled his income, he had realized a dream—a bicycle to transport his wares and widen his market.

"Yunus made several more micro-loans to craftsmen and vendors and was always repaid. Word spread. Soon he'd committed most of his own savings to this revolving fund. He saw the need was insatiable, so he decided to start a bank. But here he was up against the impracticality of accepting innumerable little loan applications, looking into them and making decisions, yet managing to keep the bank self-supporting. It couldn't be done.

"He thought how he'd made almost all his loans on the recommendation of people to whom he'd previously lent, and he concluded he must rely on borrowers' knowledge about one another. Let them make the decisions while the bank did the bookkeeping. That's the invention.

"In this system, a borrower has to be a member of a circle of five to ten members. They form the circles themselves and decide among themselves which two members will get the first loans. When those are repaid, two more members are eligible for credit, and so on, until the circle's members are all drawing credit as they need it. One member, chosen by the others, makes collections and turns them in to the bank. If there's a default, the whole circle is in default and nobody in it can draw more credit. So they keep one another behaving responsibly and prudently. More important, Yunus says, they help one another in many ways and rally around in case of emergencies, like the SHARE board helping the janitor, Ben.

"A branch of the bank, on average, serves about one hundred fifty borrowing circles. The bank staffs spend most of their time teaching. They give group lessons in accounting, usually to several circles at once. The borrowers learn to identify which parts of their work are paying off and which aren't, and to see reasons for profits and losses, in an informed, businesslike way. The classes are hard work for them after their long working days, but Yunus says once they've become borrowers and have started improving their lot, they become avid to learn and apply good accounting practices. The teachers also emphasize thrift. Most borrowers invest their savings in shares of the bank, which cost the equivalent of five dollars each, which would be like fifty dollars to us. So as the bank has grown, it has gotten infusions of capital from its own borrowers, to whom it pays dividends. Yunus raised his initial capital from philanthropists and foundations, plus a grant from the government. More about that later." Armbruster made a note.

"For all their faults—which were compounded by defaults—the traditional moneylenders had two things right and Yunus learned from them. No bureaucracy—borrowers don't have to fill out forms—and speedy response. As soon as a circle forms, credit for two of its members is available.

"The most extraordinary development—which Yunus didn't anticipate because this is a Muslim country—is the women's borrowing circles. The first women borrowers, he says, were incredibly courageous. Now eighty-five percent of borrowers are women. I asked him if the bank discriminates against men in any fashion. It doesn't, and he himself isn't sure of the reason for the imbalance. He thinks maybe it's because the men, generally speaking, are more contented with the status quo, while the women are fiercely determined that life will be better for their children."

"What sort of businesses do they go in for?" asked Hortense.

"All sorts. In total, their work makes up not only an appreciable share of manufacturing and distribution within their own villages and among adjacent villages, but also some of the exporting work of their villages: textile dyeing; clothing manufacturing; wax, fishnet, and pottery manufacturing; rice hulling—those are the most important so far. Some women's circles combine to take out loans too large for one circle to handle, like getting a new well dug or buying pipes for water supply. The men usually do carpentry, metalwork, shoemaking, construction work, and transport.

"In science," Kate went on, "the phenomenon of simultaneous discovery is well known. A discovery crops up in different laboratories about the same time, or several thinkers hit independently on the same theory. Hence the race to publish first. Simultaneous inventions occur in technology, too. We say these are ideas whose time has come, although goodness knows, they don't seem that inevitable to people who beat their brains working out the ideas. Still, it happens.

"Discoveries of how to make micro-loans haven't been quite simultaneous; nevertheless, they've come on each other's heels. About twenty years before Yunus, a little group, now called Acción International, started making loans to poor micro-entrepreneurs in Latin America. Its founders were several young Americans who were precursors of the Peace Corps, sent into Latin America to help establish schools, improve sanitation, instigate road building, and the like. They concluded this largesse was rather futile if people were unable to develop their own economies, and like Yunus they observed the economic life going on among the poor and decided to serve that. Gradually they, too, worked out the device of borrowing circles, although the circles are usually smaller, three to seven members, and when a micro-enterprise grows large enough to have employees other than family members it becomes an individual borrower. Acción has the same record as the Grameen Bank—a ninety-eight-percent repayment rate. Somewhat more than half its borrowers are women. Acción bankers teach too, putting the same emphasis as Grameen bankers on thrift, mutual responsibility, businesslike methods, and generation of new capital for productive investment as a by-product of commercial success.

"Like Yunus, Acción got its banks started with philanthropic and foundation funds and has continued to depend on these for expanding its operations into new localities and additional countries. But now here we come to perhaps the most exciting and promising developments. In 1989, it struck a micro-lender in Bolivia—who had a missionary's zeal for the work and the good it accomplished, along with a hardheaded respect for investment capital—that the need was too insatiable to be served by philanthropic capital. No conceivable aggregate of donors could spread the service far enough and rapidly enough. He and a partner worked out the economics of a profit-making micro-lending bank.

"Already micro-lending was self-supporting, with the exception of not paying a competitive return on bank capital. They figured that if they added two percentage points to the annual interest rate charged borrowers, capital invested in the bank could earn about twenty percent annually, an attractive rate. They started their fully commercial, profit-making enterprise, Banco Solidario, in January 1992 and said they hoped for competition and plenty of it, 'The more the better.'

"Simultantous discovery again. A banker in Panama, who was incredulous when he heard of Acción's methods and extraordinarily low default rates, looked into them, learned they were as represented, and concluded that 'banking on the poor is the best business in the world, both financially and morally.' Though Panama has more than a hundred banks, none made credit accessible to micro-entrepreneurs. But beginning in 1991, this already established commercial bank, Multi-Credit, started to make micro-lending, complete with borrowers' circles, its chief business."

Hortense suddenly spoke up with excitement. "These inventions could lead to a new stage of democracy. They amount to democratization of access to business capital. Democratizations don't happen by themselves. They need inventions. Political democracy needed inventions: elections, contending parties with protection for political losers so their opposition could continue to be heard, ballots . . . The invention of public libraries democratized access to literature, and invention of publicly supported schools democratized access to education. Invention of cheap but pretty and fashionable clothes, and shampoos and cosmetics, and affordable dentistry and remedial surgery for some birth defects, and so on, democratized access to personal attractiveness."

"That's in line with what Yunus thinks," said Kate. "He believes access to business credit is a basic human right. He wants the United Nations to recognize it. As things are now, entire groups of people whose members lack access to business credit are locked into poverty and the underclass."

"Democratic access to business credit has been a long, slow time coming," said Armbruster. "If indeed its time has come—no matter where—it would be a momentous development of commercial life, perhaps one of the most momentous single developments ever. Kate, as you and Ben talked, it struck me these inventions didn't come out of officialdom, or even out of already established commercial enterprises, for that matter. Mavericks thought them up; specifically, mavericks who were tired of seeing things not work out."

"That checks with my discovery," said Jasper. "I ran into this in Eugene, Oregon, some years ago, actually. I was visiting a friend who designs opera and theatrical costumes. I thought no more about it until you asked us to keep our eyes open. I put in a phone call to my friend and she put me in touch with the inventive maverick—in this case a woman named Alana Probst, with whom I am now on first-name terms after several long phone conversations."

"One of my sons is at the University of Oregon in Eugene right now," said Hortense. "Did the university have anything to do with this?"

"It did. It needed new band uniforms. But I had better take you back to the beginning, when Alana was board chairman of a small local neighborhood-development corporation in a poor part of Eugene. She'd started with them as an adviser on how to apply for philanthropic grants. The group tried to help welfare mothers get jobs, encouraged improvements in housing and nutrition, that kind of thing. Alana was young and feisty. She concluded this was futile if the economy of Eugene did not improve. It was in a long, slow decline. The region's chief industry, timber, was petering out."

"When was this?" asked Armbruster.

"In 1982. Her idea was simple: Go to several local businesses and ask what they were planning to buy from outside the city and county in the coming year. Then immediately see if there were local businesses capable of putting in bids for the work. In the meantime, while those searches were being made and bids prepared, visit more purchasers, start seeking potential suppliers for their items, and so on. In short, the program was to be made up as it went along. No expensive studies that would be obsolete before they were finished. She put together a grant of thirty-eight thousand dollars from the city and county governments and a local bank so she and a staff of two could try the scheme. The first year, the value of the grant was returned by more than five thousand percent in direct new local contracts for work formerly done elsewhere.

One match, as Alana calls finding a local supplier, was unusually large. It involved local chicken-preparation for a locally based airline-catering plant. But the first year was no fluke. The scheme continued so successful it was extended through the state as a whole.''

"Where do the band uniforms come in?" asked Hortense. "I want to surprise my son with my inside knowledge."

"Whenever Alana found a possible match, she or her assistants helped the supplier prepare a blind bid. That means that neither buyer nor bidder at this point knew the other's identity. But sometimes, as she got more experienced, Alana suggested improvements in buyers' specifications. Oregon is a great place for marching bands, but the standard uniforms they all used were imported from New England or other eastern states and were made of heavy wool, uncomfortable in Eugene's mild, rainy climate. Alana persuaded the bandmaster to consider a new prototype, which did not exist yet. She brought my friend, the costume designer, together with a woman who was doing a little clothing manufacturing for her own retail store, and a small company supplying lightweight waterproof material for fishermen's gear. They formed a joint venture and made a joint bid. After a few changes at the suggestion of the bandmaster, he gave them the contract. I saw the uniforms at their public debut because my friend hauled me to the event and on the way told me how the regalia came to be."

"This is a brokering operation," said Armbruster. "I can't understand why local businesses weren't hustling up their own customers."

"It is not only commercial brokering; it is largely self-supporting. Oregon Marketplace, as the operation is called, takes a five percent commission on the first contract when it makes a match. That fee is figured into the seller's bid. Buyer and seller are on their own after that. The reason the program is not entirely self-supporting is that it puts as much effort into making small initial matches as large ones."

"So it loses money on small matches, the same as banks do on little business loans," said Kate.

"Yes, but it is worthwhile for the economy because small initial contracts frequently lead to larger ones later. Also, even small ones add up if they are repeated.

"As for why this is needed at all, Armbruster: too many managers and purchasing agents know what ain't so. One of Alana's first visits was to a television station. Its manager said there was nothing she was buying from a distance that could be supplied locally—and if there were, it would cost more. Alana found a printer—his shop could be seen from the manager's own office window—who was able to produce the forms the station uses in great quantities to prepare news programs, and who saved the station fifteen hundred dollars on the first order alone. The printer is now supplying forms to stations throughout the region. They used to send to Los Angeles for them.

"The scheme succeeded because it saves purchasers money. It also saves them time, and they often get more exactly what they want. So convenience for the customer is thrown in. Direct savings on prices have averaged about twenty percent but have run as high as forty and fifty percent. A bicycle assembler got his wheels at a forty-percent saving. He switched from a Taiwan supplier to a small Eugene company that made custom-built bicycles for disabled people. Savings for purchasers were part of Alana's vision from the beginning because her conception included helping buyers improve their competitive positions. Another extraordinary saving, fifty percent, came on athletes' equipment bags, formerly supplied from Korea. But most price savings are accounted for by lowered transportation costs."

"Great. Basic energy saving," said Ben.

"After Alana got into this, she learned the Eugene and Portland economies used to replace former imports as a matter of course when it was feasible. But the practice had languished, almost to the point of dying out. It needed an intelligent push. When Alana asked a supermarket manager why he was trucking bottled water from Colorado when Oregon has splendid spring water, he told her nobody was bottling it. Alana suggested to a local dairy called Echo Springs, which had bottling equipment, that it add this new item. It got the supermarket contract and now its water is being widely sold.

"Now here is a dismal thing. Shows a different face of the university, Hortense. Alana met only discouragement, even harassment, from economists there. I hope your son is not studying economics."

"No, pre-med. But I'd think the economists would love this."

"They were thinking like the television manager. Maybe they'd even taught her. They believed in comparative regional advantages, that some places are better than others to make certain things: Switzerland, for example, for cheese or France for wine. I think they got it from Adam Smith. That has nothing to do with making bicycle wheels or band uniforms. The economists believed that random, happenstance diversity is inefficient per se. They were like Yunus with his head in clouds of handed-down learning before he observed the work going on around him.

"The academics reasoned the scheme must be protectionist, therefore must undermine free trade, therefore must penalize consumers. That argument collapsed when savings were demonstrated. They switched to calling it a selfish exercise in robbing Peter to pay Paul, on grounds that it subtracted work and income from exporters elsewhere, therefore harmed other economies, and so hurt the macro-economy. Alana pointed out that while some former exporters to Eugene were losing out, others must be gaining more or less correspondingly. Some of her matches had been importing new production equipment for their expanded or added kinds of work. They also imported increased quantities or new kinds of raw and semifinished materials. More people off welfare could afford more imported consumer goods. But she says she made no headway with them. Incidentally, I tried this out on an economics teacher in Kate's university. She kindly introduced me to her. I got the same reactions, in the same order. In the end she dismissed my tale as 'anecdotal.'

"The state's development experts even tried to close down Alana's office. They preached that salvation lay in using largesse to lure factories from other places. They seem to have looked on Alana's enterprise as unwelcome competition. However, opposition from the state soon melted. Legislators from Eugene liked the Marketplace because their constituents liked it. In 1985 the legislature gave a grant to the neighborhood-development corporation—remember it? Where the Marketplace scheme was started by Alana?—to find and train people in other parts of Oregon for running twelve more offices and for a computer network to link them."

"I wouldn't think you could find enough matches in little towns and rural places to make that worthwhile," said Armbruster.

"That is why the network. When any given office out in the hinterland gets information from a possible purchaser in its bailiwick, it tries to unearth possible matches. Items for which it cannot find them—often all the items—it puts into the computer for other offices. Frequently they do find matches. The office making one splits its fee with the office that turned up the purchaser. But this statewide program is a mixed blessing. It abets import replacing from outside the state, but it threatens to hamper it within the state."

"Why?" asked Armbruster.

"The state itself does not like a product produced in one part of the state—especially a poor part—to lose markets in other parts of the state. And state largesse is funding a good part of the hinterland work. So guardian attitudes and purposes that are not in harmony with commercial criteria such as competitive pricing or other production advantages creep into the process."

"Who does this hinterland brokering?" asked Armbruster.

"All kinds: schoolteachers, retired firemen. The types they have to be wary of are the overly enthusiastic and optimistic—supersalesmen. They get carried away and push impractical matches."

"I can visualize this becoming a national program, funded and promoted from Washington," said Hortense. "A program to liven up and improve local economies all over the country and therefore, in the aggregate, the national economy. Why not?"

Jasper frowned. "Oh no, Hortense. When the bottled-water company in Colorado finds that it has lost a lot of its northwestern customers all of a sudden, and a federal program is responsible, it will express outrage to its congressman, and your Federal Import Replacement Agency or Federal Local Initiatives Agency or whatever it is called will lose a congressional friend. The agency will be hassled by New Jersey politicians when the big bank-check-printing company in that state starts losing its market share of customer banks in this part of the country and that part. And so on. Fair and square competition is moral in the commercial syndrome. Not in the guardian syndrome, where largesse and loyalty take priority.

"Hortense, your agency would realize in short order that the only import replacements that are politically safe for it to foster would be imports from foreign countries. The scheme really would become protectionist. It would be one more government-sponsored economic futility, delivering a pittance of improvement, if that, at great expense. What you are suggesting is syndrome mingling. See how easy it is to slip into? A number of other western states have started trying to imitate what Oregon has done, using state sponsorship and legislation. Predictably, they tend to concentrate on the poorest parts of their states, the parts with the scantiest economic life—precisely the least fertile territories for successful, ample, and diverse import-replacing. It is the largesse point of view toward economic life.

"It would be best if largesse could become entirely unnecessary because of the commercial success of the brokering work. But the sticking point, Alana points out, is those very desirable small matches. They take disproportionate work for the income they yield the brokers, the matchmakers; yet experience has shown her that they do pay off for the economy.''

"That impasse is an invitation to more tinkering, it seems to me," said Armbruster. "Adjustments in the brokerage-fee arrangements— say, fees on repeat orders when the first one is less than a given amount—might solve at least part of the problem. Or relatively modest local grants might be provided by business associations such as chambers of commerce or even banks—which are clear beneficiaries of local economic improvement. If I remember correctly, Alana's small initial grant came in part from a bank. It turned out to be a productive commercial investment, though an innovative one. But that's exemplary commercial morality—openness to innovation.

"It occurs to me," he went on, "that the syndrome-friendly inventions and tinkerings the three of you have described were all being developed during the same years that conglomerate builders, corporate raiders, bankers, and lawyers were so busily at work demolishing the commercial moral syndrome. And in the process deconstructing much of the American economy—loading it up with debts serving no constructive purpose, setting herdsmen against herdsmen, as Kate observed, and causing so much waste of time and effort and employing so much misguided ingenuity. What a contrast!''

"When Alana summed up her program at the end of our last phone conversation," said Jasper, "she told me the basic idea is to use whatever commercial strengths and resources a locality already has, but that it has been neglecting, wasting, or overlooking. The relevant assets are its already existing imports on the one hand and its various production and service capabilities on the other hand.''

"The great principle of self-regeneration," mused Armbruster. "It runs through all the examples of syndrome-friendly inventions you've given—Kate's and Ben's, as well as yours, Jasper. I'm inclined to think that all significant and solid regeneration is self-regeneration.

"None of you came up with syndrome-friendly inventions or tinkerings for guardian work," Armbruster continued. "Ample scope exists there, too; no reason to suppose guardians have reached the end of the line either, with respect to how they can use their syndrome, while maintaining its integrity. I've got a few examples for you. They all happen to embody the same principle of tinkering, which I'll express this way: 'We guardians are decreeing you must do such-and-such, but you have to figure out for yourselves the ways and means to comply.'

"This principle was used with extraordinary ingenuity in Taiwan to help the country industrialize successfully. It began with a national land-reform policy that expropriated holdings of Taiwanese landlords and distributed them to peasant families who had previously been tenants or hired labor. The former landowners were of course paid for this land.

"Here comes the ingenious part. To further their policy of industrialization, Taiwan's guardians wanted that compensation money to go into industrial investment. They wanted to convert former agricultural landlords into industrial capitalists; small capitalists, since these had not been big landowners as such things go. So they were forestalled from using their money in other ways. They weren't allowed to send it out of the country. They couldn't use it for real estate speculation because of prohibitively high capital gains taxes on real estate transactions. The land reforms made buying agricultural land impossible for them. They couldn't revert to becoming rentiers, this time in the city, because other prohibitively high taxes made it economically impractical for them to own more than three urban dwelling units, at a maximum, and the same went for the equivalent in office space. So how could they invest their compensation money? By default, only in industry."

"Why couldn't they just put the money in the bank and take the interest?" asked Ben.

"They could, and then the bank would have invested it in industry. But if they invested it for themselves, they were challenged, so to speak, to do better than bank interest. And they had to figure out for themselves how to do that. It was made as easy for them as possible. No frustrating licensing requirements or other hampering regulations, low tax rates—in sum, an invitation to go ahead and, by using their own ways and means, make the most of their opportunity. That's just what most of them did. They found for themselves knowledgeable production partners who'd mostly gotten their apprenticeships in commerce working for foreign-owned light industries that had been exporting to Hong Kong and the United States. They started creating new enterprises at a great rate."

"Doing what?" asked Jasper.

"Supplying inputs of goods and services to already exporting light industries; going in for exporting, themselves, as competitors; supplying goods and services to domestic consumers. In the process, they did a vast amount of import replacing of producers' goods and consumers' goods both. Alana would love the import replacing they did, Jasper, and without any contrived 'intelligent push,' which, if I remember, was her expression. They also built up more capital for productive purposes. The whole churning mass was generating capital along with goods and services. At a smaller scale and a younger stage of development, the economy in Taipei, the principal city, resembles Hong Kong's. Do-it-yourself development.''

''This is news to me,'' said Kate, ''and I've been reading a lot of newspapers and other stuff. Of course I knew Taiwan had grown an important economy incredibly fast, but everything I've seen gives the bureaucracy credit.''

''That's probably because so many development experts and economists are guardian-minded,'' said Armbruster. ''In Taiwan, they're impressed by the enterprises the state itself started; and they dwell on the structures and doings of the economic-planning bureaucracy: how it gets financing for heavy industries, how it identifies foreign products it would like Taiwan to imitate and encourages companies to imitate them, and the like. But all this would certainly be no more successful than central economic planning elsewhere if it weren't underpinned by the enormously diversified and prospering Taipei economy—which has overflowed into lesser cities too, that, among other things, replace imports from Taipei. Funny thing. When the development experts acknowledge the Taipei economy at all, they figuratively shudder and call it disapproving names like 'chaos.' I just went through a development expert's book on Taiwan—big, dense thing, some four hundred pages—and couldn't find so much as a hint he'd talked with anyone there except guardians and the protégés they'd singled out to foster. All he had to say about the Taipei economy, besides the usual references to chaos and lack of attention to land-use planning, is that it's 'untrammeled' and has serious pollution problems, and that there's no check on exploitation of workers except competition for them by employers. But in less than a generation Taiwan's reached the stage where companies are transplanting work to poorer nations in search of cheap labor, and illegal immigrants are sneaking in looking for higher wages and better opportunities than they can find at home.

''I grant you, I've presented you with an exotic and peculiar example of my syndrome-friendly principle for guardians—''

"Please repeat the principle," said Ben. "I don't quite remember what . . ."

"The guardians say, in effect, 'Here's what you commercial people have to do and we'll enforce it, but how you comply is your responsibility. Find your own commercial ways and means.'

"An example of our own was the government's mandate to car manufacturers to make cars that, on average, increased mileage per gallon of gasoline to such-and-such a figure, with the figure raised as time passed. How they complied—more efficient engines, lighter weights, equipment for alternate fuels, and so on, the ways and means—was left to them.

"Looking through back issues of newspapers I found a motif, a pattern, accompanying this kind of edict. At the time it's proposed, the industries affected scream that their costs of doing business will soar. They're supported in this claim by many experts and much of the business press. Here's *The Wall Street Journal,* for instance, pronouncing 'Clean Is More Expensive,' and predicting the clean-air bill, which it called 'a dark cloud' hanging over industry, would 'cost jobs, cut into profits and slow economic growth.' The forecast was for billions in costs, at the expense of other investment and expansion."

"Zero-sum thinking," said Kate. "What goes into this must be subtracted from that."

"Yes," said Armbruster, "and the zero-sum thinking might have been valid if complying companies relied only on the guardians' ideas of ways and means to comply—all of them expensive 'mopping up' ideas. But lo and behold, soon comes good news. *The Wall Street Journal* has to eat its words. I'll quote it. 'According to conventional wisdom, sweeping clean air laws will burden U.S. industry with billions of dollars in pollution-control costs and raise prices for a slew of commodities and finished goods. Not necessarily so, more and more manufacturers say. Surprisingly, they are actually reducing some costs as they install new pollution-cutting technologies. But the benefits come from new manufacturing techniques—not the waste and emission treatment encouraged by much environmental legislation." The *Journal* goes on to report the benefits can be huge. The new processes and materials—a host of them—are aimed at avoiding pollution in the first place, rather than creating it and then mopping it up. Different ways and means, and better ones.

"Remember," Armbruster continued, "when the government mandated that ozone-destroying CFCs—chlorofluorocarbons—must be phased out over a period of years?''

"Those schedules are outrageously slow and mild," said Ben. "The ozone hole is an emergency."

"Again," said Armbruster, "we got screams about costs and job losses, et cetera. It was hard to tell which alarm was greater—alarm over the ozone or alarm over the costs of how to save it. Now, in this case, the guardians didn't even try to mandate ways and means."

"They did not have a clue what the ways and means could be," said Jasper.

"Soon the good news started trickling in. Electronics companies are major users of CFCs; they've been the standard solvents for cleaning circuit boards. In short order the chief electronics companies had switched to naturally occurring, nonpolluting solvents called terpenes. The terpenes are derived from orange peels, waste products of food processors. And what do you know? Instead of adding to costs, the substitutions saved money. By now, scores of other CFC substitutions have been adopted or are in process of being adopted, and still more are being experimented with. And again, in most cases the changes are reducing costs."

"You are such an optimist at heart, Armbruster," said Jasper. "You are determined that everything will turn out for the best in the best of possible worlds. Not necessarily so."

"Equally, it's not necessarily so that everything will turn out for the worse in the worst of possible worlds," said Armbruster, picking up a clipping. "One of the reports I have here says that in 1990 American companies were producing five times as much waste per dollar of goods sold as Japanese companies were, and more than twice as much as German companies. To me, this means there's ample room for improvement if guardians lay down the policies, are serious about enforcing them, and keep their own hands off ways and means of complying."

"To me," said Ben, "this means that commercial people need good, hard kicks in the pants, to kick-start their brains."

"Evidently they often do," said Armbruster. "I suspect it's one consequence of the common notion nowadays that the economy is the responsibility of governments. We've been through a long period when governments themselves undertook to solve commercial problems when these emerged. Consider the savings-and-loan failures and insurance fiasco, which we've already touched on. Under the principle I've been elucidating, the guardians would have decreed, 'You must insure deposits up to such-and-such an amount against risk of loss from bank failure, and we will enforce that, but ways and means are up to you.' The banks would have had the cost discipline of minimizing premiums by minimizing risk, instead of the wild indiscipline of largesse guarantees in a pinch.

"Guardianship is derived from taking, and guardians are only too willing to take commercial ways and means into their own hands. Stultification. Regimentation. All those look-alike suburban tract houses with their mortgages insured by the federal government's financial expedients—you wouldn't believe the reams of loose-leaf federal regulations about ways and means of building the houses and laying out their lots.

"Probably the most horrendous guardian aggrandizement of commercial ways and means has been the promotion of nuclear power for generating electricity." He pulled a clipping from the bottom of his little stack and placed it on top. "This is an editorial in the London *Observer*. I'll quote. 'Privatization has proved that nuclear power is hopelessly uneconomic—' "

"I always knew it was," said Ben. "All those dangerous wastes they had no idea how to get rid of except with science-fiction dreams that won't work anyway. But how did privatization prove that?"

"When the British government sold off its nationalized electricity-generating plants to private companies and investors, nobody would take the nuclear plants. Not even for free, if they'd been offered free. Besides being an expensive way to produce electricity—'hopelessly uneconomic' as the *Observer* says—they were also 'saddled with decommissioning costs,' your point, Ben, 'no private company would accept without huge guarantees from the government. . . . Had the truth been told long ago, Britain's energy policy would not now lie in ruins. For decades the promotion of energy conservation and research into clean sources of energy has been neglected while money was poured . . . down the nuclear drain.' Ways and means taken into the wrong hands, the wrong syndrome.

"Guardians have so many important and legitimate responsibilities, ones that nobody can attend to properly if they don't. We've touched on most of them. But here's this question of how to handle new types of territorial problems as they emerge. If solutions depend on commercial behavior, as they so often do, then the constructive examples of tinkering I've mentioned are both syndrome-friendly and important.

Probably increasingly important, as still more problems emerge. This is good symbiosis: guardians taking political responsibility for enacting policies into law, and enforcing them; commerce taking responsibility for innovative ways and means of complying.

"Which brings us back to your promised report, Hortense. How do we maintain symbiosis between these two syndromes and the two families of organizational offspring deriving from them—yet at the same time avoid mutual corruption? That may be the biggest problem of all. You have the floor, Hortense."

As she spread out neat sheets of lined legal-sized paper filled with notes, Hortense said to Jasper, "By the way, I was just kidding when I suggested starting a federal agency for local import-replacing. I twigged to the hash politics would make of it, and I wanted to reassure myself that you did too. A lot of people wouldn't. Just the kind of thing politicians would try to pick up for a juicy little campaign promise."

"And your other suggestion a while back about holding fund-raising benefits to ransom conquered territories whose people want sovereignties of their own?" asked Jasper.

Hortense looked wistful. "I was only half kidding on that one." She fell silent, arranging her notes.

CHAPTER ELEVEN

Hortense
on Castes
and Flexibility

E XPERIENCE OFFERS two methods for protecting integrity of the syndromes while at the same time affording symbiosis," Hortense began. "Neither method operates well over the long run. But they're what we have. At one pole is a rigid caste or class framework. At the other pole is what I'll call knowledgeable flexibility. There are many gradations from the one to the other, but a given society at a given time uses one or the other as its basis, adjusting it pragmatically. Our society bases itself on knowledgeable flexibility. I'll take up each of these methods separately.

"Plato gives us a pure—even though imaginary—paradigm of the rigid caste or class method. His proposed guardian caste was set apart by occupations and also in every other way: birth, upbringing, selection of wives, residence, uses of leisure, and the ideals with which guardians were inculcated.

"Guardians were to be so unsullied by property and trade, they were to own nothing as individuals. Internally, the caste was to be divided by merit. Rulers and administrators were responsible for deliberating, reasoning, and making plans. Police and soldiers carried out what the rulers and administrators commanded. At the top was a philosopher-king of outstanding wisdom, goodness, and selflessness. There was no avenue into any rank of guardianship except by birth, and no exit other than expulsion of cowards into commercial life.

"For their part, commercial people were to stick to trading and producing—well policed, well protected, and well ruled by the guardians. They were excluded from concerns of government, except for their obligations to pay taxes and supply material goods required by guardians."

"Allegorical. You said that yourself when Armbruster first mentioned Plato, Hortense," Jasper interrupted.

"Not as allegorical as I thought. Real caste systems resemble those arrangements. Not that they were picked up from Plato. For instance, old Japan's arrangement had a few families of ancient nobility, the kuge, who were hereditary supervisors of ancestor worship and the general moral direction of policy and propriety. Next below came the warrior caste, the samurai. Their internal ranking depended on the size of tax yields from their territorial holdings. Samurai with small tax-takings, if any, were analogous to Plato's auxiliaries, his police and soldiers. Together, kuge and samurai were hereditary guardians. Trade was absolutely forbidden them. Their code was similar to the European code of chivalry, but more stringent, if anything, with respect to loyalty, honor, and shunning trade.

"Below the guardians came the caste of farmers, most of them on samurai fiefs. Below them was the artisan caste. At the bottom, superior only to the small group of ostracized outcastes, came merchants; they were people who dealt in other people's production, rather than their own like the farmers and artisans. Plato, too, made a distinction between what he called the craft of producing and the craft of moneymaking, saying producers combined those two crafts but merchants used only the second.

"All the non-guardian Japanese castes were excluded from government. However, in times of turmoil some farmers were able to convert themselves to warriors, and if they got away with this successfully, they became samurai. So one might say that as an adjustment, the samurai caste was fed by the farming caste. But such parvenus, once established as samurai, cleaved to the ideals and values of their new station, and their families thereafter remained in it by birth.

"Each caste was set apart not only by its ordained occupations but also by upbringing and indoctrination, customs, the kinds of pottery they used, the clothing they wore, the dimensions of their houses and the types of roofs on them, and the leisure activities they engaged in when they had any leisure. Few did, except kuge and samurai, all of whom had lots that they used for rituals and ceremonials and the appreciation and practice of martial arts and competitive games—which Plato stressed too for guardians. Also, in Japan, guardians not only appreciated but customarily practiced fine arts, which Plato did not stress.

"Topping all was the figure of the divine and perfect emperor. With a few variations, all very, very Platonic.

"In feudal Europe, great landholding warrior families were at the top, and that was the group from which kings were drawn. Next, although socially within the same grouping, came lesser aristocracy and knights, including landless knights. In parallel with these battle people came the clergy, headed by the church magnates. Guardians all.

"Just as in Japan, merchants in feudal Europe were socially lower than peasants and artisans. The merchants invented themselves out of riffraff: runaway serfs, vagabonds, dispossessed peasants, wandering Jews.

"In India, the priestly caste, the Brahmins, headed—"

Ben was fuming. Now he burst out, "Power-rigging! Caste and class are tricks and oppressions to keep top dogs on top!"

"If that's all they've been, then we have an enigma, Ben," said Hortense. "The enigma of genteel poverty. In France, for instance, members of the petty provincial aristocracy eventually became comparatively poor. Their honor required expenditures that outran the meager returns from their manors, and they were helpless to mend their declining fortunes because of the trade taboo. Some of them, poor and idle, sank out of their class. In effect, others were rescued by the dole: largesse from the king.

"It was even worse for younger sons of poor samurai in Japan. They could be among the poorest of the poor. The only approach to trading permitted them was to set up schools in temples and receive tuition gifts. Some had to become beggar-monks, or make do as ronin—poor, wandering, masterless outlaws trying to pick up a precarious living by their swords. Those who were both gifted and lucky might practice a fine art or scholarship in a temple capable of feeding and clothing them and their families.

"And it wasn't as if the better situation of merchants was invisible. In France, merchants in the cities were rising while provincial aristocrats were on their uppers. In old Japan merchants were also flourishing under the caste system. They invented department stores and travel agencies that put together horse relays and inn accommodations as packages. They developed transactions in futures as an outgrowth of warehousing. They originated bills of exchange, promissory notes, branch and correspondent banking, advertising, and commercial publicity. All this was thus in existence, in place, at the time the country was finally opened to foreign trade. To be sure, the merchants couldn't parade their wealth in old Japan; the embroidery and furs of their fine clothing had to be confined to the linings. They couldn't have tiles on their roofs, or the still-more-prestigious beautiful thatch of bark, or indulge in other ostentation. But in any case, like successful commercial people anywhere, they were using wealth mainly to expand and develop their work and so, with luck, growing richer.

"If caste can be accounted for simply as power-rigging, then why would guardian castes deny themselves commercial wealth and power?"

"Remember my surmise," asked Jasper, "about the guardian trade taboo originating as a safeguard against selling out to foes?"

"What do historical accounts in caste societies say about occupational segregation?" asked Kate.

"Will or whim of the gods. The Vikings, for instance, had it that a god named Rig fathered all three of their castes by three different women. He sneaked into their beds between them and their husbands. His first bedmate, a miserable, feckless drudge, bore him a son named Thraell whose offspring, in turn, were thralls: serfs and slaves. Rig's second woman, who was ordinary but better off, bore Karl, forefather of free peasants, craftsmen, and common soldiers. Rig's third woman presided over a prosperous household with competence and grace. She bore Jarl, progenitor of noble warriors: earls and kings. The names of Jarl's ten sons bespoke obsession with family: Son, Child, Young, Noble, Heir, Lad, Kin, Lineage, Offspring, and—the youngest—King. Karl's had names like Freeman, Warrior, Brave, Broad, Smith, and Settler, and his daughters were Quick, Bride, Wife, Woman, Weaver, Ornament, and Modest."

"Didn't noble Jarl have daughters?" asked Kate.

"Presumably, but my source for the legend doesn't name them. Likely they'd have names like Lady, Heiress, Daughter, Jewel, and Queen. The thralls, children of Thraell, had dreadful names. You'll see why democratic access to personal attractiveness occurred to me this morning. The sons were Ox, Foolish, Clumsy, Grumpy, Howler, Ugly, Clot—''

"They sound like the seven dwarfs," said Kate.

"Yes, or the last names such as Cabbagehead and Mudface that some vindictive Polish landlords registered for freed serfs in the nineteenth century. Thraell's daughters were Clot, Clumsy, Fat Legs, Talkative, Cinder Nose, Quarreler, Torn Skirt, and Crane Legs. The myths and legends aren't much help. One might as well ask why the sky is blue and get the answer 'Because it was ordained to be blue.'

"Guardian castes reserved political and military power to themselves, Ben, you're right about that. But before they stultified, the great caste societies of Japan, India, and Europe—"

"Do you think it is accurate to speak of the European class system as caste?" Jasper interrupted.

"You're accustomed to associating caste only with the Orient," answered Hortense. "We all are. But almost all Europe, at the time it was reviving after the Dark Ages, was quite as caste-ridden. Even the early European attempts at something a bit more consultative or democratic were caste-ridden. As one historian put it, all the early parliaments 'from Portugal to Finland, and from Ireland to Hungary—every country of western Christendom had its assemblies based on estates'— that means on ordained occupational groupings, such as nobility, ecclesiastics, and commercial people or bourgeoisie. In Ireland, even now, the upper house, the senate, represents occupational groups, and of course Britain still has its House of Lords.

"But to get back to my point; before they stultified, the great caste societies did develop marvelous panoplies of crafts for their times; also flourishing trade in crafts and raw materials. It follows, there must have been scope and freedom for artisans and merchants to find their customers, work out their efficiencies, make their productive investments, create their innovations, put streams of new goods and services into trade."

"You sound as if you approve caste," said Jasper.

"I don't. But I'm leaning over backward trying to fathom why large parts of the human race took to it. Rigid occupational classes must have had something useful and workable going for them. I'm proposing their asset was the separation between guardian and commercial work, a separation ensured by the constraints guardian castes imposed upon themselves, for whatever reason."

"Maybe the arrangement was so advantageous that societies shaped like this proceeded to become large and influential portions of the human race," said Kate.

"I'm suggesting," said Hortense, "that by not meddling in trade except to police it more or less effectively against fraud and use of extortion or other force, guardian castes left commerce scope and leeway, by sheer default. They didn't throttle what commercial people were capable of doing—other than in agriculture—with nooses of total power. Here's a Lao Tzu poem in that book you lent me, Armbruster, about restraint and the scope it grants:

> "Thirty spokes are made one by holes in a hub
> By vacancies joining them for a wheel's use.
> The use of clay in moulding pitchers
> Comes from the hollow of their absence;
> Doors, windows in a house
> Are used for their emptiness.
> Thus we are helped by what is not
> To use what is."

"It sounds to me as if occupational castes were a way stage in our social and economic evolution," said Armbruster. "Useful once upon a time but long since outgrown."

"Then consider modern Hong Kong," said Hortense. "It has harbored one of the most rapidly developing economies the modern world has seen. The British civil servants who've run Hong Kong had almost nothing to do with this economy except to police it and supervise certain public works. The Chinese population that created the modern Hong Kong economy was so excluded from ruling that it wasn't even granted the vote."

"Why didn't all the British Empire grow rich like Hong Kong, then?" asked Ben.

"Hong Kong is a fluke. British conquerors managed the economies of their colonial possessions with nooses of total power; they were rulers in league with economic oligarchies. That's how Hong Kong was run too before the Second World War.

"Another problem with your evolutionary supposition, Armbruster," Hortense went on, "is that the knowledgeable, flexible method appears to be as ancient as caste, perhaps older. Evidence for that can be found in the Old Testament, set forth especially vividly in Deuteronomy. The text of Deuteronomy is roughly the same age as Plato's *Republic,* but it describes events already far in the past at the time it was written.''

Armbruster pulled the Bible from his bookshelves and found the place. ''Do you need this?'' he asked.

''No, you follow along in it if you want, but I made notes from my copy at home.''

''Oh, so that's why you've had your head buried in the Bible!'' exclaimed Ben.

Jasper and Armbruster swiveled their heads to Ben, then to Hortense. Kate stared at Hortense, then at Ben. Ben muttered, ''Sorry, excuse the interruption, please disregard, go on, Hortense—''

''We may as well tell them, Ben,'' said Hortense.

''Hortense and I are a pair now,'' said Ben, his confusion giving way to exuberance. ''I love her and she's let me move in with her and what we plan to do—''

''I don't mind saying this is a total surprise to me,'' said Armbruster. ''You haven't so much as hinted! Well, now I think of it, I did notice you were making dates to discuss environmental law. Well, well, one thing does lead to another. Best wishes for happiness, Hortense. Congratulations, Ben. This calls for champagne,'' he added expansively. ''Happens I have a few bottles stashed for celebratory emergencies. I'll put them on ice,'' and he made for the kitchen while Jasper and Kate were extending good wishes.

''Maybe we'd better wait until later to go into our plans, Ben,'' said Hortense as Armbruster returned. She spread out a batch of notes. ''The book opens with a recapitulation by Moses of the vicissitudes of the Jews after their escape from bondage in Egypt. Moses is trying to prepare the refugees for the time when they'll settle down in the Promised Land but he'll no longer be alive to guide and admonish them.''

''One cannot accept all this literally,'' said Jasper. ''Moses himself did not write this. It may be more legend than history. Moses as the great legendary lawgiver might be a personification of lawmaking by many precursors.''

''Perhaps. But the story itself is a fact. And the attitudes it reveals are facts too. I'll go along with the way the story's told, as if Moses is laying it out himself. He reminds the migrants that under instructions from Yahweh—there's the will or whim of a god again—they've sometimes been a military force, killing and pillaging their way through hostile territories. And he also reminds them of instances, again under divine instruction, when they sheathed their weapons and peacefully negotiated transit, using money to buy food and water instead of seizing what they needed. Proper behavior in that case, he reminded them, was to stick to the highway, invading neither to left nor right, taking heed to their good conduct.

"In one case, when they would have preferred commercial negotiations, the king of a territory refused and brought out his people to block the way. So the migrants resorted to battle. 'We smote him and his sons and all his people. And we took all his cities at that time and utterly destroyed the men and the women and the little ones of every city; we left none to remain; only the cattle we took for a prey unto ourselves, and the spoil of the cities which we took.'

"So here you see the two different syndromes, commercial and guardian. And this is the important point. They were being drawn on not by two different occupational groups but by a single group, which was sometimes pitiless and heroic and at other times bourgeois, bargaining to reach voluntary mutual agreement."

"You can hardly call it voluntary if the alternative was to be pillaged and killed," said Kate.

"No, it's rather like Commodore Perry showing up with his gunboats near Yokohama in 1853 and demanding the Japanese open their country to foreign trade. Nevertheless, in this Bible story, the same individuals are expected to bargain and buy competently when that's appropriate and to battle and plunder when that is."

"It is merely an instance of a people shifting in unison from war footing to peace and back again as need be," said Jasper.

"Right; that's why I said the flexible, knowledgeable method is possibly the older. Shifting from peace to war footing and back again by the same individuals must be as ancient as the first hunters who became ad hoc raiders and warriors. When their peace footing included exchanging goods down at the big trading rock, we have the whole nubbin of the knowledgeable, flexible method."

During these exchanges, Armbruster had been skipping ahead in Deuteronomy. Now he looked up and remarked, "Much else here supports flexibility as opposed to caste. Here's the rule for anyone who bought a bondsman or bondswoman, a slave. The person bonded was to be released after six years and liberally supplied with animals, grain, and wine, enough for an independent start in life. That sounds like an attempt to prevent formation of a permanent underclass like the thralls of the Vikings. Then there's debt forgiveness, with the same aim, one may presume. Moses tells creditors to forgive outstanding debts once each seven years, just wipe them off the books.''

"Then why wouldn't debtors hang on to the money and wait it out?" asked Jasper. "No, don't answer. They would have a hard time ever raising another loan."

"The rule assumes debtors are honest," said Hortense. "Otherwise it's nonsense, as you say. It sounds like an early form of bankruptcy law."

"It's contrary to the traditional guardian conception of what to do about defaulters," said Kate. "They were thrown into debtor's prison, the idea being ransom. The debtor's family and friends were supposed to ransom him by paying the debt; if they couldn't, he languished indefinitely."

"That reminds me of an elderly cousin of mine," said Armbruster. "She's dead now, but she was jailed in St. Paul years ago, during the Depression, for disregarding an accumulation of traffic tickets. When her son showed up and forked over the fines he asked for a receipt. 'Your mother is your receipt,' said the cop on duty."

Glancing back to where he had kept his place with his finger, Armbruster continued, "Here's a loophole for creditors. Immediately after ritually forgiving a foreign debtor, the creditor could reinstate that debt." Hortense started to speak again, but Armbruster, flipping pages, suddenly yelped, "Here it is! Chapter twenty-three, verses nineteen and twenty. A portentous distinction. 'Unto a stranger thou mayest lend upon usury; but unto thy brother thou shalt not lend upon usury.' ''

"Why portentous?" asked Ben.

"It says, first, that lending at interest is permitted; and second, it distinguishes between kinsmen and others. Jews were blamed in medieval Europe on both counts: for lending at interest to Christians and, the Christians surmised, for lending to fellow Jews without interest, putting Christians at a disadvantage."

"Illogical," said Jasper. "What was to prevent Christians from lending to each other without interest? Then they would have had the same advantage, and without disobeying their clergy."

"You're forgetting these rules and values are syndromes," said Kate. "Not random collections of do's and don'ts. The church itself was a guardian institution. In its view, surplus money should be used for charity, ostentation, and largesse—guardian ideas—not for investment for productive purposes, such as buying goods here and transporting them there; buying materials and advancing them to craftsmen, then exporting crafts made with the materials; financing equipment like forges and smelters and improved city looms to increase efficiency. Those ideas of how to put surpluses to work belong to the commercial syndrome; and the way is much smoothed by credit and loans.''

''What interested me most,'' said Hortense, ''is that Moses, or whoever was standing in for him as author, was laying down rules and distinctions everyone was meant to understand. Everyone. Not just this occupational group or that one. Both guardian and commercial ways are treated as general information—information for everyone.''

''Now I think of it,'' said Armbruster, ''nothing in this material implies that commerce is base or tainting, nor that it's inferior to public service. Commercial ways differ from heroic ways, that's plain, but 'different' carries no connotation of social or moral inferiority.''

''A major difference between caste and flexibility,'' said Hortense. ''In caste, guardians are always superior socially and their values are presumed to be superior morally.''

''Has Deuteronomy any rules about guardians' qualifications?'' asked Kate.

''None of birth, other than that the king was to be a Jew, not a stranger. That's the same qualification our Constitution lays down for the president, citizenship by birth. No qualifications of upbringing. Moses implies qualifications of merit and reputation when he says the chiefs he chose as captains were 'wise men and known,' but that's all.

''However, the moral barrier between guardianship and commerce is firmly in place. Priests—who I take it were judges and custodians of the law—are not to produce wealth or inherit it. Moses was as clear as Plato about the commercial people supporting the guardians. A bit clearer, because Moses recognized that guardians need taxes for largesse as well as for their own support. He specifies that taxes are to be drawn on for widows, the fatherless, and strangers within the gates who lack land of their own. Kate, this seems to reinforce what you said about ancient agriculture. At any rate, it assumes land is a commercial raw material for production rather than an attribute of guardian status. But taxes are to be kept in hand. The king is not to multiply horses or wives to himself, 'neither shall he greatly multiply to himself silver and gold.' I like that modifier 'greatly.' That's realism.

"The king was also instructed to write out for himself a copy of the laws maintained by the priests, and he, too, must obey them."

"Aristotle emphasized that principle," said Armbruster. "He said rulers must be subject to the law. No comfort there for absolute monarchies or the divine right of kings; those are caste ideas."

"Everyone is to understand that honest dealing is essential in commercial life," Hortense continued. "No pillaging or preying; weights and measures must be perfect and just; no cheating, because that is 'an abomination in the sight of God.' "

"Their former masters, the Egyptians, believed that too, remember?" Kate put in.

"Moses made a nice distinction between sampling and taking," said Hortense. "It's all right to taste the grapes in a neighbor's vineyard but not to carry them away in a vessel; and it's all right to pinch the heads off some of a neighbor's grain with your fingers but not to bring in a sickle. Another edict concerned fair and just payment of wages."

"You said our society uses the flexible method instead of caste," said Ben. "But that's hard to believe, Hortense. What about African Americans? If I ever heard of a caste system!"

Hortense nodded. "Racism creates castes, Ben. But not necessarily as a way of separating guardian and commercial occupations, the kind of caste I've described. Racism, like gender discrimination, lacks that one mitigating advantage; it penalizes its victims in all manner of occupations. It has no moral purpose of defending the syndromes from corruption by preventing them from mingling.

"The flexible, knowledgeable method of separating the syndromes doesn't ordain children for occupational destinies that they stick with all their lives. It permits individuals to do either guardian or commercial work without regard to birth or upbringing; also to shift between the two, as when a businessman runs for political office or a former soldier becomes a commercial accountant or a carpenter.

"So, with this method, individuals must be morally flexible enough to adapt to either syndrome as need be, and knowledgeable enough to know the difference. This makes greater demands on individuals' moral understanding than caste or rigid class arrangements. It may even cultivate the intelligence of a population by requiring, as a matter of course, a habit and practice of critical understanding. Sharpens up people's minds, in a way caste doesn't require and doesn't encourage."

Armbruster interrupted. "F. Scott Fitzgerald's dictum: 'The test of a first-rate intelligence is the ability to hold two opposed ideas in the mind at the same time and still retain the ability to function.' "

Hortense nodded. "I was planning to quote him myself. But here's another thought along the same lines by Stephen Jay Gould, the scientist Kate quoted when she talked about physical and cultural evolution.

"Gould was writing about professional baseball. On the one hand, it's a business. On the other hand, it's a game of heroes and epic achievements and mythic failures. Each mode, as he calls it, is true of the game. But the two are immiscible, and all lovers of the game must recognize the distinction. Then he goes on to draw an analogy to science and religion. I'll quote him. 'This is a supposed conflict, more accurately a pseudo-conflict that shouldn't exist at all but flares up only when one side invades the domain of the other. . . . These subjects form necessary components of a complete life. But they integrate no better than . . . oil and water. We each need to carry a jar with two layers. Yet some of the world's greatest troubles, intellectual and otherwise, arise from movements by one realm into alien territory,' as when religion improperly masquerades as science and concocts 'the oxymoronic "scientific creationism" ' to oppose evolution; or when science 'claims we can judge human values from test scores and measurements.' He calls invasions of one realm by the other a kind of intellectual imperialism."

"Right on the nose! And he's noticed that tinkering that doesn't respect the difference is nonsense or worse," said Armbruster. "What's more, he's noting that it's up to each of us to be responsible for respecting the differences—which I take it is your point, Hortense, about the flexible method, as contrasted to the caste method. But you said neither method seems to hold up well over prolonged periods. Why not?"

CHAPTER TWELVE

Pitfalls
of the
Methods

L ET'S TAKE the caste method first," said Hortense. "Caste arrangements are like snapshots, as opposed to endlessly running motion pictures. The snapshots freeze reality, but realities change. Therefore the functional utility of the caste method is transitory, and its moral utility, too."

"Plato would have given short shrift to that remark," said Armbruster. "He thought of truths as eternal and hence abiding only in static abstractions—certainly not in phenomena of the practical and material world, precisely because these are in flux."

"But notice that our idea of truth is the opposite," said Kate. "For us, truth is made up of many bits and pieces of reality. The flux and change in itself is of the essence. Change is so major a truth that we understand process to be the essence of things."

"Spoken like a scientist," said Armbruster, "but not like a religious guardian. You may be interested to know, Kate, that another Greek philosopher, Heraclitus, born about a century before Plato, said that in nature the sole actuality is change. He said processes of ending and processes of becoming, occurring simultaneously, delude us with an illusion of stability. He used fire as his chief analogy, forever consuming and being fed. Process. But you wouldn't agree with some of his other ideas. He thought fire was the primary substance and the soul itself was fire.''

"I can agree with that," said Kate, "in the sense that vitality is a manifestation of transformations of energy; also that the source of that energy is the fire of the sun.''

"Given Plato's opposite view that process and change are illusory, it was natural for him to idealize static arrangements for society," said Armbruster. "Your point, I take it, Hortense, is that caste arrangements grow obsolete."

"They do. One way of handling this is to make adjustments. Remember the idle French aristocrats I mentioned? While they'd been growing redundant and obsolete, the regime was admitting new people into the ranks of the high aristocracy. These were called 'nobles of the robe,' as distinguished from the grander 'nobles of the sword.' Nobles of the robe were high civil administrators recruited from the upper ranks of the commercial bourgeoisie because reality was now demanding guardian administrative skills that the nobles of the sword couldn't supply, no matter how much time they had on their hands. The new people were admitted reluctantly; it was a grudged caste adjustment.

"Neither the castes of India nor those of ancient Rome made allowance for merchants. That was typical of caste arrangements elsewhere, with merchants inventing themselves and their services down at the bottom of society. But in both Rome and India we get a different wrinkle. Wealthy Roman merchants, with far-flung operations, arose out of the equestrian class, the knights, originally guardians who were just below the highest caste, the patricians. In India, similarly, a merchant class emerged from warrior caste members who abandoned their old role; this is also the group from which India's educated professional people, such as lawyers, emerged. Gandhi came of such a family. These were caste adjustments.

"But typically, caste adjustments come hard and unevenly, and often too little and too late, as in the Old Regime of France. Often they don't happen. Back in the Middle Ages, after the Saracens defeated the Christian crusaders and drove them from the Middle East, hereditary European warriors and commanders who would otherwise have gone on crusade were redundant. But they and their descendants couldn't reconcile their self-respect with commercial pursuits, as the Hindu warriors and Roman equestrians had done. They had been too rigidly programmed as warriors by heredity and upbringing. So for generations some picked horrendous fights in Prussia and Lithuania—a much larger territory than it is now—to no purpose but to fulfill their ordained destinies. Others took up war against suspected heretics at home, as in the Thirteenth Crusade, against the French count of Toulouse and his people. 'How can we tell the heretics from the Catholics?' the commander is said to have asked the pope, Innocent the Third. The reply that has come down to us was 'Slay all, the Lord will know his own.' ''

"Don Quixote is the famous symbol of hereditary caste minus function," said Armbruster.

"Yes, so gratified to find windmills for his onslaughts. He also symbolizes another pitfall of caste, extreme social ignorance, although Marie Antoinette is our great symbol of that. Machiavelli understood this pitfall and its relationship to tax yields. He urged the Prince not to lose touch with the commercial classes. He advised that 'since every city is divided into guilds or other corporate bodies,' the Prince ought to assemble with them occasionally, 'thus giving proof of his affability and munificence, yet never failing to bear the dignity of his position in mind, for this must never be lacking.' The Prince must encourage citizens to pursue their own affairs peaceably so that no one would hesitate to improve his possessions for fear they would be taken from him—that is, lost to robbers or other criminal predators—and also so a citizen wouldn't hesitate to open 'a new avenue of trade' for fear of taxes. This was unusually enlightened advice for his time.

"Even centuries later, no such enlightenment prevailed in the imperial court of China under the regal descendants of its Manchu conquerors. In the 1880s, a radical provincial viceroy took to benign treatment of industry and shipping in his domain and encouraged their development. The imperial mandarins were then astonished to learn that tax revenues increased under his policy. Weird naïveté. But the educational programming of mandarins omitted all acquaintance with trade figures or other commercial information; these were not fit concerns for scholars trained to serve equally ignorant rulers."

"Do you think caste and class arrangements can be overcome only by revolutions?" asked Ben.

"Insurrections and revolutions are among their hazards. People eventually get fed up beyond toleration with the old snapshots, and the oppressions, injustice, incompetence, and stultification their very obsolescence imposes. You said a great historical theme of our times, Armbruster, still unfinished and mounting, is take-backs of territory and creation of new sovereignties. Prior to that, and still unfinished, too, the great historical theme was demolition of caste, primarily by using parliaments and their growing legislative powers as the instrument.

"No matter how it's done, whether by revolution or by incursions from parliaments, it's innately difficult for caste guardians to accept either overthrow or whittling away of caste. They venerate tradition, they cultivate loyalty to one another, and their impulse is to rely on prowess and vengeance when they are confronted by serious dissent. Their normal virtues, in other words, tend to hamper minor caste adjustments and rule out radical revisions unless and until these are forced upon them.

"However—although it almost never happens—it's possible for caste guardians themselves to dispose of occupational castes. After Japan was opened to foreign trade in response to Perry's gunboats and demands in the 1850s, the samurai feared foreign conquest if the country didn't rapidly modernize. Or rather, a faction among the samurai took this tack, and it triumphed over more traditional-minded factions. The modernizing samurai collaborated closely with the merchants to jettison caste itself. The key to the success of their policy was, paradoxically, the revival of a moribund and ancient tradition. They reinstated the emperor as de facto head of state. For many centuries, the emperors had been rusticated as dim and isolated figureheads while the country was actually being ruled by shoguns, military dictators. The emperor gave his imprimatur to the radical changes. At the same time, his restoration signaled that although the caste structure was demolished, respect for government was being affirmed and stability and continuity were to be retained. One is reminded that democratic countries such as the Netherlands, Denmark, and Sweden have maintained their ancient traditions of monarchy to the same purpose.

"Once the new course was set, it was respectable for former caste warriors to work in trade and production. The change seems to have been accepted matter-of-factly. For instance, here is what the aged son of a samurai had to say about his family history as he looked back on his life in the 1980s. 'My father was a samurai in the [local lord's] service and had spent some time as a governor. . . . But after the Meiji emperor's Restoration the samurai lost their stipends so, in order to make a living, he and his former master decided to set up a company, and in 1871 they founded the Mitsuwa Trading Company. Mitsuwa wasn't just a bank in those days; it also traded in rice, beans and general wholesale goods.'

"It quickly even became the fashion among many samurai to place their daughters, until they married, in factory jobs. Descendants of merchants, and merchants themselves, became as socially respectable as descendants of kuge and samurai. Japan's present empress is from an old merchant family. All unthinkable under caste, but all perfectly natural under the flexibility method.

"Now for a pitfall of the caste method that is the opposite of revolution. It's the reason I didn't lump in Britain with the Netherlands and the Scandinavian countries a few minutes ago. Britain, in spite of many adjustments, retains a remarkably rigid class structure descending from the old European caste arrangements. Its class system seems to be a kind of museum piece within modern Europe.

"The pitfall it exemplifies is what I'll call self-subversion of commerce and industry. Remember that in all caste or rigid class systems, guardians are much loftier socially than members of commercial classes. Therefore guardians are socially enviable. Successful commercial people may thus hanker after socially superior guardian educations, customs, pastimes, and ideals. If they are able to afford them, they take these on, provided class rigidities have loosened enough, as they have in Britain, to permit that adjustment.

"If successful industrialists, shippers, and bankers with such aspirations had confined their guardian ways to private life or to the public duties they assumed, little harm to commerce would have resulted. But their new casts of mind infected their commercial responsibilities. The result of that, in Britain, is sometimes called 'the British disease' by European observers, or, as one American analyst has it, 'the decline of the industrial spirit.' The subverted commercial people took to venerating tradition over innovation and efficiency in their commercial work. They found ostentation, largesse, and achieving the status of patrons more satisfying than attending to productive investment. Their own industriousness suffered in favor of guardian pastimes—horses, hunting, maintaining landed estates, becoming engrossed in arts, connoisseurship, and scholarship in the immemorial way of aristocratic amateurs. They found hobnobbing with guardians more congenial than keeping in close touch with suppliers, customers, and competitors. Yet at the same time they retained control over commercial enterprises. That was the more harmful, since enterprises they controlled were leading businesses and in many ways set the country's patterns of commerce. Gradually, these higher reaches of commerce also attracted some hereditary gentry and aristocrats, but they did not need to adjust to commercial values when they took to commerce. The commerce they entered had already made so many adjustments to them.''

''When did this self-subversion begin?'' asked Jasper. ''A century ago Britain led the world industrially.''

''In retrospect, analysts of the decline of British industry from its mid-Victorian eminence place the start of the process somewhat more than a century ago. They identify the first signs of weakness as neglect of innovation. By the turn of the century, for instance, Germany had decisively forged ahead of Britain in the new fields, at the time, of optics and chemistry-based products. Then it soon became evident scant attention was being paid to comfort and convenience. For instance, farm labor-saving devices, central heating, modern refrigeration and kitchen equipment of other kinds, modern plumbing, and telephones as ordinary household conveniences were all slow to arrive in British life. In the meantime, productive investment even in equipment for traditional products was being neglected, so that by the time of the Second World War, British textile plants, shipyards, machinery manufacturing, coal mining, and steel making—work inherited from the great English industrial revolution of the past—were saddled with obsolete, inefficient equipment and plants.''

''Hortense, are you trying to argue that social envy has been responsible for Britain's decline!'' exclaimed Jasper.

''No, it's just one factor. Big empires almost always decline industrially and commercially. But perhaps most important, self-subversion of commerce and industry is an obstacle to regeneration. The British seem to like their subverted commercial values. What others call 'the British disease' they consider marks of cultural superiority.

''Britain isn't unique. In some recently liberated colonies—and in some liberated long ago in South America—big commerce, big industry, and government have become all but indistinguishable, the proprietors of all three together forming a dominant class with guardian values and casts of mind. A great gulf yawns between that mélange and little commerce. A social lid separates them. The borrowers' circles of micro-entrepreneurs Kate told us about dwell under the social lid. But democratic access to business capital may in time help them bridge the gap and become a regenerating force.''

''If I understand you,'' said Armbruster, ''you're telling us that occupational castes can suitably and fruitfully segregate guardian and commercial work for a time. But in the longer run, the method is too static and institutionalized to absorb necessary adjustments easily, quickly, plentifully, and flexibly. The method also leads to social ignorance. And it carries the hazards of insurrections on the one hand or self-undermined commercial values and competence on the other hand. Any other disadvantages?"

"Only the obvious, which brings misery to many an individual. Ordained occupational destinies ensure that many square pegs are forced into round holes."

"In a backhanded way, you've already made an argument for the knowledgeably flexible method," said Kate. "Why do you say this method doesn't hold up well over prolonged periods?"

"I implied its greatest pitfall when I said it makes greater demands on individuals' moral understanding. Kate, you said early on that you thought the master virtue, if there is one, is cooperation, because we're social animals. I'll accept that. But cooperation is another two-edged sword. Cooperation turns rancid when it becomes cooperation with immorality or with inappropriate functions and values.

"Here's a little instance, but it's instructive. Generations ago, the Philadelphia antique and secondhand dealers formed collusive bidding pools in their various specialties, such as jewelry, furniture, and china. How the practice started seems lost to memory but, as I picture it, it began with informal ways of helping one another out. 'I can't make it to the auction next Wednesday, but here's what I'd like to get. Will you bid for me up to such-and-such a figure?'

"However the collusion began, it became institutionalized in bidding pools and events called knockouts. One member of a given pool was delegated to bid at a given public auction. This profitable privilege was rotated among pool members. The others attended but didn't bid against their delegate. Then immediately after the public auction came the pool's knockout, its own private auction. A desk that brought, say, $1,235 at the public auction might bring the pool delegate $5,000 at the knockout. The desk's former owner was thus defrauded of $3,765. That plum went to the pool delegate who got his bargain because of the rigged bidding."

"Were the public auctioneers in on the racket too?" Jasper asked.

"No, they detested it. Besides gypping their clients, it defrauded them by reducing their commissions on sales. Finally, for a wonder, the guardians took action; in this case the U.S. Department of Justice made an investigation and indicted twelve prominent dealers. Eleven pleaded guilty to acts in restraint of trade. The twelfth went to trial and was convicted by a jury. Here's the detail that caught my attention. An elderly dealer in business with his daughter had obviously prided himself on his and his daughter's reputations. He said, 'The day I was allowed to go into the pool'—some forty years previously—'was a banner day. If you weren't in a pool, you weren't considered much of a dealer.'

"What can we say of this man? He fell into bad company. He took illegal behavior to be normal because every successful dealer was engaged in it. Armbruster, you made much the same point our first evening when you told us about people who should know better buying pirated software. Rancid cooperation.

"Sometimes falling into bad company and going along with it doesn't entail personal wrongdoing. Just the same, it blurs moral understanding, entails loss of bearings, if I recall your phrase. After the Lockheed bribery scandals of the mid-1970s, *The New York Times* had a reporter interview a number of office workers outside the company headquarters in Burbank, California, to learn how they were reacting to the company's disgrace. Without exception, the workers defended the bribe-giving. Some did so aggressively, like a woman who said, 'Everybody's doing it. That's the name of the game. That's the way business is done all over the world these days. Why do they have to pick on Lockheed?' Her assumption, by the way, was mistaken. Lockheed wasn't merely adopting, through rancid cooperation, the well-established customs of corrupt foreign regimes into whose bad company it had fallen. It was an active corruptor. The bribes it dispensed in the Netherlands and Japan stirred up greater national outrage, shame, and astonishment in those countries than the revelations did here.

"Other employees defended the bribery sadly, even with pathos. One woman said her fourteen-year-old son was 'a real idealist' and had questioned her about the bribes. 'I told him that what the company did wasn't right, but that it had no choice . . . and he said, "How could you say that?" I told him you wouldn't be asking those questions if you were forty-four years old and had to pay bills.' "

"Let me repeat what I said earlier," Jasper remarked. "In a corrupt context, the moral and scrupulous man or woman is a misfit."

"Cooperation is esteemed across the board," said Hortense. "If rancid cooperation is the only kind offering itself, then rancid cooperation is what almost anyone will practice. Cooperating is a powerful impulse."

"Except for whistle-blowers," said Armbruster.

"Yes, rare individuals with exemplary moral courage who usually suffer in consequence. They are ostracized. They may lose their jobs. They are apt to get bad recommendations and to be mistrusted as misfits and troublemakers when they seek other employment.

"I'm taking up where you left off, Armbruster, when you expounded your Law of Intractable Systemic Corruption. Once a given organization breaches its syndrome, and the breach becomes institutionalized, the resulting conversion of normal virtues into vices wins cooperation among management and workers. Now their work experience is blurring their moral understanding instead of clarifying it.

"Over the course of time, corrupted organizations accumulate in a society. Without correction, the accompanying rancid cooperation blurs moral understanding in more than the afflicted organizations. People carry their blurred and blunted morality with them if they move into other organizations. The toxins, so to speak, the rancid spoilages, spread and accumulate. With the passage of time, knowledgeable flexibility loses its necessary knowledgeability. The method becomes rickety and slovenly instead of growing firmer and sturdier with time. This is the great pitfall of the method."

Armbruster adopted his summing-up manner. "You argue that the flexible method is spared structural flaws that are built into the caste method. Instead, its weakness is the fact of human imperfection. You contend that random transgressions become entrenched. Then they magnify themselves because the people involved—and, I would add, people outside the organization proper with whom it deals—take the corruption for granted."

"I shouldn't have omitted that point," said Hortense. "For instance, a municipal buildings-inspection department accustomed to receiving petty bribes simply to push the work along expeditiously and not keep architects and contractors waiting has the peripheral effect of getting the architects and contractors to take the corruption for granted too. Members of the relevant public. They may grumble, but they cooperate and, in blurred fashion, accept the situation as normal."

"Your thesis, then," said Armbruster, "is that as time passes, the flexible method weakens and perhaps ultimately fails. A depressing scenario."

"And so frighteningly matter-of-fact," added Hortense. "Each breach of integrity, as it occurs, can seem so logical, so harmless, even beneficial. No red lights flash. No riots follow. Life just continues, a little more corrupt. It's supposed to be the job of guardians to nip initial transgressions and breaches in the bud. But the guardians are doing the same things themselves: randomly breaching their syndrome in their own organizations, converting virtues to vices and becoming morally blurry.

"Hannah Arendt was deeply interested in the terrible matter-of-factness of institutionalized wickedness and rote cooperation with it. In her famous phrase, she called it 'the banality of evil.' She was writing about horrible war crimes carried out matter-of-factly. But her observation also applies to humdrum breaches of integrity, as she was aware. In her last work before her death she argued that each by each, everyone should habitually be aware of the moral implications of what he or she is asked to do and, each by each, should stand up for the right to be moral. She thought that was a basic human right."

"Like the fourteen-year-old son of the Lockheed employee? He was following the Arendt prescription even if his mother wasn't. Good for him," said Ben.

"Yes, but the Arendt prescription is no panacea," said Hortense. "That mother's likely got all she can handle keeping her own little establishment afloat, and in any case she has no way of reforming her employer. It's the same with an engineer given the job of designing a piece of fancy equipment and also given to understand that cost is no object, it's all on the taxpayer.

"All the same," she went on, "I do agree that widespread moral understanding and respect for the syndromes are the only reliable buttresses of the flexible method, in place of the rigidities of caste. I also agree with Arendt that we cannot rely on an intelligentsia to make critical and discriminating judgments for us. In fact, some tenured and certified intelligentsia maintain we shouldn't make moral judgments at all; they're extreme moral relativists."

"I don't place much faith in schemes that presuppose, for their success, widespread reform of human beings," said Armbruster. "Especially when the momentum is at odds with that aim, as your scenario depicts it to be."

"Here's a thought from Richard Nielsen, a professor in the Carroll School of Management at Boston College," said Hortense. "He argues that a major cause of corruption in business organizations is 'managerial isolation.' He advocates that managers at all levels in an organization should habitually think about the enterprise's legitimate values and the morality of what it's doing or planning to do. That's Arendt's advice, as he acknowledges. But then, in addition, he thinks managers should habitually discuss these matters with each other. The purpose would be to forestall ethical mistakes when they threaten, or nip them quickly, supposing they do occur.''

"Wouldn't they be scared to do that, Hortense?" asked Ben. "Lose their jobs maybe?"

"Feeling alone is what scares managers, Nielsen says. If they find they have allies—or can persuade allies into existence—moral courage becomes more practicable. In effect, he proposes invoking wholesome cooperation to combat rancid cooperation.''

"He's fantasizing," said Jasper.

"What he suggests isn't impractical in itself," said Hortense. She waved a clipping. "I see here that a big investment-banking firm has instructed its people to comb their operations for transgressions and bring them into the open. There's a reason for this, of course. Some of its securities traders were criminally indicted for breaking the laws and several top executives resigned because of documentary evidence that they knew about the illegalities but didn't report them to government regulators, as they should have, and by keeping hands off let them continue.''

"Your point, I suppose, is that the management should have gone in for serious self-examination earlier, and all this wouldn't have happened," said Jasper.

"No, that's not the point I'm making, although what you say is true, of course. After indictments came down and various resignations were accepted, a new chief executive was installed. He ordered the various departments to unearth all illegalities not yet discovered so they could be reported and corrected.''

"Were they really that scared of the guardians, Hortense?" asked Ben.

"They were more scared, it seems, of losing customers," Hortense answered. "When the scandal broke, the firm did lose important customers. A series of continuing scandals would send the firm's reputation totally down the drain and—along with it—the firm itself and its thousands of employees. That was already clear to everybody concerned.

"What's more, according to this news account, practically all the firms handling securities—stocks, bonds, Treasury bills—promptly began to scrutinize themselves for illegalities, trying to beat the investigators to it. That was because the guardians had already issued subpoenas to officials or workers in more than a hundred and thirty other firms, so they, and others that hadn't been subpoenaed so far, scrambled to clean up their acts.

"My point, Jasper, is that if serious self-examination because of fear is a practicable measure, which it demonstrably is, then self-examination to maintain moral standards is also practicable."

"This is like constructing a boom after the oil has spilled," said Jasper. "You cannot skip that lightly over the motive of fear. Fear of guardians, fear of customers, fear of losing jobs. Doing right only because of fear, that is not what I understand you to be proposing."

"Well, but listen to this," said Hortense, consulting another clipping. "The professional foresters' association in British Columbia—this is a cheering note for you, Ben, and maybe for PPOWW—has revised its code of ethics. The revision calls on members, I'll quote, 'to recognize and report practices detrimental to the stewardship of the forest land.' Revisions like this don't happen of themselves; they require discussions about moral standards. Members who want to uphold them evidently found they weren't alone.

"This same clipping mentions that forestry students have formed an organization called Students for Forestry Awareness—I like their using that word 'awareness'—to combat conventional but bad logging practices. Whether their taste of moral courage and wholesome cooperation as students can fortify them against rancid cooperation later in life when they get jobs, we can't know. It's a start.

"Now here's an interesting item," she went on. "Some companies give written question-and-answer honesty tests to job applicants. Sometimes employees are tested, apparently to learn which ones are actually ignorant of differences between honest and dishonest behavior. What interested me was that a convenience-food-store chain with several hundred employees and a bad inventory-theft problem didn't require its employees to hand in their tests for marking. Instead, employees kept their papers and were supplied the correct answers so they could mark their own tests. The report says of this experiment, 'Exposure to the test and the process of self-correction . . . prompted an immediate two-thirds reduction in inventory theft.' "

"But in that case," said Jasper, "it was clearly in the management's own interest to promote moral education and self-examination. Quite a different proposition from using self-examination to reform a company that is dishonest through and through, or from the top down.''

"Yes, I have something depressing on that," said Hortense. "Back in 1986, after a series of defense scandals, the Pentagon instituted a project it called the Defense Industry Initiatives on Business Ethics and Conduct. Forty-six military contractors, including most of the largest, agreed to establish internal codes of ethics and to give ethics training to all employees, with management receiving more extensive training. Employees were provided confidential hot lines to report abuses or suspected abuses."

"Did it do any good?" asked Jasper.

"Well, the forty-six contractors did confess voluntarily to ninety-six cases of fraud or waste during the next two years and returned $43,000,000 to the Pentagon."

"Hmmm, let's see," said Armbruster, squeezing his eyes closed while he did mental calculations. "I make that less than $450,000, average, per transgression. Peanuts."

"Peanuts is the least of it," said Hortense. "Of those forty-six contractors, thirty-nine were shortly afterward investigated for abuses they failed to report. And scandals even worse than frauds and waste— or anyhow bigger—continued: collusion between corrupt Pentagon officers and contractors in making contract awards. The results led one congressman to say the government was kidding itself with the self-policing idea, and an aide to the House Armed Services Committee concluded that 'self-governance is really a public relations strategy.' ''

"It probably merely demonstrates what we already know," said Armbruster. "That the military-industrial complex is irredeemably corrupt."

"Now here's something I don't know whether to consider hopeful or depressing," said Hortense. "A poll of Canadian office workers on the quality of their working life turned up a response by eighty percent that they consider it very important for management to be honest and ethical. That sounds pretty good. Now for the bad news. Only thirty-six percent thought it was clearly evident that behavior in their companies was honest and ethical. Indeed, overall, the largest single dissatisfaction with work was bad ethics."

"That sounds as if the dismal scenario you depicted for us earlier has much truth to it," said Armbruster. "But it also sounds as if people aren't happy with it. Resigned to it, maybe, but not happy."

"We're all frightened of overbearing governments, and no wonder," said Jasper, "but isn't depending on this fantasy of organizational moral self-examination pretty unrealistic in comparison with beefing up the law and its enforcement?"

"I thought we'd already agreed guardians are necessary to keep commercial life in line," said Hortense. "But Arendt and Nielsen argue that isn't enough. So do I. Guardian organizations don't even keep themselves in line without guardians of guardians, if then. They need self-examination and moral awareness as much as commercial enterprises do, and managers in the bureaucracies can feel as morally alone as commercial managers.

"Furthermore, the formal guardianship that you speak of, Jasper, can't anticipate novel transgressions. For example, how could guardians even recognize and start combating computer crimes until after they already existed and had come into the law's ken? Monopolistic trusts and related acts in restraint of trade preceded the laws on that subject and their enforcement. Not until the close of the 1980s did a few states attempt to outlaw some of the novel practices of corporate raiders. Whoever the ancient traders first using dishonest weights may have been, we can be sure that laws and penalties were responses after the fact. In the nature of things, the law is forever running at the rear of inventive types of misbehavior.

"Therefore, only organizational self-examination—based on adhering to whichever is the appropriate syndrome for its work—can forestall clever and novel malfeasance, nip it in the bud before it becomes well rooted as it waits for the law to catch up—if it ever does.

"Nielsen, like Arendt, assumes that many people—perhaps most people—given the choice and chance, prefer not to be corrupt and dislike seeing their organizations and society go rotten. The alternative to that faith is despair. What can I say? We must try our best, even if in our hearts we do despair. What else? Give in with resignation or become rancid ourselves?"

"Let's take a break for a quick but relaxing lunch," said Armbruster. "I've got something for everybody. And then I'm sure we have questions about your report, Hortense."

"I haven't even finished yet," said Hortense. "I told you the advantages of the caste method for protecting moral syndrome integrity. But apart from saying the flexible method is a motion picture instead of a snapshot, I haven't told you its advantages and therefore why it's worth every effort to make it work well."

CHAPTER THIRTEEN

Hortense's Defense of Moral Flexibility

W HERE DEMOCRACY means more than having the vote, many citizens engage part-time in public affairs," Hortense resumed after lunch. "Some push causes or movements, like Ben's battlers in the forest. Some serve on boards of quasi-public institutions. Some serve on citizens' advisory boards to municipal agencies, all that kind of thing. This work demands the guardian syndrome, especially the precept to shun trading. Yet great numbers of people who take on public responsibilities part-time happen to make their livings in commercial work. Therefore they must be flexible and knowledgeable enough to understand the differences and abide by them.

"When they don't, public good succumbs to private gain. That hazard lurks everywhere, even in as genteel, high-minded, and public-spirited a body as a museum board of directors. Once in a long while we hear shocking hints that deacquisitioned museum possessions, ostensibly sold because they weren't valuable enough to keep, were actually sold because board members or their friends wanted the items for their private collections. That seems to be rare, but only because most museum boards, curators too, are loyal to the purposes of their institutions.

"On the other hand, some types of 'public service' institutions are so frequently corrupt, it's tiresome. Perhaps the worst are those entailing real estate interests. We also all know of honorary degrees, or other guardian accolades such as 'outstanding citizen of the year,' that have been bestowed on mediocrities or even rascals because they've coughed up a contribution to the institution or are being wooed so they will."

"That is like the corruption of the medieval church, when clergy used to sell indulgences for contributions," said Jasper. "I belong, by the way, to an advisory board for a public library upstate."

"How come?" Armbruster asked.

"My old hometown. I still go there for family visits. The librarians do a good job, but sometimes they need us. The town has its quota of zealots, would-be book burners, not many, but the trouble they make is why the library established an advisory board. We get complaints that books are racist or sexist, pornographic, politically subversive, too religious or antireligious, unpatriotic."

"The zealots are self-appointed guardians, aren't they? Censors?" Armbruster interrupted again.

"Yes. Very occasionally they make a sufficiently good case that we advise that a book be moved from the circulation to the reference department. Budget decisions can be controversial. We are not the Library of Congress. We cannot get everything. The librarians' judgments are good, and mainly we back them up against unsuitable pressures."

"I suppose you're valuable when it comes to advising on crime books," ventured Kate.

"Absolutely not. Conflict of interest. In this role I am strictly a generalized library guardian. I am loyal to the library as an institution based on freedom of information and the arts, and put all other considerations out of my mind."

"What do you turn down?" asked Armbruster.

"The most recent thing we advised against was actually a staff proposal. The library board—we advisers are an adjunct to the board—was split on adding a comic-book section to the children's department. The argument for it was statistical. It was expected to increase library traffic and so make the annual reports look splendid. We advised against it as an inappropriate diversion of funds. We could have been more withering, called it a self-inflating, careerist-motivated diversion of funds."

"Do you get paid?" asked Ben.

"An appointment without pay. The board makes the appointments.

Its members serve without pay too. They are mostly concerned with budgets and fund-raising: lobbying for tax contributions, soliciting other contributions, raising money for renovations and building expansion. It is like your SHARE board, Ben; without these volunteers, administrative costs would soar, at the expense of acquisitions.

"But even if we or the board were paid, it would still illustrate your point, Hortense," Jasper went on. "It is ordinary for the same individual to do both guardian and commercial work, yet keep the two distinct. Almost all board members get their livings commercially. One sells building materials. But as far as I know, no one uses board positions to snag commercial work for himself or friends."

"Now take labor unions," said Hortense. "When the union's battling for a contract, maybe out on strike, it has to shift into its guardian mode and behave more or less like Ben's battlers. But when a contract is signed, those workers have to shift into a commercial mode. If the battle morality infuses everyday production or service work—which it sometimes does in companies with bad labor relations—it's disastrous for the work.

"The union leadership is always guardian; if it sells out the workers, that's corrupt. Just the same, the leadership must respect the commercial values of innovation, competition, and efficiency, and the necessity for productive investments. Otherwise, the leaders may become closet Luddites, to the detriment of the industry in which their membership works."

"You're saying the leadership must keep its eye on getting a fair share of the pie for members, a guardian concern," said Jasper. "But it has to recognize the members are making pies, a commercial preoccupation with all that this entails morally. Two casts of mind here, and both the union leadership and the company leadership need knowledge of both syndromes and respect for the integrity of both."

"Yes, to the point that individuals can knowledgeably shift between the two syndromes if a change in jobs demands it," said Hortense. "That can happen if a union member doing factory or commercial service work takes a new job as a union organizer, for instance, or a floor shop steward is promoted into company management. In Yugoslavia, under its Communist regime, workers' councils running factories failed to understand or respect the commercial syndrome, even though their management duties demanded it. A common breach of the commercial syndrome—and a disastrous one—was to vote on how to use company surpluses at the end of the year as distributive largesse; factory-financed worker junkets around the country were a favorite, to the neglect of productive investments. Pretty soon there weren't surpluses.

"Now consider newspapers and magazines," Hortense went on. "Those that take investigative reporting seriously are assuming responsibility for being guardians of guardians—a chief reason that a free press is valuable. Yet most periodicals are commercial. Selling advertising is how they stay free to be guardians of guardians. Except for public broadcasting, which looks to grants and to donations from viewers, the same is true of television stations and their broadcasts of documentaries and news. However, commercial income opens the possibility, likely the probability, of editorial pressure from advertisers. Bad, because it undercuts guardianship of commerce or exposing instances when governments and commercial interests are in corrupt collusion."

"Good periodicals maintain a barrier between their editorial and advertising departments," interrupted Armbruster. "You don't necessarily need the flexible method for that. In a caste or rigid class society, editorial people can be drawn mainly from an elite indoctrinated as guardians, while the advertising people can be recruited from the commercial hoi polloi."

"Even so, at the top must be a publisher who knows what both the left and right hands are doing and can help them both," said Hortense. "The barrier has to be in his head.

"Still another point. Government agencies are entangled in commerce, the more complex a society, the more so. It's simpleminded to suppose privatization can eliminate that. To be sure, where governments have inadvisedly taken on commercial functions, privatization of those enterprises makes sense morally and financially. Nevertheless, governments have to let contracts, buy goods and services for their own needs and other clearly public purposes. We've noted how the Pentagon took to subverting commercial morality. The Pentagon-supported manufacturers aren't owned by government; they're private enterprises. Furthermore, if guardians are not morally flexible enough to understand the commercial syndrome as well as their own, they can't do a decent job of policing commerce or legislating for it. For instance, how good will guardians be at legislating and policing against monopolies if they ignore or take lightly the necessity of commercial competition?

"In sum, a complex and democratic society needs knowledgeable flexibility for many, many practical reasons. But my most important reason for thinking it valuable is this: if it's true we're the only creatures with two fundamentally different ways of getting a living, it follows that to be as fully human as we can be, we should all be capable of using our two syndromes well. They belong to all of us because we're human, no other reason. They don't merely belong to this or that ordained group, as if we were social insects.

"This finishes my report, Armbruster, but there's something else I'd like to get off my chest while I have the floor.

"I'm sick of cant about the family being the bedrock of society. The reverse is true." She waved a clipping. "Here's an item about a Pathan who cut off his wife's nose because he was jealous. That was his right in his society. After second thoughts he took her to a doctor. When he learned nose repair would cost thirty rupees he said no, not worth it, he could buy a new wife for eighty rupees."

"Icky story, but what does it have to do with the subject?" Jasper asked.

"Society itself is the bedrock of society, and it's also the bedrock of the family, not the reverse," said Hortense. "Families are fragments of their societies. The bedrocks are the ways people get their livings, and the institutions and organizations formed to that end: guardian and commercial. Society, including the family, is in their keeping, not only materially and politically but morally as well."

"That sounds an extreme view," said Armbruster. "The family is an institution too, after all."

"What is a family, institutionally speaking?" asked Hortense. "Its nature depends on its society—that is to say, on its place and time like that Pathan's family—not on the fact and functions of family per se. A family can include multiple wives and concubines. It can practice selective infanticide of daughters. It can radically differentiate the upbringing of boys from that of girls, and the expectations of each."

"It can even radically differentiate the upbringing and expectations of a first-born son from younger sons, as well as daughters," put in Kate.

"Yes," said Hortense, "or the destinies of the youngest son and daughter. In the old yeoman rule of inheritance, called 'borough English,' the youngest son—not the oldest son but the youngest—inherited the homestead and farmstead. The older sons left to make their way when they became capable, leaving the youngest, finally, who not only remained thereafter to take care of his elderly parents and the property but was the destined heir from birth—or rather, because of last birth.

In some times and places the custom has been for the youngest daughter not to marry while her parents are alive, so she can stay home and take care of them.

"There are nuclear families, extended families, families that incorporate apprentices and servants, families that supply dowries and those that don't," Hortense went on. "If a society's means of getting its livings are stagnant over a long period of time, the forms its families have taken remain stagnant too. In that case, it is easy to conclude those stabilized families represent the foundations of their society. But it is an erroneous conclusion. As soon as such a society experiences economic changes, its families change in response, maybe for better, maybe worse.

"Everywhere, birth rates drop with prosperity. Consider the effects on families of shifts from craft to industrial production; chronic unemployment; long commuting by fathers; both parents becoming breadwinners outside the home; selective migrations of men, or of young people, to find work.

"Social context easily and drastically reshapes families. Give welfare aid to mothers with dependent children only if no able-bodied man is in the household, and watch how fast the number of fatherless families soars. Give generous pensions to old people, and watch three-generation households dwindle. Reduce premature mortality rates of adults, and notice how divorce rates rise. Is bastardy socially disgraced or not? Is the family-run farm an economic success or not? Are children counted on to help with family income or not?

"Immigrant families in our country change very rapidly in their new contexts. Children take to insisting on choosing their own mates instead of submitting to arranged marriages. They may rebel against the father's decisions on other matters; the wife may too.

"How can a unit so malleable, so vulnerable to changes in context, so easily manipulated, be the bedrock of society? Face it—if the guardian and commercial organizations of a society are corrupt, the society is corrupt, whether that pleases or displeases families. But if the guardian and commercial organizations respect and adhere to good moral standards, they supply a moral social context for the family.

"Societies shape and reshape the family and blow it about for better or worse." Hortense had now risen, as if she were addressing a jury. "Passing the buck to the family for the corruption and other shortcomings of society is a cop-out on the part of institutions and their managements who make messes out of the moral syndromes."

"But good personal morals and good character are surely related to family upbringing," said Jasper. "You decided, Armbruster, we're not to stray into personal and private morality, but it does intersect with our concerns about workplace morality and maintaining integrity there."

"I willingly grant," said Armbruster, "that what we call good personal character—responsibility, capacity to resist harmful temptations, compassion, courage—such qualities certainly intersect, as you say, with performance in the workplace.

"But personal morality doesn't explain as much as we like to suppose, and not only because of its limitations within larger contexts, as Hortense was just pointing out, if a bit elliptically. Consider Quincy, for instance. I know from long acquaintance that Quincy is a man of fine character. Suppose this were also true of everyone in his bank. It would be to no avail in preventing them from making messes with largesse—"

"—in which many innocent bystanders were hurt, especially poor people in poor countries," Kate interrupted.

"Yes, it would be to no avail if these people of good character and good upbringing failed to realize that distributing largesse under the name of productive loans is immoral for the organization in which they find themselves."

"Oh, I almost forgot," said Hortense. "I have a parting gift. It's from Lao Tzu again.

> *"When people lost sight of the way to live*
> *Came codes of love and honesty,*
> *Learning came, charity came,*
> *Hypocrisy took charge;*
> *When differences weakened family ties*
> *Came benevolent fathers and dutiful sons;*
> *And when lands were disrupted and misgoverned*
> *Came ministers commended as loyal."*

After a few seconds of silence as they took this in, Jasper said, "That is a real downer you have given us, Hortense. I will add two lines:

> *"When society's workplace morals were deranged*
> *Came talking heads telling of ordered syndromes."*

"So you think we're just a symptom!" said Kate. "That is a downer!"

CHAPTER FOURTEEN

Plans and Champagne

"THAT WINE must be chilled," said Armbruster.

Setting down his glass after the toasts to Hortense and Ben, he said, "I'm more than casually interested in your plans, you two. After all, Hortense is my niece. Are you thinking of marrying?"

"Yes," said Ben.

"Maybe," said Hortense.

"We have work plans, anyway," said Ben. "I'm going to concentrate more on helping groups with fights on their hands. Victories are more influential than arguments."

"Ben's gotten me interested in environmental law," said Hortense. "It can help win the victories. I plan to give up my family-law practice—"

"Isn't that rather rash?" asked Armbruster. "You still have those sons to educate. You've built a dependable practice."

"I'm burnt out, Armbruster. Cantankerous divorce settlements; bitter, tragic child-custody disputes; separations; delinquent child-support payments; child abuse; child neglect; juvenile delinquents; wife beaters; alcoholics; drug addictions; infidelities. Every morning I grit my teeth and climb back on the treadmill. Oh, I realize it needs doing, but I've had it with loused-up personal morality. I won't leave my clients in the lurch, but I won't accept new ones. While I'm phasing out, two old law school friends swamped with environmental litigation cases will pass me assignments and help break me in. Don't worry about me, Armbruster. I'm being rescued by loused-up commercial and guardian morality.''

"We'll both be doing a lot of weekend work and traveling," said Ben. "We've talked it over and I'm afraid you can't count on us for more of these sessions. I'm glad I was in on them for all kinds of reasons, but continuing is too much.''

"What are your plans, Jasper?" asked Armbruster. "Like to do another report? If I could drum up another member or two?''

"'Thanks, but no. However, I am grateful too. I had gotten so bored with crime writing I could not go on. I made an abortive try at autobiography, partly, I suppose, to learn why I was bored.''

"And did you?"

"Simple, really. Bored with repeating myself. Now I have a renewed itch to get back to crime novels, have already started a new one. I am going to put our syndromes to work in it.''

"Watch out. No didactic talking heads.''

"No talking heads. Interesting background contradictions. New twists and characters with more depth.''

"Kate? I've a favor to ask you, but do you feel like making another report?''

"Not really, although all kinds of material suggests itself. What's the favor?''

"Helping with the transcript. It's going to need another eye in the editing, and second opinions. Weekend work for you.''

"What transcript?" Kate asked.

"The transcript of our conversations. What else? We'll see if it adds up to a book.''

"I don't like the sound of that," said Ben. "If you propose to circulate stuff I said here off-the-record—''

"Not to worry. If you want anonymity, we'll change your name and the few facts advertising your identity. You can turn into a fiction. We all can. The usual disclaimer about none of these characters being living persons. Like to work on it, Kate?''

"Sure, I'd enjoy it. But what makes you think anyone else will be interested? We've had our discoveries and amusement but—''

"That remains to be seen." Armbruster made a tent of his hands and tapped his forefingers while he thought. "I realize that most of us after our formative years resist revising our views of how the world works. Most of us have a bit of the Bourbons in us. Probably a good thing or we'd be butterfly-brains forever flitting from one intellectual fad to another. But I've revised some of my views since we began these talks.

"I used to think of government—meaning good government—as the major force at work in the civilizing process. Now I'm inclined to think of government as being essentially barbaric—barbaric in its origins and forever susceptible to barbaric actions and aims. But don't get me wrong. We need it. So now I see government as being incapable, on its own, of civilizing even itself.

"Some other civilizing agent must therefore be necessary. This, I now think, is the guardian-commercial symbiosis that combats force, fraud, and unconscionable greed in commercial life—and simultaneously impels guardians to respect private plans, private property, and personal rights. Mutual support of morally contradictory trading and taking; it tames both activities and their derivatives. So perhaps we have a useful definition of civilization: reasonably workable guardian-commercial symbiosis.

"We still have another bottle of champagne here." He popped the cork and poured. "To civilization!" he said, raising his glass.

The cold bubbles glinted. They all laughed except Kate, who hesitated and forced a smile. Jasper patted her shoulder. "So chancy," he murmured. "Such a tightrope act. Always has been, of course. All the more reason to cross your fingers and drink to it."

"Before you leave, you can help Kate and me by telling us why you accepted my first invitation," said Armbruster. "We'll insert what you tell us right at the beginning of the transcript. Think back now, and be honest."

APPENDIX

THE COMMERCIAL MORAL SYNDROME

Shun force
Come to voluntary agreements
Be honest
Collaborate easily with strangers and aliens
Compete
Respect contracts
Use initiative and enterprise
Be open to inventiveness and novelty
Be efficient
Promote comfort and convenience
Dissent for the sake of the task
Invest for productive purposes
Be industrious
Be thrifty
Be optimistic

THE GUARDIAN MORAL SYNDROME

Shun trading
Exert prowess
Be obedient and disciplined
Adhere to tradition
Respect hierarchy
Be loyal
Take vengeance
Deceive for the sake of the task
Make rich use of leisure
Be ostentatious
Dispense largesse
Be exclusive
Show fortitude
Be fatalistic
Treasure honor

NOTES

Epigraph—This is from an oration, "The American Scholar" (1837), by Ralph Waldo Emerson. *The Harvard Classics* 5 (New York: P. F. Collier, 1909).

The following abbreviations are used in chapter notes:

> *G&M*—*The Globe and Mail,* Toronto
> *NYRB*—*The New York Review of Books*
> *NYT*—*The New York Times*
> *WSJ*—*The Wall Street Journal*

The note sequences follow the chapter texts.

1/*Armbruster's Summons*

The pirated-software episode is drawn from life; a visiting scientist at the meeting gave me a careful eyewitness description. The university is not identified for the reasons Armbruster gives.

The list of white-collar crimes has been compiled from press reports of investigations and prosecutions; also from press releases concerning successful prosecutions or settlements by New York City's Department of Consumer Affairs.

The garment district thefts and raid: *WSJ,* November 5, 1982, "Operation Furtrap—Police Uncloak Burglary Rings Stealing Apparel in New York's Garment Center" by Stanley Penn; and accounts of the same operation, *NYT.*

The foreign debt default crisis referred to occurred in 1982. In 1987, the large write-downs of defaulted loans began. The comment about the American banks' accounting was made by an unnamed financial vice president of a German bank, quoted in *WSJ,* June 18, 1987, "German Banks Avoid Worst of Debt Crisis," a dispatch from Frankfurt by Thomas F. O'Boyle.

Various other financial finaglings were contemplated, including "recycling" the loans into the World Bank, a taxpayer-supported institution: *WSJ,* March 9, 1989, "Another Round—Bush Aides Are Likely to Offer a Plan Soon on Third World Debt—U.S. Fears Political Turmoil May Hit Latin America—Banks May Pay Big Price" by Walter S. Mossburg and Peter Truell. For an overview: *Banks, Borrowers and the Establishment* by Karen Lissakers (New York: Basic Books, 1991).

The "PPOWW" story is fictional. However it incorporates much factual material: the description of a threatened valley in the West Kootenays of British Columbia; logging-company practices and deceptive justifications; the ever-looming but seldom-used threat of tree-spiking; confrontations between protestors and loggers; inane comment by a distant logging-company executive while television pictures are giving him the lie; televised pictures stunningly contrasting logged and unlogged tracts. I have drawn my information from personal inspections, interviews, and scenes from television news and documentary programs broadcast by the Canadian Broadcasting Corporation.

In spite of Ben's gloomy assessment that nothing has changed, it may have. In November 1991, the government that had ruled British Columbia for all but three of the past forty years was defeated in elections. The new administration seems to be taking initial steps to reform forestry policies and practices. More significantly perhaps, during protests against a logging road in the summer of 1991, protestors were for the first time supported by loggers (two locals of the International Woodworkers of America, the loggers' union) because they recognized that the long-term future of their industry depends on reformed practices. "The last people to understand that will be the logging companies," one of the protestors has told me, "but eventually they'll understand too."

The Great Bear as "Keeper of the Game" is a bit of folklore circulating among environmentalists.

2/A Pair of Contradictions

The precepts are a compilation and refinement of "esteemed behavior" notes I've made over a period of some fifteen years. Initially, I conceived of the two precept groups as embodying "trader" and "raider" morality, and was laggard at recognizing that "raider" precepts are as morally valid as traders', and are grounded in legitimate territorial concerns.

The edition of Plato's *Republic* from which quotations are drawn is a translation by G. M. A. Grube (Indianapolis: Hackett, 1974).

The discussion on justice is in Book IV of the *Republic.* The commentator referred to is Nicholas P. White, *A Companion to Plato's Republic* (Indianapolis: Hackett, 1979).

3/Kate on the Commercial Syndrome

The bit about the English navy is drawn from *Guilds and Companies of London* by George Unwin (London: Methuen, 1909).

Stuart Piggott, in *Prehistoric India* (Harmondsworth: Penguin, 1950), describes the meticulously standardized stone weights, c. 2500 B.C., in two cities and many towns and villages throughout an ancient empire of the Indus.

The Egyptian self-recommendations to the gods are quoted from *The Book of the Dead: Papyri of Nai, Hunefer, Anhai,* commentary by Evelyn Rossiter (Miller Graphics, distributed by Crown, New York).

The traveler in Asia Minor was John G. Bennet. The fragment of his book that has come into my hands (which I deduce was called *Witness*) does not indicate who published it or when. Bennet was apparently a surveyor and entrepreneur-adventurer.

Mariam K. Slater made her perceptive comment on social and commercial life in Nairobi in *African Odyssey: An Anthropological Adventure* (New York: Anchor/Doubleday, 1976).

The contrast between bourgeois cosmopolitanism and courtier insularity is drawn from *The Court Society* by Norbert Elias, translated by Edmund Jephcott (New York: Pantheon, 1983).

The Custom of Merchants is also known as *jus mercatorum,* the term used by Henri Pirenne in *Early Democracies in the Low Countries* (New York: Harper and Row, 1963). Pirenne comments that apart from charging commercial people a high price for protection, territorial authorities ignored them and their settlements during the whole of the tenth and early eleventh centuries. Rulers "did not give them any institutions of their own, but . . . did not hinder them from providing them for themselves." Once a man passed through medieval town gates then, and for long thereafter, he "escaped from territorial law and came under an exceptional jurisdiction," both politically and economically. Although town inhabitants were socially unequal, they were nevertheless legally equal, "all with the same title and the same rights."

Assimilation of the Custom of Merchants into rulers' law varied from place to place and occurred slowly. Nathan Rosenberg and L. E. Birdzell in *How the West Grew Rich* (New York: Basic Books, 1985) comment that rulers' official courts "were not likely to be presented with commercial disputes so long as their decisions were made unpredictable by lack of precedent, by medieval concepts of discretionary justice, and by possible bias against foreigners. The impasse was broken here and there, in the courts of the trading cities, by the late Middle Ages. But it was not until the latter part of the eighteenth century that the royal courts in London had accumulated enough experience in deciding disputes over insurance, bills of exchange, ships' charters, sales contracts, partnership agreements, patents, arbitrations and other commercial transactions to make English courts and law seem a factor contributing positively."

The Roman Law of Foreigners was despised by Roman lawyers, according to Sir Henry Sumner Maine, *Ancient Law* (London: John Murray, 1905; first published in 1861), who notes that "social necessities and social opinion are always more or less in advance of the law." The Law of Foreigners was based on a principle called *jus gentium,* meaning law of all peoples; it was creative, says Maine, in getting at the essence of contracts.

The Fourteenth Amendment provides, among other things, that no state may deny to any person within its jurisdiction the equal protection of the laws; and that Congress has power by appropriate legislation to enforce the provision. The amendment was preceded by the post-emancipation Civil Rights Act of 1866, providing that "all citizens of the United States shall have the same right, in every State and Territory, as is enjoyed by white citizens thereof to inherit, purchase, lease, sell, hold, and convey real and personal property." Congress reenacted this statute upon ratification of the Fourteenth Amendment in 1870.

Huxley's tribute to "science and her methods" was addressed to the Rev. Charles Kingsley in 1860; quoted from Volume 2 of *With Great Pleasure,* a compilation of tidbits by the British Broadcasting Corporation, edited by Alec Reid (London: Arrow, 1989).

Circumstances of the lawsuit by Stanford University against the National Heart, Lung and Blood Institute of the federal Department of Health and Human Services were reported in *Science News,* November 16, 1991.

Kate's worries are also reflected, for example, in *WSJ,* July 12, 1985, "Competition in Science Seems to Be Spawning Cases of Shoddy Work— Plagiarism and Data Faking, Though Still Rare, Sting a Field That Needs Trust—Medicine Is the Hardest Hit" by David Stipp. The competition referred to is for grants (patronage) and honors. *Scientific American,* June 1985, reports in its Science and the Citizen department the chilling effects upon scientific collaboration of the Export Administration Act of 1979. The magazine also reports numerous types of inappropriate restrictions attached to many government research grants; perhaps the most odious are "change" clauses, permitting the federal funding agency to change "without notice the content and/or scope of the research contract without the researcher's agreement."

For discussion of the Protestant work ethic, I have drawn mainly upon *Protestantism and Capitalism: The Weber Thesis and Its Critics,* edited and with an introductory essay by Robert W. Green (Boston: D. C. Heath, 1959).

Richard Baxter (1615–91) was an English Nonconformist clergyman. Weber regarded him as the outstanding writer on Puritan ethics. I have taken his killjoy remarks from an essay by Kemper Fullerton in *Protestantism and Capitalism.*

Oliver MacDonagh, in *States of Mind* (London: Allen and Unwin, 1983), points out that despite many restrictions with respect to trade and the professions imposed upon Irish Catholics, by 1750 a Catholic middle class engaged in export trade to the Continent and retail trade at home had arisen in Ireland, and that its members, though Catholic, exhibited "the classic characteristics of Protestant Nonconformist capitalism—frugality, the ploughing back of profits, the networks of cousinhoods providing investment capital, the modest, withdrawn style of life."

"The golf links lie so near the mill" was popularized by crusaders against child labor. Bergen Evans, *Dictionary of Quotations,* says it is by Sarah Cleghorn.

4/*Why Two Syndromes?*

Fewer than 5 percent of Israeli citizens live in kibbutzim.

William McCord, *Voyages to Utopia: From Monastery to Commune* (New York: Norton, 1990), surveys past and present communal experiments.

The information on some current Swedish economic problems is drawn from *G&M,* September 13, 1991, "Giant firms taking a one-way street," dispatch from Stockholm by Peter Cook.

Conflict between the Swedish government's concepts of forest stewardship and those of private owners of forests are drawn from *WSJ,* August 25, 1989, "Save the Forests—Sell the Trees," by Lawrence Solomon. "Because governments around the world have such an abysmal record, environmentalists like the World Resources Institute have come to favor returning state lands to private landowners and local communities, which, on the whole, have maintained their [woodlands] far better." (The World Resources Institute is a UN-funded organization in Washington, D.C.)

5/*Jasper and Kate on the Guardian Syndrome*

For information on chivalry, here and in later references, I am heavily indebted to *Chivalry* by Maurice Keen (New Haven: Yale University Press, 1984).

Meiji 1868 by Paul Akamatsu, translated from the French by Miriam Kochan (New York: Harper and Row, 1972), describes taboos against trading by samurai in old Japan, and the penalties. *The Idea of Nationalism* by Hans Kohn (New York: Collier, 1944) touches on the trade taboo for Polish aristocrats. The French marquis who gets the tax break for promoting cultural events comes from a news story about how modern aristocrats keep up their expensive inherited houses. I have misplaced the citation.

In *The Code of Hammurabi,* introduction by Percy Handcock (New York: Macmillan, 1920), the sections discussed are 34, 38, and 39.

Information on the disobedient policeman's trial and appeal is taken from *G&M,* November 21, 1987, "Obedience is vital, police hearing told" by Deborah Wilson; and *G&M,* December 12, 1988, "Officers don't have the right to disobey orders, hearing told" by Charles Shank.

J. Glenn Gray, author of *The Warriors* (New York: Harper Torchbooks, 1970), had the duty of interrogating captured Nazi and Fascist police and functionaries in 1944 and 1945. With "nauseating regularity," he says, they protested, "My conscience is clear." Gray assumed at first that they were masking guilt for heinous crimes, but eventually he became convinced they meant exactly what they said. "Guilt was an empty word; they had done what they were told to do." Later, he observed the weight American civilian soldiers placed on the soldier's oath. He heard, " 'I'll do what they tell me and nobody can blame me.' Their satisfaction at sloughing off responsibility and conscience was often plain. Even if at first it was a bit unnatural, it quickly became a habit."

U.S. Navy Secretary John Lehman expressed his view of treason in an interview by John McLaughlin on NBC television, June 16, 1985, quoted June 17, 1985, in *G&M,* "Entire U.S. catches espionage fever," by William Johnson.

The treason penalty under China's last imperial dynasty turned up in *G&M,* July 25, 1987, "China rubs out crime with a vengeance," dispatch from Beijing by James M. Rusk. Keen, in *Chivalry,* calls penalties for treason "solemn sadism."

The edition of *The Prince* by Niccolò Machiavelli that I have used is translated, edited, and introduced by Daniel Donne (New York: Bantam, 1981).

!Kung and Gebusi murder rates are taken from *Science News,* February 6, 1988, "Murder in Good Company—Cooperation, camaraderie and a dizzying homicide rate distinguish a small New Guinea society" by Bruce Bower. An insight into traditional Eskimo views of murder is given by Raymond de Coccolo, *The Incredible Eskimo: Life Among the Barren Land Eskimo* (Surrey, B.C.: Hancock House, 1987). A hunter could kill another "without fear of being punished by other Eskimos, who consider it his own business so long as it does not injure their community as a whole." When this book was originally published in 1954, the author omitted some of his observations and self-censored his manuscript in anticipatory deference to his religious superiors; the work was then further bowdlerized by these superiors and by editors at Oxford University Press. The Hancock House edition editors and the author have restored omitted material and excisions.

A comparison of murder rates for 1986–87 in twenty-two industrialized countries, by the U.S. National Center for Health, Washington, showed the U.S. rate was so high as to be in a class by itself, ranging from more than two and a half to eight times the rates in the twenty-one other countries surveyed. *G&M,* August 24, 1990, Reuters news dispatch.

The usual form of "the Peace of God" appears to have been the Truce of God, cessation of warfare and violence during specified holy days. The penalty for breaching the truce was excommunication. *A History of French Civilization* by Georges Duby and Robert Mandrou, translated by James Blakely Atkinson (New York: Random House, 1964).

G. N. Clark's dismissive discussion of the social contract is to be found in

The Seventeenth Century (Oxford: Oxford Paperbacks, 1960; originally published by Clarendon Press of Oxford University, 1929).

Elias, *The Court Society,* notes that in the reign of Louis XIV, for example, dueling was in clear defiance of the king and his chief minister, Cardinal Richelieu, who were extending their central control over the French aristocracy. Nobles who dueled regardless, Elias says, were asserting their individual freedom "to wound or kill each other if they are so inclined." This may have been a residue of the earlier right of nobles and aristocrats, as warlords, to levy private war in their legitimate exercise of vengeance and prowess. Keen, *Chivalry.*

The murder of the New York murder witness and its consequences were reported in *WSJ,* October 8, 1984, "Intimidation to Silence Witnesses of Crime Worries Law Enforcers" by Stanley Penn.

Smashed-in-the-Head Buffalo Jump is about a hundred miles south of Calgary, near Ft. MacLeod, Alberta.

The boys with the egg-white money-traps were reported in *NYT,* July 14, 1970, "Thieves and Vandals Still at Work on Pay Phones, But So Is Company" by Richard Phalon.

One facet of the difficulty of maintaining legitimacy of deceit among those entrusted with legitimate deceit is described in *WSJ,* November 4, 1985, "Undercover Jobs Carry Big Psychological Risks After the Assignments—Agents' Personalities Change, They Botch Prosecutions and Even Commit Crimes—Resuming the False Identity" by Anthony M. DiStefano.

Information on the abundant leisure of !Kung hunters and a generalization about the leisured life associated with hunting and gathering is drawn from a paper by Patricia Draper, "Crowding among Hunter Gatherers: The !Kung Bushmen," *Science,* October 19, 1973.

The uses of leisure in a Bushman hunting-and-gathering group (not the !Kung, for once) are recounted by Laurens van der Post and Jane Taylor in *Testament to the Bushmen* (New York: Viking, 1984).

The Franklin quotation is from *The Autobiography of Benjamin Franklin,* edited and annotated by Leonard W. Labaree et al. (New Haven: Yale University Press, 1964).

Stephen Jay Gould discussed co-opted epiphenomena in "Cardboard Darwinism," a review essay, *NYRB,* September 25, 1986. He also now and again refers to the subject in his wonderful monthly essays for *Natural History* (American Museum of Natural History, New York).

Cross-use by commerce of technologies taken from the arts is explored in the paper "On Art, Invention and Technology" by Emeritus Professor Cyril Stanly Smith, *Technology Review* (Massachusetts Institute of Technology), June 1976.

Kissinger's announcement of largesse cutbacks was reported in *G&M,* January 9, 1976, "U.S. cutting back aid to nations that vote against it at the UN" by Leslie Gelb, NYT Service. Twelve years later, members of Congress were justifying U.S. nonpayments of UN dues because the small nations chiefly benefiting from the funds "ignored the wishes of [the] largest benefactor, the U.S." This was reported in *WSJ*, September 14, 1988, "Aid to Poor Nations Has Been Disrupted by U.S. Failure to Pay Over $500 Million." The funds being withheld were owed to the UN Food and Agricultural Organization, the World Health Organization, the International Seed Testing Association, and also the Organization of American States.

Benzuiin Chobei, a Japanese Robin Hood, turned up in *WSJ*, October 19, 1984, "Japan's Yakuza Gangs Extend Their Reach, Worry U.S. Lawmen" by Steven P. Galante.

The comment about dependency enjoining both conformity and defiance is by MacDonagh, *States of Mind*.

I was the tourist who didn't know what to pay the sexton. My husband was the bridegroom who didn't know what to pay the minister.

The Japanese businessman quoted on business philanthropy is Kazuo Watanabe. The occasion was an Atlanta conference organized by Craig Smith, editor and publisher of *Corporate Philanthropy Report* (Seattle). Watanbe's remarks were reported in *The Sun* (Baltimore), September 23, 1991, "Japanese Business Begets Japanese Philanthropy" by Neal R. Peirce. The traditional avenues for Japanese patronage of the arts and aid to worthy causes have been religious temples and government.

"We all have exactly the same habits" is drawn from *WSJ*, December 1, 1988, "Rich Poles Revert to an Old Manner: Living in Manors" by Barry Newman.

The scientist who compared throwing the bones with rational choice by hunters was Omar Khyyam Moore, "Divination—A New Perspective," *American Anthropologist* No. LIX, 1957.

6/*Trading, Taking, and Monstrous Hybrids*

Characteristic values of large, successful U.S. street and housing-project gangs include pride in prowess, vengeance, hierarchy, obedience, loyalty, largesse distribution, all in service to control of territories. But, in common with the Mafia, the gangs do not shun trading. For instance, *WSJ* of September 30, 1988, "Chicago Street Gangs Treat Public Housing as Private Fortress—The Black Gangster Disciples [name of gang] Menace Tenants, Use Units to Store Guns, Sell Drugs—Co-opting Kids and Old Folks" by Alex Kotlowitz.

A study of English youth gang culture, *We Hate Humans* (Harmondsworth: Penguin, 1984), reports that members seek employment for the purpose of stealing from employers; favorite takings are money from the till and clothing from stock. Income, from whatever sources, is spent largely on ostentatious clothing representing gang "uniforms," train fares, and industrial shoes for kicking victims and enemies. The English gangs do not run organized illegal businesses, a main difference from American gangs. They emphasize the values of loyalty, hierarchies, and ostentation and take pride in their art form, graffiti. Their chief preoccupation is invasion and defense of territories.

Scores of books on the Mafia are available. *The Honoured Society* by Norman Lewis (London: Collins, 1964; paperback edition, London: Eland, and New York: Hippocrene Books, 1984) traces the organization's Sicilian history. *A Man of Honor: The Autobiography of Joseph Bonanno* (New York: Simon and Schuster, 1983) is interesting in portraying the way a successful don wishes himself and his organization to be seen. *The Fortunate Pilgrim*, Mario Puzo's first (and, to my mind, best) novel, gives a fictionalized account of the early, poor Mafia on Manhattan's West Side, victimizing other poor Sicilians.

The rule of *omerta*, silence, has occasionally broken down in recent years, when charged or convicted members have cooperated with law enforcement officials to obtain mitigated sentences or other advantages. A notable recent instance is the testimony of Salvatore Gravano, a formerly trusted and highly placed underboss, during the trial of his don, John Gotti, in New York; his testimony began March 2, 1992, and continued thereafter, extensively reported in *NYT* and other papers. An interesting feature of the trial was the elaborate precaution taken by the judge to prevent the intimidation or bribery of members of the jury. They were identified only by numbers; their names and addresses were sealed in a court safe. Outside court, they were kept in a secret place and when not in the jury box were accompanied at all times by federal marshals. Even so, after hearing Gravano's first day of testimony about murders, reprisals, and vengeance, one jury member became so fearful that the court permitted her to resign. Later two more were permitted to resign.

The Mafia convention, of which I was a discreet but fascinated observer for two days from breakfast to nightfall, occurred in St. Martaan, the Dutch West Indies, in early 1970. The gathering lasted three days in total, and ended in a grand shopping spree in Philipsburg. Apart from the wives of the two dons, the only woman at the gathering was a young beauty in clothing that can only be described as fantastically high-style. She not only looked like an inanimate fashion mannequin, but literally behaved like one. She was in the charge of the most unattractive man present, and she did not move except upon his orders, standing immobile for long periods of time, sitting immobile at others, walking only as he ordered for as long as he ordered. She never spoke or changed facial expression. Later in New York I was informed that she had probably been guilty of some infraction, and this humiliating ordeal was her punishment.

The story of the threatened photographer is from life. He told me his experience several months after it occurred.

Acquaintances who are not Mafia members themselves but who, through their upbringing, have personal connections with members, have told me— omitting names—of offspring who've defected. This phenomenon is corroborated by reports in the United States and Canada of more or less continual recruitment of Mafia personnel from Sicily, necessitated in part because appreciable numbers of offspring born and raised in America choose to reject the criminal life.

The President's Commission on Organized Crime estimated that such organizations employ a total of about 500,000 persons and generate some $47 billion in revenue annually, amounting to about 1 percent of the country's economy. *G&M,* October 27, 1986, "Trial in Manhattan opens window into world of mob" by Martin Mittelstaedt. A group of eight New York dons ("There would have been a ninth man on trial but he was shot dead by disgruntled associates in front of a Manhattan steak house last year") being prosecuted was alleged to be entrenched in shipping, construction, several unions, commercial garbage collection, drug smuggling and selling, extortion, loan-sharking, and money laundering—as well as the garment industry, notwithstanding the previous successful police action (see Chapter 1).

The quotations from Gorbachev are from his speech on January 27, 1987, to the Communist Party's Central Committee, distributed in translation to the foreign press by Tass, the Soviet news agency. *NYT,* January 28, 1987.

Fidel Castro's speech, with an introduction by Lee Lockwood, was published in *NYRB,* September 24, 1970.

Gitkasan and Wet'suwet'en Indian trade information comes from *The Spirit of the Land: The Opening Statement of the Hereditary Chiefs in the Supreme Court of British Columbia* (Gabriola, B.C.: Reflections, 1989).

Many prehistorians have now come to believe that trading was an ordinary feature in many pre-agricultural hunting-and-gathering groups. Anthropologists are now also reassessing contemporary foraging bands from this standpoint, noting evidence of trade not only in recent times, but evidence (previously overlooked or ignored) that trading had extended far into their pasts. *Past and Present in Hunter-Gatherer Societies,* edited by Carmel Schrirer (Orlando, Fla.: Academic Press, 1984).

The ancient Peruvian cotton-growing and manufacturing city was described by Jeffrey Quilter in *Science,* January 19, 1991.

Scottish-English border raiding, along with its moral, economic, and political contexts, is vividly described in *The Steel Bonnets* by George MacDonald Fraser (London: Pan Books, 1974).

I am indebted to Clark, *The Seventeenth Century,* for the information about the mapping of European national frontiers as lines.

Isaiah Berlin's wise remarks about conquered ethnic groups were given in an interview by Nathan Gardels, published in *NYRB,* November 21, 1991.

An interesting sidelight on long-conquered portions of modern European nations reemerging as regions asserting various degrees of autonomy is a map by Kristina Ferris and an accompanying essay by Neal Ascherson in *The Independent* (London) of February 9, 1992. Ascherson concludes that the map "of the real Europe which counts, as opposed to the conventional lines and colours—is changing utterly."

John Holt's description of ten-year-olds is from *How Children Fail* (Pitman, 1964; paperback edition, New York: Dell, 1988).

7/Anomalies

Stewart E. Perry's comments on military medical priorities are drawn from *Communities on the Way: Rebuilding Local Economies in the United States and Canada* (Albany: State University of New York, 1987).

The story of the wounded Civil War soldier was told me by my father-in-law, Robert H. Jacobs, Sr. (1870–1959). The soldier was his father, Ferris Jacobs, Jr., of Delhi, N.Y., a Union cavalry officer. The doctor was Ferris Jacobs, Sr. Robert had the story from a close friend and fellow soldier of his father's; Ferris junior never spoke of his war experiences to his children.

The CIA-corrupted psychiatric clinic was the Allan Memorial Institute in Montreal; its director was the late Dr. Ewen Cameron. A joint lawsuit on behalf of victims and their families was brought against the CIA but was dragged out by delays until many victims were dead. An account by the son of one of the victims, who became a psychiatrist himself, is *A Father, a Son and the CIA* by Harvey Weinstein (Toronto: James Lorimer, 1988).

The current practices of English barristers respecting fees and the historical meaning of their gowns' black bags were described in *G&M,* November 1, 1986, "The ins and outs of Inns of the Court" by Penelope Johnston.

A historian who is particularly good on southern slaveholders' moral code and its cultural power to transcend countervailing economic considerations is Eugene D. Genovese, *The Political Economy of Slavery* (New York: Pantheon, 1965) and *Roll, Jordan, Roll: The World the Slaves Made* (New York: Random House, 1975; Vintage paperback, 1976). Much about the southern moral code as revealed in the literature of the South can be found in *Patriotic Gore* by Edmund Wilson (New York: Oxford University Press, 1962). I am also indebted to *Yankee Saints and Southern Sinners* by Bertram Wyatt-Brown (Baton Rouge: Louisiana State University Press, 1985).

Arno J. Mayer, in *The Persistence of the Old Regime* (New York: Pantheon, 1980), deals with, among other things, the ubiquity of guardian agriculture in Europe until very recent times. In a curious review essay of Mayer's book, in *NYRB,* April 2, 1981, A. J. P. Taylor seems bent upon pinning these economic injustices and gross economic inequalities upon capitalism. While granting that private ownership of land was almost a monopoly of the European aristocracy until the twentieth century, he says the bulk of aristocratic wealth came not from agricultural land use but from urban land rents (e.g., the great wealth of the Duke of Westminster), coal royalties from mines under landholdings, and railways, which "brought fortunes to those over whose land they passed." True enough in later times, but this does not negate the fact that agricultural land was long in the hands of royalty, aristocracy, and hereditary gentry (in England it still is) and was managed less by commercial values than by guardian values.

On the unique economic problems of artists, Lewis Hyde's book is *The Gift: Imagination and the Erotic Life of Property* (New York: Random House, 1983).

8/*Casts of Mind*

The newsletter is from the *International Eco-technology Research Centre,* Issue 4, January 1990 (Cranfield, Bedford, U.K.).

Information about the mycorrhizal fungi and ecological niches of animals closely related to its presence is drawn from "The Ancient Forest" by Catherine Caufield, *The New Yorker,* May 14, 1990; and from *Seeing the Forest Among the Trees* by Herb Hammond (Vancouver: Polestar, 1991), a marvelous text on forestry issues, informatively and beautifully illustrated.

I have lifted the quotation by Francis Bacon from Clark, *The Seventeenth Century.*

9/*Armbruster on Systemic Moral Corruption*

Sir Lewis Namier's astute remark about men in office is from a collection of his essays, *Crossroads of Power* (New York: Macmillan, 1962).

Information on the Ik is drawn from Colin M. Turnbull's remarkable book *The Mountain People* (New York: Simon and Schuster, 1972).

The destruction of communities and pauperization of people victimized by World Bank megaprojects is described by Patricia Adams and Lawrence Solomon in *In The Name of Progress: The Underside of Foreign Aid* (Toronto: Energy Probe Foundation, 1985); and in *Odious Debts: Loose Lending, Corruption and the Third World's Environmental Legacy* by Patricia Adams (London and Toronto: Earthscan, 1991).

Unfortunate results of the IMF's attempts to reform the economies of poor defaulting countries have been reported frequently in the press; for example, *WSJ* of March 23, 1989, "Brazil's Poor Get Hungrier on Bare Bones IMF Menu" by Alexander Cockburn.

A historical account of why the taxpayers are on the hook for savings-and-loan failures can be found in *High Rollers: Inside the Savings and Loan Debacle* by Martin Lowy (New York: Praeger, 1991).

Quincy's worries about the bad precedent set by the expedient of dishonest accounting (see Chapter 1) were not unfounded. *WSJ* of November 2, 1990, "Hall of Shame—Besides S&L Owners, Host of Professionals Paved Way for Crisis—Auditors, Advisers, Officials Took Narrow View of Jobs or Were Led by Ideology" by Charles McCoy, Richard B. Schmitt, and Jeff Bailey.

The "gruesome little poem" is put together from phrases in an article in the *G&M* business section, November 16, 1985.

The deplorable "definition" of investment banking was an advertisement for Citicorp Investment Bank, *WSJ,* April 28, 1987.

For the material on solvency letters I am indebted to *WSJ,* January 14, 1988, "Legal Time Bomb—Big Accounting Firms Risk Costly Lawsuits by Reassuring Lenders—Their 'Solvency Letters' Say Company Can Pay Debt; No Court Cases So Far" by Lee Berton. Also edifying is *WSJ,* January 12, 1987, "Tricky

Ledgers—To Hide Huge Losses, Financial Officials Use Accounting Gimmicks—Farm Credit System Plans Two Sets of Its Books; Insolvent S&Ls Stay
Open—But Few Expect a Real Crisis" by Jeff Bailey and Charles F. McCoy.

The pie-shaped diagram of junk bond ownership appeared in *WSJ,* December 22, 1988.

Among the chief defenders of leveraged buy-outs and hostile takeovers have
been Harvey N. Segal, *Corporate Makeover: The Reshaping of the American Economy*
(New York: Viking, 1989); Michael Jensen, a Harvard University economist;
and (much of the time) the anonymous editorial writers of *The Wall Street
Journal.* But there were many, many other defenders of these practices.

The excitable advertisement for Sun Tzu's *The Art of War,* translated and
introduced by Samuel B. Griffith (Dorset), appeared in the Barnes & Noble
(New York) book sales catalogue of March 1991.

Antony Jay's book of advice to managers is *Corporation Man* (New York:
Random House, 1971). Jay is also the author of *Management and Machiavelli*
(New York: Holt, Rinehart and Winston, 1968; New York: Bantam, 1969).

The *Wall Street Journal's* equation of business with an army and its managers
with military officers led off a special section, "Medicine and Health," April
22, 1988. The metaphor was particularly misguided in view of the profound
moral differences between civilian and military medicine (see Chapter 8).

Information on the false arrests by transit police is from *NYT,* November 24,
1987, "New York Transit Police Officers Accused of Unlawful Arrests" by
Richard Levine and Elizabeth Neuffer.

Lockheed's financial troubles and its rescue are described in *NYT,* October
17, 1976, "Lockheed Gets Off the Ground—Problems Linger, but Defense
Money Pours in for Biggest Military Contractor" by Robert Lindsey.

Seymour Melman's views on the corruption of engineering capabilities by
lack of cost discipline were set forth in a long interview with Robert Matas,
"Military spending: route to ruin," *G&M,* June 27, 1988. Melman has also
written a book on the subject, *The Demilitarized Society* (Montreal: Harvest
House, 1988).

Neglect by military contractors to make productive investments is addressed
in *WSJ,* October 8, 1987, "Antique Arsenals—Many Defense Firms Make
High-Tech Gear in Low-Tech Factories—Pentagon's Flawed Ordering, Role
of Congress Cited; Waste, High Costs Result" by Cynthia F. Mitchell and Tim
Carrington.

Information on the United States' declining share of the world market in
machine tools (as well as various other technological products) comes from
WSJ, January 28, 1991.

Plato on justice and injustices (see Chapter 2 note).

Information on Kopinor is from an interview with John-Willy Rudolph by
H. J. Kirchhoff, *G&M,* March 30, 1988.

The teacher (of undergraduates in business administration and community
development) who made photocopies of an out-of-stock book for his students
is Stewart E. Perry. He is an author himself (see note for Chapter 7) and also

the director of a community economic-development center in Sydney, Nova Scotia. It was one of my books he copied, so he sent the payment to me, and I sent it on to my publisher.

The ancient Chinese poem is from *The Way of Life According to Lao Tzu,* a version by Witter Bynner (New York: Capricorn, 1962).

10/*Syndrome-Friendly Inventions*

I am indebted to personal communications from Susan Witt and Robert Swann, to newsletters from SHARE and the E. F. Schumacher Society (both of Great Barrington, Mass.), and to press reports for information on the SHARE program. Instructions covering the legal instruments necessary for such a program are available from the Schumacher Society, as well as much other information pertaining to local economic development (e.g., land trusts, issues of local currency).

For information on the Grameen Bank over a period of years, and for the opportunity to hear Dr. Yunus speak in Toronto and to ask him questions, I am immensely grateful to the Calmeadow Foundation of Toronto.

A catalogue, "Principal Providers of Very Small Loans," and an article, "Micro-loans to the World's Poorest," by Clyde H. Farnsworth, were published in *NYT,* February 21, 1988.

For information about the first commercially capitalized micro-lending banks—in Bolivia and Panama—I am again indebted to the Calmeadow Foundation, which has given technical advice to the Bolivian bankers; and to Acción, which has done a similar service in Panama.

An Operational Guide for Micro-Enterprise Projects (Acción International, Cambridge, Mass., and Calmeadow, Toronto, 1988) is available from both its publishers. Acción International also publishes a newsletter.

The Other Path: The Invisible Revolution in the Third World by Hernando de Soto (New York: Harper and Row, 1989) describes how micro-entrepreneurs are fettered politically and economically in Peru (and by extension in many other places).

The Marketplace Manual: A Practical Guide to Import Replacement, prepared for publication by Glen Gibbons (NEDCO, Eugene, Ore., 1987) relates the experience of Oregon Marketplace, gives short case studies, and includes model contracts and other documents. I am also indebted for information to Alana Probst, personal communications; to "Oregon Marketplace" by Alana Probst and Glen Gibbons, *Economic Development Commentary,* Winter 1987 issue (Northwestern Council for Economic Development Institute, Evanston, Ill.); and to Probst's slide lecture explaining how the program works.

The "flexible networking" program (not mentioned in chapter text) of the Emilia-Romagna region of Italy, centered in Bologna, is not, strictly speaking, a new commercial invention. But it has been wonderfully ingenious and effective at reviving competition-cum-cooperation urban clusters of small businesses, which have always been indispensable to prospering economies, and in helping them incorporate highly advanced techniques, skills, and equipment. It is also a splendid example of constructive, non-corrupt commercial and guardian symbiosis. It is credited with having raised per capita income in its region from seventeenth up to second place in Italy during the past twenty years. It is now being imitated in Denmark, and is in process of being instituted in Oregon. *Transatlantic Perspectives* (The German Marshall Fund of the United States, Washington, D.C.), Issue 22, Winter 1991, "The Power of Manufacturing Networks" by Richard Hatch; and Issue 24, Autumn 1991, "European Economic Development Ideas Take Root in Oregon" by Wayne Fawbush and Joseph Cortright. "A New Idea from the Old World," a video, is available from the German Marshall Fund.

For information on the Taipei economy, I am indebted to personal reports from Canadian visitors there and immigrants to Canada from Taiwan; to news dispatches, especially *G&M,* June 20, 1979, "Taiwan feeling pains of industrial growth" by John Fraser; and *WSJ,* February 8, 1980, "Taiwan Still Thrives a Year After the Loss of U.S. Recognition" by Barry Kramer. For information on the part played by tax laws I am indebted to *Governing the Market* by Robert Wade (Princeton: Princeton University Press, 1990).

The *WSJ* articles anticipating exorbitant costs of the Clean Air Act were by Rose Gutfeld and Barbara Rosewicz, October 29, 1990. The subsequent *WSJ* article appeared December 24, 1990: "Industrial Switch—Some Companies Cut Pollution by Altering Production Methods—Clean Manufacturing Avoids Many Problems at Source Rather Than Mopping Up—Change May Trim Costs Too" by Amal Kumar Nz.

Terpene substitution for CFCs by electronics companies was described in a *WSJ* Technology item by John R. Wilke, May 18, 1990. A plethora of other CFC substitute materials and methods was reported in *G&M,* February 22, 1992, "Phaseout of CFCs induces ingenuity" by Marcus Gee.

The London *Observer* editorial, "Nuclear Fantasy," appeared November 12, 1989.

11/*Hortense on Castes and Flexibility*

Plato's caste scheme is set out in the *Republic.*

Information on old Japan's caste arrangements is from *Meiji 1868,* from *Japan: An Interpretation* by Lafcadio Hearn (New York: Macmillan, 1904), and from the generous assistance given me by Toshiko Adilman of Toronto.

The intensifying poverty, as time passed, of the French petty provincial aristocracy is described and analyzed in *The Court Society.*

Temples in old Japan resembled seignorial fiefs, comparable to many European monasteries in this respect.

The legendary origin of Viking castes is from *The Vikings,* by Johannes Brøndsted, translated by Kalle Skov (New York: Penguin, 1965). I have made one minor correction of a mistranslation ("ox" in place of "cattleman").

The comment on early European parliaments' embodiments of caste (estates) is from *The Seventeenth Century.*

The poem is from the Witter Bynner version of *Lao Tzu.*

The Deuteronomy quotations are from the King James version of the Bible.

"Your mother is your receipt." This story was told me by the late Wilbur Strong Broms of New York and St. Paul. He was the son who paid the traffic fines.

Stephen Jay Gould's comment on the separateness of science and religion is from a review essay, "The H and Q of Baseball," *NYRB,* October 24, 1991.

12/Pitfalls of the Methods

I have taken my information about Heraclitus from the *Encyclopaedia Britannica,* 1949 printing.

According to Elias, *The Court Society,* who takes this information from Saint-Simon (a duke himself, and the confidant of Louis XIV and his son, the dauphin), relationships between nobles of the sword and of the robe were tense, regardless of friendships or arranged marriages, because of the unabated contempt for men of bourgeois origin.

Roman equestrians became so closely associated with trade that eventually any rich and worthy merchant was given—or took—the courtesy title of Equus. *Roman Imperialism in the Late Republic* by E. Badian (Ithaca, N.Y.: Cornell University Press, 1968).

Keen, *Chivalry,* remarks on the redundant knights who turned to war-making in Lithuania and Poland. Later, many such warriors, redundant in Europe, turned to conquest in the New World, and subsequently to imperial adventures in Asia and Africa.

Pope Innocent III's order to slay all (he was asked what to do with prisoners) is drawn from *The Children's Crusade* by George Zabriskie Gray (1870; reissued New York: William Morrow, 1972).

The mandarins' astonishment at increased tax yields is taken from *The Dragon Empress: Life and Times of Tz'u-hsi, 1835–1908, Empress Dowager of China* by Marina Warner (London: Hamish Hamilton, 1972).

The reminiscence of the aged son of a samurai is taken from *Memories of Silk and Straw: A Self-Portrait of Small-Town Japan* by Dr. Junichi Sago (New York: Kodansha International, 1990). This is a marvelous oral history, telling, among other things, how the ingenious old crafts were traditionally carried on.

English attitudes toward commerce can hardly be avoided in contact with anything English. They are extensively quoted and analyzed in *English Culture and the Decline of the Industrial Spirit 1850–1980* by Martin J. Wiener (Cambridge University Press, 1981).

The tale of corruption among Philadelphia antique dealers is from *WSJ*, February 19, 1988, "At Many Auctions, Illegal Bidding Thrives As a Longtime Practice Among Dealers" by Meg Cox.

The quotations from interviewed Lockheed workers are from *NYT*, February 17, 1976, "In Burbank, Many Workers Defend Lockheed Payments" by Robert Lindsey.

Hannah Arendt's last work was *The Life of the Mind*, uncompleted but posthumously published, edited by Mary McCarthy (New York: Harcourt Brace Jovanovich, 1978).

Richard Nielsen's papers on managerial morality and self-examination include: *Journal of Business Ethics* 3, 1984, "Toward an Action Philosophy for Managers Based on Arendt and Tillich"; *California Management Review*, Spring, 1984, "Arendt's Action Philosophy and the Manager as Eichmann, Richard III, Faust or Institution Citizen"; *Journal of Business Ethics* 8, 1989, "Negotiating as an Ethics Action (Praxis) Strategy"; *The Academy of Management EXECUTIVE*, 1989, "Changing Unethical Organizational Behavior"; and *Journal of Business Ethics* 9, 1990, "Dialogic Leadership as Ethics Action (Praxis) Method."

Self-examination from fear is noted in *G&M*, September 12, 1991, "Honesty begins at home—with the number of scandals rising, firms are sniffing for any whiff of wrongdoing in their closets before the regulators find them," a dispatch from New York by Jacquie McNish. The same phenomenon, in one company, is described in *New York* magazine, December 9, 1991, "Saving Salomon" by Bernice Kanner.

Revision of the B.C. foresters' ethical code and the Awareness organization formed by forestry students were reported in the *Vancouver Sun*, October 16, 1991, "The Value of Ethics—Scandals force business on to new path" by Carrie Nishima.

The self-corrected honesty test was reported in *WSJ*, July 11, 1985, "More 'Honesty' Tests Used to Gauge Workers' Morale" by Thomas F. O'Boyle.

The sortie of military contractors into ethics was reported in *WSJ*, July 21, 1988, "Defense Contractors' Ethics Programs Get Scrutinized" by Eileen White Read. Military-industrial scandals surfacing since that time are so numerous, horrendous, and complex that they would make a book in themselves. Examples can be found in *WSJ* of June 27, 1988; July 7, 1988; September 2, 1988; December 22, 1988—and on, and on, and on. This is from *WSJ* of March 29, 1990: "William Galvin, until recently one of the most influential and highly paid defense industry consultants, pleaded guilty to bribing the Navy's top acquisition official and another Pentagon manager during the late 1980's. . . . More than 30 other individuals have been convicted in the scandal, but prosecutors consider Mr. Galvin to be an essential link to seeking possible [additional] charges."

The office-worker poll, conducted by Louis Harris and Associates, was reported in the *Vancouver Sun*, October 16, 1991.

13/Hortense's Defense of Moral Flexibility

The library Jasper advises portrays no one library. Details are picked up from several and combined.

The Pathan who cut off his wife's nose is lifted from *WSJ*, July 16, 1974, "Visit to the Past—Waziristan Is a Land Where Change Comes Very Slowly—If at All—In Remote Pakistan Area, Every Man Has a Gun and Is Ready to Use It—How a Wife Lost Her Nose" by Peter R. Kann.

The poem is another from the Witter Bynner version of *Lao Tzu*.

ACKNOWLEDGMENTS

Although the characters in this book, as personalities, are wholly fictional, many real people have contributed to their information and viewpoints. Some of these are acknowledged in notes for specific items.

Criticism by my editor and publisher, Jason Epstein, has been indispensable. His constructive skepticism and requests for clarifications and amplification have made him an unpersonified participant throughout the book.

I am especially indebted to faculty members of the philosophy and theology departments and the Pulse Program of Boston College who in 1987 generously afforded me an opportunity to present a preliminary version of my ideas at a Lonergan Workshop seminar, the proceedings of which have been published as *Ethics in Making a Living,* edited by Fred Lawrence (Atlanta: Scholars Press, 1989), and who subsequently reviewed with me an early draft of the dialogue. Information and suggestions by the following Boston College people have been extremely helpful: Professor Patrick Byrne, the Reverend Joseph F. X. Flanagan, S.J., Glenn Hughes, Richard Keeley, Professor Frederick Lawrence, Sue Lawrence, Professor Francis McLaughlin, Professor Richard Nielsen, Dr. James Rurak, Mary Donley, and students Peggy Bedevian, Cindy Kang, Sheila Lynch, Sara Marcellino, and Nancy Soohoo. I am also gratefully indebted to the Reverend T. P. O'Malley, S.J., who in 1986 afforded me an opportunity to present much of the material appearing in Chapter 10 for comment and discussion at John Carroll University in Cleveland.

I owe a special debt also to Patrick Lawlor, organizer of an informal report-and-discussion group which, over a period of several years, gave me a feeling for informal reports and the kind of give-and-take they occasion.

Others who have aided me wittingly or unwittingly by supplying pieces of information, ideas, and germs of ideas, or by reviewing, criticizing, or correcting the manuscript, include: Patricia Adams, Sid Adilman, Toshiko Adilman, Jeffrey Ashe, Virginia Avery, Charles Bergengrin, James I. Butzner, Dr. J. Decker Butzner, Judge John D. Butzner, Pete Butzner, Mary Ann Code, Martin Connell, Marcel Coté, Robert A. Crosby, Benjamin Dreyer, Robert Fichter, Mary Ann Glendon, Paul Golob, C. Richard Hatch, Linda Haynes, Mary Houghton, Burgin Jacobs, Edward D. Jacobs, Dr. James K. Jacobs, Dr. Lucia Ferris Jacobs, Leticia Kent, Alex Kisin, Professor Marvin Lunenfeld, S. H. MacCallum, Mel Manchester, Elizabeth R. Manson, Doris Mehegan, Maryam Mohit, Mary Perot Nichols, Dr. Alan Powell, Alana Probst, Mallory Rintoul, Norm Rubin, Lawrence Solomon, Henry Stern, Robert Swann, John Tulk, Barbara Weisl, Susan Witt, and Jane Zeidler. I am grateful to all of them. Most of all, I am grateful to Robert H. Jacobs, my husband, chief encourager, and best friend.

ABOUT THE AUTHOR

JANE JACOBS was born in Scranton, Pennsylvania, and now lives in Toronto.

ABOUT THE TYPE

This book was set in Perpetua, a typeface designed by the English artist Eric Gill, and cut by The Monotype Corporation between 1928 and 1930. Perpetua is a contemporary face of original design, without any direct historical antecedents. The shapes of the roman letters are derived from the techniques of stonecutting. The larger display sizes are extremely elegant and form a most distinguished series of inscriptional letters.